VIRTUAL CLASSROOMS

VIRTUAL CLASSROOMS

Educational Opportunity
through Two-Way
Interactive Television

VICKI M. HOBBS
Director
Missouri Interactive Telecommunications Education Network

J. SCOTT CHRISTIANSON
Technical Coordinator
Missouri Interactive Telecommunications Education Network

TECHNOMIC
PUBLISHING CO., INC.
LANCASTER · BASEL

Virtual Classrooms
a **TECHNOMIC** publication

Published in the Western Hemisphere by
Technomic Publishing Company, Inc.
851 New Holland Avenue, Box 3535
Lancaster, Pennsylvania 17604 U.S.A.

Distributed in the Rest of the World by
Technomic Publishing AG
Missionsstrasse 44
CH-4055 Basel, Switzerland

Printed in the United States of America
10 9 8 7 6 5 4 3 2 1

Main entry under title:
   Virtual Classrooms: Educational Opportunity through
   Two-Way Interactive Television

A Technomic Publishing Company book
Bibliography: p. 291

Library of Congress Catalog Card No. 96-60519
ISBN No. 1-56676-312-6

**PART THREE: THE I-TV CLASSROOM:
THEORY, PRACTICE, AND REALITY**

A quiet revolution is occurring in rural education in the United States. So quiet, in fact, that few people really know the extent to which telecommunications technology is redefining the geographic barriers of schools and communities, broadening limited educational opportunities for rural youth, and closing the gap in rural school inequity. At the heart of this revolution is two-way interactive television, a distance learning technology that links two or more geographically separated classrooms so that students and teachers in these classrooms — although miles apart — can see, hear, and interact with each other. In essence, two-way interactive television allows teachers and students from different school districts to meet in a "virtual" classroom where they interact as though they were in the same classroom.

Two-way interactive television, or I-TV, can best be described as the linkage of three to ten school districts over fiber optic, coaxial cable, or dedicated copper telephone lines, which enables participating schools to share teachers and electronically combine students. The major advantage of I-TV technology over other distance learning methods is the ability of students and teachers to simultaneously see and hear each other and to spontaneously interact. Unlike other distance learning technologies, I-TV preserves the dynamics of the traditional classroom, allowing students to ask and immediately respond to questions, to pick up essential visual cues in teaching and learning, and to interact with other students.

I-TV has much to offer rural schools that are economically unable to provide advanced science, math, or foreign language courses through traditional means. Many small schools cannot offer advanced courses because of limited enrollments, their inability to attract and retain quality teachers, or their inability to hire teachers multi-certified in diverse curricular areas. By banding together with surrounding school districts in an I-TV network, a small school can greatly expand its course offerings, usually at an annual cost roughly equivalent to that of hiring one beginning teacher. For the rural student hoping to enroll in college in this time of increasing admissions requirements, I-TV can provide a life-changing opportunity.

In addition, I-TV can be an important tool for community and economic development, since 24-hour availability of the network allows for significant after-school usage. From medical and legal continuing education courses, adult evening courses, EMT and Private Industry Council job training programs to extension community development, 4-H, or agri-business meetings, the opportunities for inter-community usage are only limited by one's imagination.

The potential for immediate and full interactivity is the difference between interactive television and other distance learning technologies and is why more than half of all states have significant, ongoing efforts in two-way interactive television. Few educational technologies have been of sufficient importance to claim a role in reinventing rural America. Through the provision of advanced secondary and dual-credit courses, and by interlinking institutions, agencies, organizations, and businesses through "telecommunities," two-way interactive TV may indeed live up to that promise.

THE authors gratefully acknowledge the patience and philosophical contributions of their respective spouses and families, as well as the significant contributions and insights provided by the students, teachers, and administrators of the Missouri Interactive Telecommunications Education (MIT-E) network and Central Methodist College. The authors would like to especially thank Ava Fajen for diligently reviewing the manuscript and Technomic Publishing Company for publishing *Virtual Classrooms.*

Numerous reviewers and sidebar contributors greatly improved the quality of this book with their insight and wisdom. These include Pete Royer, Ron Stammen, David Hart, Don Hays, Dan Wendling, Bryan Leimkühler, Eldon Wahlers, Daryl Hobbs, Kathleen Olivieri, Joy Dodson, Carol Swinney, Sheryl Melton, James Chadwick, Al Race, Richard Kenshalo, Leigh Anne Rettinger, and Denise Coldwater.

VIRTUAL Classrooms provides the reader with a comprehensive review of two-way interactive television (I-TV) and its use as a tool in rural education and community development. The book is divided into sections that reflect the many different aspects of I-TV networks. Although many I-TV issues are steeped in technical jargon, we have done our best to write *Virtual Classrooms* in easy-to-understand, non-technical language. Where specific technical verbiage is unavoidable, the reader will find a comprehensive glossary to which to refer.

Sidebars and guest essays from pioneers in two-way interactive television and educational technology have been included to provide additional insights and real-life examples of I-TV usage and complement the perspectives of the authors. Due to the rapid growth of two-way interactive television and the regulatory turmoil in the telecommunications industry, this book cannot be all inclusive of I-TV issues. We have tried, however, to cover in depth those issues most crucial to the success of I-TV.

The first part of the book, "Crossing the Miles," explains the why and how of distance learning and interactive television. Chapter 1 discusses how distance learning, and specifically I-TV, can help meet the growing needs of rural school districts. Chapter 2 provides an overview of several different technologies and transmission mediums that can be used in an I-TV network. In this context, the chapter provides information on the four major I-TV transmission technologies, and addresses basic concerns such as cost effectiveness, ease of operation, quality of transmission, and availability.

The next part of *Virtual Classrooms* — "Bricks, Mortar, and Imagination: Building an I-TV Network" — contains information for those considering or currently attempting to establish an I-TV network. Chapter 3 presents the authors' recommended steps for establishing a school-based I-TV network, while Chapter 4 presents a model of I-TV administration in a way that brings together all parties with a vested interest in the success of the network and those with the necessary technical and educational expertise. The last chapter in this section discusses paradigms for the evaluation of two-way interactive television networks.

"The I-TV Classroom: Theory, Practice, and Reality" —Part Three of *Virtual Classrooms*—focuses on the experience of teachers and students in I-TV classrooms. The two chapters in this section address the issues surrounding teaching and learning in an I-TV classroom, as well as the effective use of the instructional resources available in an I-TV classroom.

Part Four—"Is It Worth It? Assessing Investment and Returns" — takes the reader through the process of determining the economic justification for involvement or non-involvement in a two-way interactive television network. Chapter 8 provides a discussion of the diffusion of I-TV technology and its relationship to the production of social and human capital. Chapter 9 assists the reader in conducting a cost-benefit analysis, with a computer spreadsheet available from the authors (on disk or via the Internet).

"Realizing the Potential of I-TV," the fifth and final part of *Virtual Classrooms,* explores the possible uses of school-based I-TV networks for economic and community development, as well as the current regulatory and legislative impediments to widespread adoption of I-TV.

Appendix 1 lists I-TV networks which would welcome visits from potential adopters of I-TV technology. The second appendix provides information on print and electronic resources for I-TV, including information on how to participate in the I-TV Internet discussion list and how to access the I-TV worldwide web site. Appendix 3 is a glossary of terms and Appendix 4 provides a bibliography of works cited in the text and other useful references.

PART ONE

CROSSING THE MILES

CHAPTER 1

The Need for Distance Learning:
An Introduction to Two-Way
Interactive Television

MANY small school districts do not have the financial and instructional resources to offer advanced math, science, or language courses. However, the ability to expand student access to advanced curriculum offerings is essential if a district is to meet the needs of all its students and increase college-bound students' chances for success.

Many small school districts attempt to meet the needs of their students by adjusting course offerings each year, but they are often unable to find part-time certified teachers in needed subjects or multi-certified teachers appropriate to the district's curricular needs. In addition, in order to meet student demand for courses, small schools may be forced to eliminate or shift positions in one year, only to reinstate them in subsequent years—the situation is less than ideal. Despite the problems small districts face in providing advanced courses, the need to provide them continues to grow. Indeed, mandated curriculum requirements in a number of states have already led school districts to search out alternative means of providing needed courses.

Thus distance learning was born of necessity.

Distance learning allows districts to offer courses when the number of students enrolled in the course at a single school does not justify the hiring of a full-time teacher. Distance learning or distance education has become the byword in rural education circles, but it is important to differentiate among the various technologies included under the broad label of distance learning. All distance education methods are not created equal. Distance learning encompasses a variety of technologies for instructional delivery, including: correspondence classes, in which interaction is dependent on the mail; audiographic tele-learning classes in which teachers interact with remote students by means of a computer; instruction by satellite, in which the interaction is largely one-way, i.e., from teacher to student; and two-way interactive television in which the level of student-to-teacher and student-to-student interaction approximates that of a traditional classroom.

AN OVERVIEW OF DISTANCE LEARNING TECHNOLOGIES

Instruction by Satellite

This technology was popularized by both the Texas TI-IN Network and Oklahoma State University Arts and Science Teleconferencing Network. In satellite instruction a course originating in a distant studio/classroom is broadcast via satellite uplink to subscribing school districts that have satellite receiving capabilities (downlink sites). Reception of satellite courses is not bound by distance, that is, a downlink site can be located anywhere in the country. Instruction is provided by a remote teacher who may simultaneously teach to hundreds of students; at each downlink site, on-site coordinators are responsible for supervising students and equipment. In most satellite courses, broadcasts fill only a portion of the time students spend in class. Broadcasts are commonly received two to four times per week, with the remainder of the class time devoted to local labs or computer-assisted instruction (CAI). Instruction by satellite, as it is operated today, is not fully interactive; it does not allow the students and teacher to spontaneously interact, visually and audibly, as in a traditional classroom. The level of interactivity varies by course provider; while video and audio from the teacher is transmitted one-way, students can sometimes interact with the teacher via telephone or through a digital keypad.

Audiographic Tele-Learning

Audiographic tele-learning, introduced in Pennsylvania and Utah in the 1980s, has quickly evolved from a relatively primitive technology to a much more sophisticated format. Through the use of a computer, modem, and telephone line, students at multiple sites are taught by a teacher located at one of the sites. The teacher sends computer screen images (text and graphics) to each student's computer via modem. The screen image is accompanied by a telephone audio link. Students may respond to questions appearing on the computer screen through the computer keyboard. Individual responses are relayed by modem to the teacher's computer screen. Through the use of video cameras, still video images may accompany the audio instruction, but full audio and video interactivity is not yet feasible with this technology.

Photograph 1.1.   *Audiographic tele-learning. Audiographic tele-learning uses telephone lines to transmit voice and computer graphics. Participants in audiographic courses can talk with the instructor and each other as well as share computer images such as graphics, text and charts. Audiographic systems, such as WisView shown here, require two phone lines, a personal computer with a high-speed modem, color monitor, electronic writing tablet, microphone and speakers (photograph courtesy of University of Wisconsin-Extension).*

Two-Way Interactive Television (I-TV)

Begun in 1980 in a cluster of schools surrounding Eagle Bend, Minnesota, the simplest form of two-way interactive television involved the two-way transmission of video and audio signals from a host site to one or more remote sites. Full interactivity was possible with the technology, but its reliance on new and emerging transmission technologies made it very expensive. With the assistance of the Minnesota Technology Demonstration Sites program in the mid-1980s, the first fifty-eight Minnesota school districts installed two-way interactive systems, paving the way for cross-district course offerings. Today, fiber optic telephone lines are the transmission medium of choice and more than 150 districts in Minnesota have implemented two-way interactive

TV systems. Most other states have now implemented or are experimenting with two-way interactive systems to some extent.

Clusters or networks usually involving three to ten schools serve as the joint decision-making entity by which needed classes are identified, teachers are recruited, and student needs are met. At the secondary level, I-TV technology provides high school, advanced placement, dual credit, and/or college courses to high school students within a network. A teacher located at any one of the network schools provides instruction to students at that site as well as to students located at one to four additional sites. Teacher-student communication is two-way and instantaneous — students and teachers can both see and hear each other at all times. The potential for immediate and full interactivity is the key difference between interactive TV and other distance learning technologies such as audiographics or instruction by satellite (see Table 1.1).

Photograph 1.2. Teacher perspective of an I-TV classroom. The teacher in a two-way interactive television sees both the local students and the remote students. The system shown here uses one large monitor to show remote sites in quadrants of the screen. In this class remote students are located at three different sites. Two-way I-TV allows the teacher to see, hear, and interact with students at all sites, local and remote (photograph by J. Scott Christianson).

Photograph 1.3. *Remote student perspective of an I-TV classroom. Remote students in an I-TV classroom can see, hear, and interact not only with the teacher and students at the originating site, but also with the students at other remote sites; note teacher in upper left-hand quadrant (photograph by J. Scott Christianson).*

Photograph 1.4. *Perspective of students at originating site. The students attending an I-TV course at the same site as the teacher can interact with the students at the remote sites as well as the local teacher (photograph by J. Scott Christianson).*

Table 1.1. Interactivity, Cost and Availability of Distance Learning Technologies.

Distance Learning Technology	Level of Interaction	Relative Cost	Availability
Correspondence	Delayed Two-Way Written Interaction	Least Expensive	Worldwide; dependent on mail service
Instruction by Satellite	One-Way Interaction[a] • Teacher to Student		Anywhere within satellite range, e.g., Northern Hemisphere
Audiographic Tele-Learning	Two-Way via Computer Screen and Telephone		Access to phone lines required
Two-Way Interactive Television	Simultaneous Two-Way Interaction • Teacher to Student • Student to Teacher • Student to Student	Most Expensive	Dependent on phone company or other copper or fiber optic line providers

[a]Student to teacher interaction can be increased by using telephones.

Because of its immediacy, two-way interactive television can be an exciting and highly effective instructional methodology. The level of student-to-student and student-to-teacher interactivity increases the amount of instructional time-on-task beyond that seen in other distance learning technologies. As a result of the instantaneous interactivity afforded by I-TV, students can immediately receive teacher (or student) response to questions as they arise. Thus, student frustration, often apparent in less interactive forms of distance learning, is greatly decreased.

DISTANCE LEARNING EVALUATION: A NORTH DAKOTA CROSS-TECHNOLOGY STUDY

During the 1989–1990 academic year, a study in North Dakota evaluated the effectiveness of different distance learning technologies

(Hobbs, 1990). Twenty-eight school districts were involved in the study, each using some form of distance learning: twelve utilized instruction by satellite (two with the TI-IN Network in Texas, five with the Satellite Educational Resources Consortium in North Carolina, and five with Oklahoma State University); nine utilized two-way interactive television (four with an analog system and five with a digital system); and seven of the school districts used an audiographic tele-learning system.

With the assistance of the North Dakota Department of Public Instruction and Mayville State University, questionnaires were mailed to (1) the administrator at each school who was most familiar with the program; (2) the program coordinator for each course—the person in the local school responsible for coordinating or supervising the course; (3) all students enrolled in each distance learning course; and (4) the remote instructors involved in each course originating from North Dakota. In addition, national standardized tests were administered to all North Dakota distance learning students enrolled in Spanish I and German I. (The two language courses were chosen because of the large number of students enrolled in those courses, the existence of a national standardized test in those subjects, and the offering of the courses across multiple distance learning technologies.)

The study reported several major conclusions:

- Students do not all experience the same level of success in a given distance learning format, just as all students do not succeed equally well in a traditional classroom.
- The degree to which the technology mimics a traditional classroom—that is, allows for immediate or nearly immediate student-teacher verbal and visual interaction—reduces the level of student frustration and increases the willingness of students to enroll in other distance learning courses.
- In order to insure maximum student success in distance learning courses, three elements must be in place: (1) full implementation of the technology and all instructional components; (2) an adequate student support system in the remote classroom; and (3) high student motivation.
- When considering the issues of cost, student achievement, coordinator and administrator satisfaction with the technology, frequency of student-teacher interaction, and existence of technical or other problems, two-way interactive television emerged as the preferred technology, followed by audiographic tele-learning and instruction by satellite.

While a statistically valid comparison between distance learning and traditional instruction was not possible, the North Dakota study provided strong evidence that distance learning *per se* appears to be neither inferior nor superior as an instructional methodology. However, its use is most logical where curricular needs exceed the capability to provide needed courses by traditional means. The question most relevant to the rural school considering distance learning is not "How does distance learning compare with traditional instruction?" but rather "What benefits are accrued by being able to offer a particular course at all?"

The study further concludes that statewide promotion of one method of distance learning over another may not be in the best interest of any district or its students. All technologies are not created equal; for a school to gain maximum educational benefit from a distance learning technology, it must be fully implemented both technically and instructionally and be designed to meet local needs under local conditions. In other words, the technology must be driven by, and responsive to, local need.

Sidebar 1.1. Course Interest Survey (CIS) Conducted across Missouri I-TV Districts

Three clusters of rural Missouri high schools formed I-TV networks during the summer of 1993. These were the first fully interactive networks in the state. A total of twenty-three high school and dual-credit classes were offered to approximately 300 students during the first year of operation— including twelve advanced science and math courses.

John Wedman of the University of Missouri, Columbia, Department of Education, administered a Course Interest Survey (developed by John M. Keller and Raja Subhiyah) to participating students. The survey was designed to measure how students perceive the motivational aspects of a specific course in four basic constructs—attention, relevance, confidence and satisfaction.

"Motivational reaction as measured by the CIS show that [I-TV] students were generally motivated, with the composite mean at 3.46 on a 5-point Likert scale" (University of Missouri, 1994). Confidence was the only component in which there was a statistical difference between the responses of remote and home-site Missouri I-TV students, leading to the conclusion that physical proximity of teacher to student has no effect on attention factors, perceived relevance of instruction, or course satisfaction.

When compared with CIS data from other studies the composite score for attention, relevance, confidence and satisfaction ranked two-way interactive television (3.46) above one-way satellite (3.43), correspondence with text and media (3.29), and correspondence with text only (3.12) (Wedman, 1994).

Similar studies have concluded that among the distance learning technologies available today, the interaction in a two-way interactive television system most closely resembles the dynamics of a traditional classroom (Johnson, O' Connor, Rossing, 1984; Ellis and Mathis, 1985; Garrison, 1987).

POTENTIAL OF I-TV FOR REVITALIZING RURAL EDUCATION

While small schools have not always been widely appreciated, certain advantages of attending and teaching in small schools are well documented (see Table 1.2). These and other assets of smallness are important reasons why diversity in school size should be encouraged. However, the educational limitations of smallness are significant.

I-TV technology can enable small schools to overcome many of the limitations of smallness while retaining their assets. Table 1.2 lists

Table 1.2. Advantages of Small Schools and Limitations That Can Be Overcome through I-TV.

Advantages of Small Schools	Limitations Addressable through I-TV
Higher potential for community-based education and an integrated learning environment	Inability to offer advanced science, math, and foreign language courses due to cost and limited student demand
High student achievement, controlling for socio-economic status (Hobbs, 1989)	Difficulty in meeting increased course requirements for college admission
Potential for high level of individual attention	Inability to attract or retain quality teachers due to non-competitive salary schedule
Small class size	
High levels of student participation in school activities	Inability to find or hire teachers certified in multiple curricular areas
Good conditions for organizational creativity	Problems associated with matching qualifications of existing teachers with changing curricular demands
High level of parent and community involvement	
Strong sense of belonging among students and teachers	Inflexibility of course schedule; only one section of advanced courses available to students
Low level of administrative bureaucracy	

several of the limitations facing schools in rural America that can be addressed by two-way interactive television technology.

Two-way I-TV can bring enhanced course offerings to any school regardless of small size or remote location. In addition, the ability to link high schools to higher education institutions via I-TV creates unprecedented opportunities for dual credit college courses for high school seniors, expert teaching input for advanced high school courses, special programming opportunities for teacher inservice, and a wealth of guest lecture and other ''virtual'' learning experiences.

While distance learning has more applicability to smaller or rural districts, two-way I-TV capabilities can allow larger or urban districts the flexibility to offer multiple sections of any course taught by one or several different teachers. This could potentially eliminate student scheduling conflicts and allow students to take many more advanced courses not traditionally taught because of low enrollments. With the eventual linkage of I-TV clusters it becomes possible to have a different inter-cluster configuration of schools participating in each class. This would enable districts to link with other schools wishing to offer a particular class at a particular time of the day, regardless of whether the schools were members of the same original I-TV network.

Sidebar 1.2. A Rural Student's Perspective, by T. Bryan Leimkühler

I am very happy to have participated in the Interactive Television program offered at Slater High School. It has given me opportunities that I never would have thought possible at a small rural school. It has also had a significant effect on my college plans and career plans.

When I entered high school, I knew I wanted to try new subjects in addition to the standard courses which were required to graduate. One particular interest of mine was to learn the language of my progenitors—German. Unfortunately, Spanish was the only foreign language course available at our poorly funded high school, and I was forced to settle for training in that language.

By some wonderful circumstance, the interactive television network was installed in our school. This offered high-ranking students a chance to escape the standard curriculum and to pursue more interesting and demanding subjects like German language, chemistry, anatomy/physiology, and physics. Naturally, I applied for a position in the German 101 class right away.

My experiences in the dual-credit German 101 and German 102 courses conducted by Professor Eldon Wahlers were very positive. The pace and gravity of the classes were more academically stimulating for me than those of any other class I had taken in high school. Dr. Wahlers pushed me hard and taught me lessons in the conduct of a more serious classroom that proved valuable once I began taking classes at Southwest Missouri State University (SMSU). The most valuable lesson he taught me was to take responsibility for myself regarding my education. He was a kind and patient professor, but he was not interested in excuses!

Interacting with students from other high schools and from Central Methodist College via I-TV was also an interesting aspect of the network. Besides coming to know people from other areas, we came to know the idiosyncrasies of the system. It was a bit strange at first to start class by "training" (initializing) the system and by adjusting the cameras and the volume. Occasionally, we would come to class able to hear the professor, but not able to see him . . . or vice versa.

The biggest change from the normal operation of class, I believe, was all the correspondence we handled—by mail and by facsimile. Our greatest problems came not from the physical absence of the instructor, but timing the correspondence and eliminating "echo" (audio feedback) from the system.

Overall, I would rate the interactive television network and the instruction I received highly. I did miss having the teacher physically present, but the images and sounds produced through the network were adequate.

Upon adjusting to the system, I found the German language course to be my favorite class. This had a profound effect on my goals and plans for my higher education here at SMSU. Based on my experiences in German 101 and German 102, I have decided to continue my studies in German language. I even plan to study abroad for a year in Marburg, Germany. All this, plus the pleasure I derived from studying the German language and becoming fluent in this language, would not have been possible without Professor Wahlers and the interactive television network.

Interactive television is one of the best things that has ever happened to Slater High School. Not only has it greatly enhanced the curriculum and made learning more worthwhile at the Slater School District, it has broadened the horizons of its students.

SUMMARY OF I-TV ATTRIBUTES

Some common attributes of two-way I-TV instruction include:

- It promotes formation of school district clusters that band together to offer a common set of advanced or low-enrollment courses to their students.
- Each I-TV classroom is equipped to send and receive continuous full-motion video and audio signals, resulting in an environment

which closely approximates a traditional classroom—the remote teacher and all students can see and hear each other at all times.

- Because teachers can see all students simultaneously at all times, it is not necessary to have continuous supervision by a classroom coordinator at the remote site(s).
- Because all two-way I-TV sites can both send and receive audio and video transmissions, each school within the cluster can originate one or more classes, thereby equalizing the relationship among cooperating districts.
- Outside high school class hours, additional uses of the I-TV system can include adult education, business and agency seminars, teacher in-service workshops, school administrator meetings, athletic directors' meetings, etc.; the use of the system is only limited by the user's imagination.

GLOBAL TECHNOLOGY, LOCAL INITIATIVE

I-TV is a valuable educational technology, but it should not be viewed as a solution in itself. As Terry Woronov (1994) explains in "Six Myths about the Uses of Educational Technology," technology alone cannot be the means for school reform. Administrators, parents, and teachers can be easily seduced into believing that technology will cause desirable changes in their school; that message is often conveyed by technology manufacturers. However, technology alone will not necessarily ensure desired results. For example, I-TV will not improve a teacher's performance or infuse new teaching methods into the curriculum. An instructor who performs poorly in a traditional classroom will be just as uninspiring in an I-TV classroom.

New technology, when coupled with well planned and supportive implementation, can facilitate radical change. For example, I-TV is an ideal medium in which to experiment with moving away from lecture oriented teaching methods toward more innovative techniques such as cooperative learning and authentic instruction. However, if teachers are not given the appropriate training and support to integrate these methods into their classrooms, they will likely resort back to the methods with which they are most familiar and comfortable. This may be satisfactory for many schools, but the opportunity to couple adoption of I-TV with teacher training in new instructional methods should not be overlooked.

Sidebar 1.3. Six Myths about the Uses of Educational Technology, by Terry Woronov

Computer Technology is fast becoming an almost universal presence in education. Ninety-eight percent of U.S. schools now have at least some computers. The ratio of computers to students is increasing across the country, and continued growth is expected in purchases of hardware, software, and related equipment such as videodisk players and CD-ROM technology.

The push to get more and more computers into schools has been fueled in part by the belief that their mere presence will make good things happen (and by aggressive marketing by hardware and software manufacturers). A variety of studies, however, tell us that computers in themselves do not automatically change the nature of teaching and learning; rather, it is the way teachers integrate computers into classrooms, the content of technology-aided lessons, and the quality of software programs selected that determine whether and how computers in schools really benefit students.

Computers have proved valuable in supporting inquiry-based science teaching, inclusion of students with disabilities in regular classes, interdistrict collaboration, distance learning, and the dissemination of professional development materials. At the same time, certain myths about the magic of technology persist. Six widely held beliefs, in particular, are worth examining closely.

Myth #1: Computers are here to stay, so we have to get as many of them as possible into classrooms, as quickly as possible.

Larry Cuban of Stanford University argues that computers are merely the most recent in a long line of technologies that have been promoted in schools, beginning with radio and television. As with these earlier technologies, decisions to integrate computers into education are often made without much thought about the reasons for doing so—that is, how they fit into the wider goals of education—and without a clear understanding of the benefits they are supposed to produce.

"Before technology can be used effectively," says Martha Stone Wiske of the Educational Technology Center at Harvard, "everyone involved in education—teachers, students, principals, school board members, parents, and communities—needs to think carefully about why we want to use technology, and what we hope to accomplish with it."

Myth #2: Educational technology would be used more widely, and more effectively, but for resistance from technophobic teachers.

A "phobia" is an irrational fear. But there is nothing irrational about teachers being afraid of looking stupid in front of students who know more about computers than they do; similarly, the difficulties of integrating computers into daily classroom practice with no system support are not imaginary.

Blaming teachers for the failure of technology to change education is a common historical theme, says Larry Cuban. The blame usually centers on the teacher's inability to integrate the technology into classroom practice. But many teachers face formidable barriers in learning about computers. Relatively few pre-service programs for new teachers include more than a cursory introduction to technology. Neither is time generally available for in-service education about technology. Equipment and services that industry takes for granted—such as a computer and phone on every desk, access to a systems manager to help with programs and questions, and time on the job to learn new systems—generally do not exist in schools.

Myth #3: Using and programming computers teaches children "thinking" and "problem-solving" skills.

The research jury is still out on this claim. In 1992, Aqeel Ahmed reviewed 21 empirical studies on the effects of students having learned to program computers. Each of the studies attempted to measure the students' "cognitive abilities." Ten of the 21 studies showed no effect on students' "cognition," while the other 11 detected some benefits. But in every case, "cognitive abilities" was defined differently. Moreover, Ahmed found significant problems of methodology and reporting in all 21 studies.

Similarly, there is as yet no definitive evidence of the cognitive benefits of other uses of computers, such as multimedia, "edutainment," or hypertext (a computerized form of text that provides multiple options for calling up related texts and annotations). Indeed, researchers are still trying to determine what kinds of cognitive benefits may result from using new technologies and how to measure those benefits.

The authors of a longitudinal study of high school students enrolled in a "high access to technology" program conducted through Apple Classrooms of Tomorrow argue that, by using computers extensively in class, students acquire cognitive skills other than those measured by traditional indices. For example, they found that students had learned how to integrate graphics, animation, and hypertext into their written texts. The authors also assert that these students had improved ability to work in groups and to integrate large amounts of information, and had increased self-confidence. But did these activities and skills help the students to understand and reflect on important ideas, or to communicate clearly in speech and writing? No answer.

Myth #4: Wider use of technological resources like the Internet will help remedy inequities in U.S. education.

While the Internet provides unprecedented access to information and resources around the world, only selected students currently have access to these computer tools. Henry Jay Becker's 1989%1991 study of computer use across the country found inequities based on race, gender, tracking, urban versus rural districts, and subject area. In an earlier study, Becker also found that students in lower tracks were often restricted to drill-and-practice work on computers, while "brighter" students were more frequently taught to use computers as tools for accomplishing other educational tasks.

The latest data show that the hardware gap is closing, with minimal differences in numbers of computers and student-computer ratios in schools across the country—except in Hispanic-majority schools. The new equity gap, according to Becker, is in the use of telecommunications and in computer expertise. Poorer school districts and black-majority schools have largely been "left out of the loop" when it comes to telecommunications, he says.

Myth #5: Increased use of technology in classrooms will inevitably bring about systemic school reform.

Many advocates of educational computing claim that computer use will, by itself, cause a dramatic change in teaching and learning by promoting critical thinking and inquiry-based problem solving. But simply putting a computer in a classroom does not necessarily change anything. Computers are commonly used in traditional, unconstructive ways—for drill and practice, as electronic worksheets, and as rewards for good behavior.

Some innovative schools are using technology to support efforts to reexamine the purposes and potential of education, but it is a mistake to assume that the technology itself is driving the process of change. Michael Eisenberg, director of the ERIC Clearinghouse for Information and Technology, warns educators not to have unrealistic expectations for technology. "Schools are complex institutions," he says. "Learning and teaching are complex processes. Technology is essential because it pervades our society. But it is only a means. Technology itself will not change or reform education."

Myth#6: Kids love to use computers—so they must be learning.

Until relatively recently, most adults assumed that serious learning in school had to be unpleasant. Only in recent decades have educators come to believe that learning can and often should be fun. Computer use in schools is sometimes justified because students enjoy it. But just being engaged by computers doesn't necessarily mean that students are learning anything important from them.

Excerpted with permission from *The Harvard Educational Letter,* Vol X, No. 5, September/October 1994, pp.1 – 3. Copyright © 1994 by the President and Fellows of Harvard College. All rights reserved.

To be sure that educational technology is selected and used appropriately—that it meets local needs and priorities—administrators and teachers need to invest time in learning about its capabilities and limitations. Recently, schools have shown a frenzy of interest in gaining access to the Internet, sometimes with the presupposition that if they are connected to the "information superhighway" they will no longer need to maintain their current libraries or acquire new reference materials. Internet access, however, cannot replace a school library. If administrators were to learn about the true capabilities—and liabilities—of the Internet, many might choose to invest their resources, human and financial, in other ventures.

The point is not that Internet access is undesirable, but rather that the adoption of any new technology for education is best undertaken with full awareness of user needs and the capabilities and limitations of the technology available.

As potential users of new technological tools, educators and administrators must continually upgrade their knowledge base regarding educational technologies. In the next chapter, we explore in detail the technology behind two-way interactive television.

CHAPTER 2

I-TV Technology Options

AN I-TV network is an integrated technology system with two main components—the classroom equipment and the transmission network. The classroom equipment includes the video, audio and control devices found in the I-TV studio. The transmission network encompasses all the lines, switches and other devices required to transfer signals between sites. This chapter provides a general overview of several common I-TV technologies starting with the classroom equipment and then covering several types of transmission networks.

CLASSROOM EQUIPMENT

All I-TV studios have the following essential pieces of equipment: cameras, microphones, television monitors, speakers, and a control unit. Figure 2.1 shows a diagram of a typical room layout. Optional pieces of equipment include a facsimile machine and telephone, VCR, laserdisk player, computer, audio tape player, additional cameras, and other video inputs.

Most I-TV networks are designed to be symmetrical. That is, each I-TV classroom is capable of being both a teaching, or originating, site and a receiving, or remote, site. In addition, all I-TV classrooms in a network should have identical pieces of equipment placed in approximately the same position at each site.

Cameras

Each I-TV classroom typically has three cameras: one focusing on the teacher (teacher camera); one focusing on the class (student camera); and one showing what is displayed on the teacher's desktop (graphics or

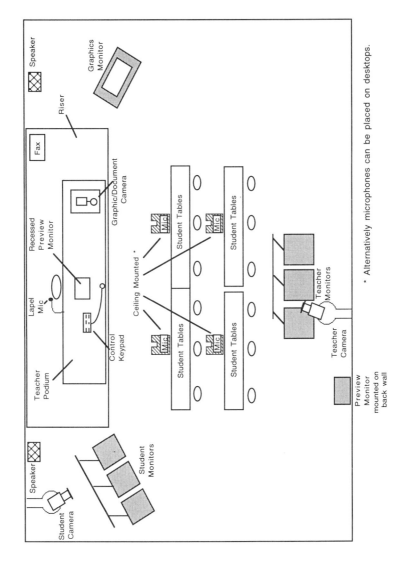

Figure 2.1. Diagrams of two classroom layouts: (a) a typical classroom arrangement in a network that uses a multi-monitor system (remote sites are viewed on banks of monitors).

20

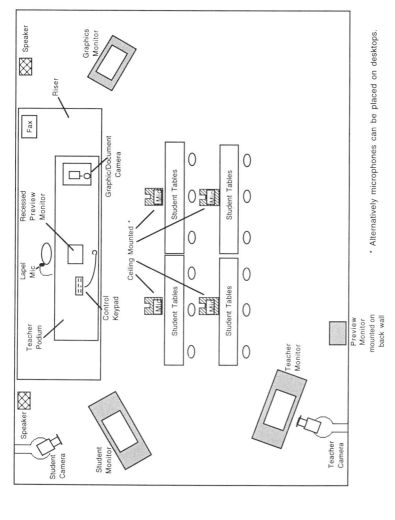

Figure 2.1 (continued). Diagrams of two classroom layouts: (b) is different in that all remote sites are viewed in quadrants on one large monitor.

* Alternatively microphones can be placed on desktops.

21

0156417

document camera). The graphics camera is seen by many I-TV teachers as one of the greatest assets of I-TV technology—it allows students to clearly see anything that is written or displayed on the teacher's desktop [see Photograph 2.1(a)].

The teacher at the originating site can control where the cameras are pointed, and can zoom in on one student or zoom out to view the entire classroom. [With certain systems, the teacher can control cameras only at the local site; other systems allow teacher control of camera functions at all sites, both local and remote.] Cameras are controlled by the use of pan, tilt, and zoom (PTZ) units on which the cameras are mounted, as shown in Photograph 2.1(b). The PTZ units can be controlled through a teacher control pad. PTZ units can also be purchased with a "Follow Me" feature. With the "Follow Me" system, the teacher wears a marker on his/her collar. The PTZ units sense the marker and follow it as the teacher moves, aiming the cameras so that the teacher is always in view.

The graphics or document camera does not need panning and tilting capabilities. Camera focusing is handled by specialized lenses that can either focus automatically or be focused remotely by the teacher via a control pad. Through the use of the desktop control pad, the teacher also has full control over which video source—student, teacher, document camera, or other source—is displayed over the system, see Photograph 2.2(b).

Monitors

The number and placement of monitors in an I-TV studio will depend on the technology chosen and the design of the transmission network. Borrowed from videoconferencing design, some educational applications (most often involving post-secondary use) have used a single monitor per classroom on which all other sites can only be viewed on a timed, sequenced, or intermittent basis. Often, the last site from which audio was received remains in view until a student from another site speaks. Most K−12 applications, however, make it possible for the teacher and all local and remote students to see each other simultaneously.

Most I-TV systems that allow for simultaneous viewing of all sites use a multi-monitor setup of two banks of four or five TV monitors in each classroom, see Figure 2.1(a). One of these monitors shows the teacher, while each of the remote sites is displayed on a separate monitor. The

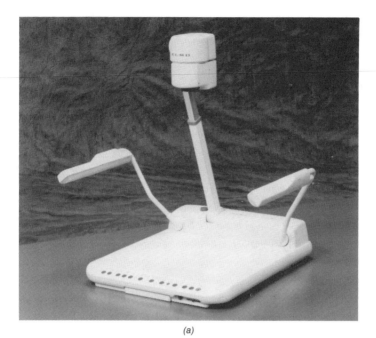

(a)

(b)

Photograph 2.1. *Document camera and pan, tilt, and zoom unit. The document or graphics camera (a) allows the instructor to show a wide variety of text and graphics; in the I-TV classroom, the document camera replaces the traditional blackboard (photograph courtesy of ELMO Corporation). Cameras in I-TV classrooms are mounted on pan, tilt, and zoom (b) units, allowing for a full range of movement control by the instructor (photograph by J. Scott Christianson).*

(a)

(b)

Photograph 2.2. I-TV control system and I-TV control pad. The equipment in the
I-TV classroom is controlled by a "master" computer (a) (photograph courtesy of
AMX corporation). This device communicates with the other pieces of I-TV equipment—the video switcher, CODEC, echo canceller, and PTZ units. Control pads
for this type of control system can be customized to meet the needs of local
conditions and equipment (b) (photograph by J. Scott Christianson).

restriction of four to five student monitors (and therefore four to five sites) is an educational, rather than a technical restriction. Beyond four to five total sites, it becomes difficult to visually maintain contact with all of the remote students.

The monitors that allow students to view the teacher and each other are usually located below the teacher's desk or podium, or are suspended from the ceiling in the front of the room. The second bank of monitors is usually mounted overhead and behind or above the students to allow the teacher to view all remote site classrooms.

A small additional monitor, usually located on or in the teacher podium, allows instructors to preview the outgoing video to ensure that it appears as intended. In some systems, an additional preview monitor is located in the back of the room. This enables the teacher to maintain eye contact with students throughout instruction (and still be aware of the outgoing signal) without feeling "tied" to the preview monitor inside or on the podium.

A relatively recent technology which allows for the continuous viewing of all remote sites on a single monitor is the quad-split system. In this design two very large (35 to 45 inch) monitors are placed in position for student and teacher viewing [Figure 2.1(b)]. During a class involving more than two sites, the image at the originating site is split into four quadrants, each showing the image of a different remote classroom. At the remote sites the teacher appears in the upper left-hand quadrant and the other remote classrooms appear in the other quadrants (see Photographs 1.3 and 1.4 in Chapter 1). In this situation, the teacher usually has the ability to display any one of the quadrants, including his/her own image, as a full screen image at any time. This configuration allows simultaneous viewing – all sites being able to see all other sites at all times – in some digital technologies in which multiple monitors cannot be used.

In addition to the monitors displaying images of the teacher and remote students, a "graphics" monitor is usually included in the classroom. This medium-sized television displays either still images or a live feed from the document camera. This allows the teacher to display an item – for example, a dissected frog or a course outline – on the graphics monitor, while remaining visible to remote students. The capability to simultaneously view the teacher and a graphic can dramatically increase the interest and attention of remote students. (A picture in a picture device can also be used to simultaneously display graphics and the teacher on a signal monitor; one video source is viewed in a small window, while the other is projected full screen.)

Audio Components

In Figure 2.1, there are two types of microphones in the I-TV room. Usually four to six student microphones are positioned to pick up student voices. These can either be mounted in the ceiling or on the table or desktops. Neither option, however, is without potential problems. Some students may tend to talk with their heads angled down, and depending on their confidence, too softly for a ceiling microphone to detect. Microphones on the desktops have the advantage of being able to pick up student voices well, but they also detect all paper and book movement, often causing a distracting level of background noise. (Desktop microphones are usually mounted on a table-top stand to reduce the amount of noise they pick up.) Ceiling microphones have the advantage of being placed out of the way, but can be less satisfactory at picking up softer voice levels or in the margins of the room.

A lapel microphone is usually worn by the teacher; in some cases a desktop microphone may also be used. In order to compensate for differences in the tone and pitch of voices, the lapel microphone should be adjusted by the teacher at the beginning of each class. Lapel microphones can either be wired to the console or wireless. Wireless microphones are often preferred because they allow the teacher to move freely about the room without having to remove the microphone. However, that same mobility can allow a teacher to unknowingly walk out of the I-TV room after class, still wearing the microphone.

A minimum of two speakers is located in the I-TV classroom. They are placed away from the student microphones to reduce audio feedback into the system. When the audio is improperly balanced or where speaker and microphone location is not optimized, the room microphones may pick up the audio from the speakers, amplify it and resend the signal out over the system, creating an audio loop-back. Depending on how the audio is transmitted, an imbalance in the audio system will show up as either feedback (a loud buildup of sound) or as an echo. Thus, it is vitally important that the volume of the speakers be properly balanced with the sensitivity (gain) of the microphones in the room.

In networks where audio is transmitted without delay, that is, in real time, the audio systems may experience feedback if the microphones are set too high or if the speakers are too loud. This is fairly easy to correct by calibrating the levels of speakers and microphones at all sites on the network, after which, only the lapel or teacher microphone will need to be readjusted as the teacher changes from class period to class period.

For I-TV networks in which the audio signals are compressed, and therefore delayed, echo can be a significant audio problem. A signal can echo back and forth several times until it eventually fades away. It is almost impossible to teach over a network that has severe echo problems – one cannot concentrate when being constantly interrupted by the words that were spoken two seconds before.

Echo cancellers (Figure 2.2) are devices that eliminate echo by comparing the audio being broadcast over the speakers with the audio introduced into the microphones. The echo canceller then attempts to eliminate duplicated signals. Echo cancellers can be either separate, self-contained units, or integrated into the CODECs (part of the transmission system, see below) or microphones. Echo cancellation technology has progressed in recent years and is now very operator friendly and reliable.

Auxiliary Video and Audio Sources

In addition to the three basic cameras in an I-TV classroom, any video source can be displayed over an I-TV system. Live satellite input, interactive laserdisk, CD-ROM, or videotaped programming can be displayed by the teacher while still maintaining a full view of each remote classroom.

NTSC (National Television Standards Committee) composite video is the standard in the United States for video sources and displays such as VCRs, videodisks, and video monitors. Most video formats can be easily converted into NTSC composite video. For example, the video of a

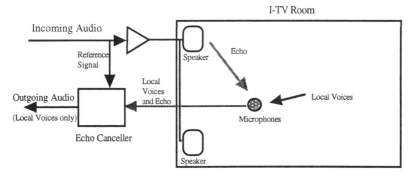

Figure 2.2. Echo canceller operation. Echo cancellers sample the incoming audio and subtract it from the outgoing audio, thereby allowing both microphones and speakers to be active at the same time. Systems without echo cancellers sometimes use "push to talk" microphones, i.e., the remote students must press a button on the microphone to talk to the teacher, or use some other means of determining when the speaker is active.

computer screen, which is often transmitted as a set of signals known as RGB (Red Green Blue — the three primary colors of transmitted light), can be translated to an NTSC signal through the use of a device called a scan converter. Converters (both internal and external) are available for almost every type of computer.

[Note: In some compressed networks, a device called a Time Base Corrector will be required to synchronize the video from auxiliary sources with the CODEC (see below).]

Additional audio sources, with or without accompanying video, can be sent out over the network as well. Audio sources used as inputs to the system should be "line-level," not amplified outputs such as would be used for speakers.

Video Switchers

A video switcher is used to select which video and/or audio source is sent out from any I-TV site. The video switcher is usually controlled by the teacher through a desktop control unit or through a hand-held remote control device.

Switchers are designated by the number of inputs and outputs. For example a 10 × 1 switcher is capable of switching between ten different inputs and sending the designated source through one output. A 10 × 2 switcher sends signals to two outputs simultaneously. These simple switches offer the user only one selection at a time and limit the flexibility of the system.

A matrix switcher is a much more flexible — and expensive — solution for dedicated I-TV rooms. A matrix switcher may actually consist of several simple switchers that are specially wired and controlled or it may be a single device. When properly installed, matrix switchers allow any video or audio input to be sent to any output or to multiple outputs. Most matrix switchers automatically amplify and distribute the video to the designated number of sources, eliminating the need for a large group of external distribution amplifiers.

Classroom Control Unit

To simplify the operation of classroom equipment, all the essential controls are consolidated into a single control unit. The unit consists of a programmable computer capable of controlling other pieces of equipment in the room. The user can then control this "master" unit via a control pad. Photograph 2.2 shows a control system and a custom-built keypad. These systems are flexible and can be expanded relatively easily to control additional pieces of equipment. However, a general rule of thumb is that the more a control unit is consolidated and simplified for the operator to use, the more sophisticated and expensive the control system will be.

Facsimile Machine

A fax machine located in each classroom can transmit and receive paper copies of tests or homework, reducing or eliminating the use of mail or courier as a delivery system. Depending on the restrictions imposed by the technology or the transmission line provider, I-TV networks may be designed with the capability for "in-line" fax transmissions. This allows the school to use the same line for I-TV transmission and for delivering and receiving fax transmissions. Otherwise, a dedicated phone line is placed in the room for the fax machine. This has the advantage of providing the teacher with a telephone for contacting principals and technical personnel, should a problem arise.

SYSTEM DESIGN

Engineering

Obviously, a school district, or even most small telephone companies, will not have the capabilities within their organization to engineer and install an I-TV studio. However, the school's role in system design should be one of an informed consumer. An outside engineering firm should be retained to design and install the classroom equipment and control system. This may often be a service which is contracted for by the telephone company or other transmission line provider. In order to determine what system features will be most useful, potential adopters of I-TV are encouraged to visit several operating networks and to talk with their personnel. Ask both technical and instructional staff to discuss not only the capabilities of their systems, but also which features they most value and which features they would add. (Appendix 1 lists sites willing to host visits from those considering I-TV adoption.)

(a)

(b)

Photograph 2.3. *Example of a turnkey I-TV system. Several companies manufacture videoconferencing and I-TV systems that come "out of the box" ready to connect to the transmission line (a). Most of these systems come with a preconfigured operation system and control pad or remote (b) (photograph courtesy of Compression Labs Incorporated).*

30

Turnkey Systems

Several companies now manufacture "turnkey" I-TV systems; that is, a complete system with the control unit, cameras and monitors all in one integrated unit that is ready to be tied into the transmission line. Photograph 2.3 shows a turnkey system from Compression Labs Incorporated. While this eliminates a lot of the necessary engineering for an I-TV site, it also limits the user to the functions and features designed into the product. Turnkey systems can also be difficult to upgrade because of their integrated design. However, for many applications, a turnkey system will function very well.

Companies offering turnkey systems include:

(1) Interactive Communications International, 26 Wavecrest Ave., Unit A, Linden, NJ 07036
(2) PictureTel Corporation, 222 Rosewood Drive, Danvers, MA 01923
(3) VTEL, 108 Wild Basin Road, Austin, TX 78746
(4) Datapoint, 8400 Datapoint Drive, San Antonio, TX 78229-8500
(5) Compression Labs, Incorporated, 2860 Junction Avenue, San Jose, CA 95134-1900
(6) GrassValley, 13024 Bitnet Springs Road, Nevada City, CA 95959-9017

Sidebar 2.1. Designing an Interactive Distance Learning System, by Richard Kenshalo, Matanuska Telephone Association, Palmer, Alaska

The major participants in a distance learning system design will be the system designer, public or private network supplier of the communication links between facilities (i.e., fiber-optic links, satellite links, microwave links, T1 lines, ISDN, Switched-56 etc.) and the videoconference equipment supplier or systems integrator. Since existing classrooms are normally converted to distance learning classrooms, and many times can not be dedicated to this purpose, careful consideration must be given to the facility location and preparation, as well as to the equipment selection for the audio system, lighting, cameras, and codecs used.

Video Cameras

Camera placement in the distance learning classroom must be given careful consideration. The primary consideration is providing eye contact with the video subjects, giving a "natural" appearance to the video. The instructor camera should be placed in the middle or rear of the room, at a height allowing a natural viewing angle to the instructor's eyes. In a like manner, the student camera should be placed at a location the students will be normally viewing, which will be the monitor displaying the incoming video. Camera height will be naturally placed if the camera is placed at the same height as the incoming video monitor. The camera should also provide a natural "heads up" look for the participants, which can be provided by locating the student's camera as central to the student's seating area as possible. This effect can also be enhanced by providing seating arrangements central to the camera placement. Often, this will result in seating arrangements that may not be traditional (equal rows, etc.), but skewed to fit the room's dimensions and camera placement.

Modern video cameras are typically chip cameras, rather than vacuum tube cameras. All video cameras are not alike, but the most popular are charged-coupled devices (CCDs) that replace the image pick-up tubes and photo conductive sensors of tube cameras with photo diodes. CCDs provide several advantages over tube cameras, including better stability, no image burn, low power consumption, smaller, lighter, and lower cost. Disadvantages of CCDs are that the cameras have lower resolution, and may have image smear problems when shooting a very bright object. The degree of these disadvantages varies according to the quality and cost of the particular camera.

Current chip cameras use either one-chip or three-chip technology. One-chip cameras are smaller and less expensive than three-chip cameras, but typically provide lower performance than three-chip cameras. Chip size also plays a factor in camera performance. One-half inch and two-thirds inch chip sizes are available, with the two-thirds inch chip providing more space for picture processing, resulting in higher resolution and better color detail.

Video camera resolution determines the camera's ability to see fine detail. A resolution of 450 – 600 lines is considered very good, while 330 – 450 lines is considered acceptable for distance learning applications. Overall system resolution (cameras, monitors, codecs) needs to be considered since a high resolution camera used with low resolution monitors or highly compressed video wastes the cameras resolution, and is an unnecessary expense.

Video camera sensitivity, which is measured in lux, is another important consideration. Lux is a measurement of illumination per unit area, and represents the camera's ability to see under low light conditions. Most modern CCD video cameras have the ability to see under low light conditions at 3 lux or below. Under extremely low light conditions, a "faster" lens may be used.

Video Camera Lenses

Video cameras need a lens that covers the subject at the viewing distance available. This is defined as the lens capture angle. For distance learning applications, capture angle for covering students will be larger than the capture angle needed to cover the instructor. Depending on room geometry, a wide angle lens may be required.

In two-thirds inch cameras, the capture angle is calculated by dividing 450 by the focal length of the lens (in mm). In one-half inch cameras, the capture angle is calculated by dividing 320 by the focal length in millimeters. These are only approximations to help find the nearest size lens available. The actual angle will vary as much as 5 degrees. The calculated capture angle can then be used with a dimensional layout of the distance learning classroom to determine the suitability of camera "look angles" at proposed camera placements using proposed lenses.

Zoom lenses can provide variable capture angles. The size of a zoom lens is expressed in focal length ratio and wide angle focal length. For example, a 10 × 8 zoom lens is a lens with an 8 mm wide angle setting that zooms in to ten times that focal length (80 mm). The lens has a focal length ranging from 8 mm to 80 mm (with a capture angle ranging from 46 degree to 4.6 degree for a two-third inch chip camera).

Other lens characteristics will be expressed in terms of focal length and f-stop. The lower the f-stop number for a lens, the more light it can pass. An f-stop number of 1.4 is considered to be good for any video camera. A lens with a number above 1.4 might work, depending on the sensitivity of the camera and how well the facility is illuminated. Lenses with maximum f-stops in the 1.8−2.3 range will work effectively with cameras with 25 lux sensitivity in a very well lit room.

Automatic or remote lens control is also useful. Automatic iris (f-stop), and remote focus and zoom should be considered when there is no easy way to manually control lens settings. Most lenses offer automatic iris control for varying illumination situations. Lens control, paired with camera control, provides the maximum flexibility for pan, tilt, focus, and zoom to enhance distance learning dialogue. Both local and remote camera controls are desirable.

Video Monitors

It must be kept in mind that video monitors are different from most household televisions that receive VHF/CATV modulated video and audio (broadcast or CATV). Video monitors display unmodulated, or baseband NTSC video, and audio must be provided separately.

Video monitors primarily use picture brightness and picture clarity as measures of monitor quality. Picture brightness is measured in foot-lamberts, and is a measure of viewing quality in a well lit room. Monitor brightness of 200−350 foot-lamberts is considered necessary when viewing in a well lit room. Picture clarity is a function of monitor resolution, and is a measure of the monitor to display fine detail. Horizontal resolution of 350−450 lines is considered ideal, with 300−350 lines being acceptable. Again, camera and monitor resolution, and video compression, should be used to determine the monitor resolution required.

Video monitor picture size is related to the participant's viewing distance, which is a function of the room's dimensions. The recommended monitor viewing distance is 2 to 5 times the picture size, measured diagonally. A total viewing angle of 45 degrees will also allow fairly undistorted viewing, and matches a lens capture angle of 45 degrees, if the camera is placed very close to the monitor. Standard picture tube, or direct view monitors, can be found in diagonal sizes up to about 40 inch.

Monitors should be placed at a height that allows the participants to see without being blocked by other participants, while being low enough to not cause undue neck strain and discomfort. Step seating in the participant area can help mitigate these tight constraints on monitor placement, allowing lower monitor placement, along with unobstructed viewing.

In summary, the specifications of brightness, picture size, and horizontal resolution can be used to narrow down comparisons of video monitors. The remainder of the decision is subjective, based on room dimensions, and viewing arrangements. Correct monitor choices with emphasis on correct placement will significantly enhance the distance learning process.

Video Codecs

Inter-operability of video codecs can be an issue of concern, if links to other distance learning networks or videoconference networks are to be eased. The ITU (CCITT) H.261 videoconference standard for codecs, also known as Px64, recommends a set of algorithms for video compression, based on Discrete Cosine Transform (DCT) technology. The standard compresses the video to a variety of data rates from 64 K-bps to 2.048 Mbps, in increments of 64 K-bps. Higher data rates result in better quality video. The compressed video resolution standard specified in H.261 is the Common Intermediate Format (CIF). Full CIF (FCIF) has a frame rate of 30 frames per second, each with a resolution of 288 lines by 352 pixels. A second format, Quarter CIF (QCIF), can be used for small screens, and specifies a frame rate of 15 frames per second, each with a resolution of 144 lines by 176 pixels. Compressed video rates at or below 384 K-bps, will generally use QCIF. Based on pixels and frame rates, FCIF represents an approximate 10 to 1 improvement over QCIF in terms of picture quality.

The H.261 standard for video codecs is part of a family of standards known as H.320, which is made up of five individual standards. The family of standards covers video and audio compression, graphics, multi-point videoconferencing, encryption, and other features such as far-end camera control. The five standards cover techniques for video and audio compression, display resolutions for video, and where the digitally compressed information is placed in the digital bit stream. The five standards that presently make up H.320 include: H.261 which defines the video coding algorithms; H.221 which covers frame placement of the compressed digital video and audio; H.242 which defines the communications protocol; H.230 which defines control and administration information structure; and H.231 which defines a Multi-point Control Unit (MCU) and allows links of three or more H.320 compliant codecs to participate in a multi-point videoconference. A complement to H.231, H.243 defines the control procedures between a H.213 compliant MCU and other H.320 compliant codecs for multi-point videoconferences.

New standards are also being developed, such as G.728, defining 16

K-bps audio, a necessary addition for low bit-rate codecs. Present methods of audio compression specified by G.711 and G.722, provides for toll quality, audio compression at 64 kbps (3 kHz or 7 kHz). When H.320 codecs are used at data rates of 112 to 128 kbps, audio can take up one half of the available data rate. G.728 will fill a void in H.320 by providing a much needed common method of compressing audio for low data rate codecs.

Encryption techniques are also being specified by H.233. This defines both the encryption technique to be used, and how the encryption key is passed from one site to another.

The H.320 standard is the building block for video codec interoperability. Non-compliant video codecs can create islands of user groups, isolated from compliant codecs. Higher bandwidth digital codecs (DS-3), and non-compliant video codecs require the use of gate-ways, or back-to-back video codecs, to link systems utilizing different coding and compression techniques.

The selection of a video codec is a very subjective process, and must be accomplished by considering the distance learning environment, network infrastructure available, and weighing the costs involved with the equipment and transmission facilities. Distance learning environments, particularly $K-12$, require video codecs with good motion-handling capabilities. Better motion-handling capabilities require higher bit-rates and larger transmission bandwidths, with simpler compression algorithms (DS-3), and less expensive codecs. The advantages of DS-3 encoded video are superior quality of video and audio, low codec cost, and the overhead capabilities that can include embedded T-1 and other sub-rate data circuits. These are highly useful for facsimile, voice, and interactive computer networking, greatly enhancing distance learning capabilities. Higher transmission costs continue to limit wide-spread application of high bit-rate codecs, while high codec costs continue to limit wide-spread application of T-1 "near broadcast" quality codecs.

In summary, video codec cost is a direct function of the complexity of the compression algorithm, which should be weighed against the cost of the required transmission facility for the digitally encoded video signal. Standard-compliant video codecs offer internetworking advantages, which must be weighed against the amount of compression that can be tolerated for the distance learning environment, and the cost of the video codec. The amount of video compression used, also determines the resolution required of video cameras, and video monitors.

Audio Systems

The most difficult problem in the design of distance learning classrooms is the design of the classroom's audio system. Since these classrooms are nearly always converted from existing classrooms, feedback, noise, echo, and hollowness can present problems to the audio system that can be very difficult to overcome. Careful planning, and expenditures for acoustic treatment, can provide low cost solutions for the distance learning classroom. Alternatively, consulting with acoustic experts could prove to be a wise choice.

Three types of audio mixing/amplifiers are generally used in the distance learning classroom. These are microphone mixing amplifiers, line-level mixing/pre-amplifiers, and power amplifiers. These audio amplifiers and sound mixers allow the classroom designer the needed flexibility to properly engineer the room's audio system, and also provide flexibility needed to deal with the many acoustic problems that will exist in the distance learning classroom.

Microphone mixing amplifiers allow the designer to control the many microphones required in the distance learning classroom, and usually allow adjustments for sound gating thresholds, multiple gating attenuation, and frequency/gain attenuation of the individual microphones. Because of the large number of microphones that exist in the distance learning classroom, microphone mixing amplifiers quickly become necessary items.

Line-level mixing amplifiers/pre-amplifiers provide the ability to mix the many audio sources (mic-mixer output, VCRs, audio recording equipment, etc.) with frequency/gain attenuation for each source for presentation to the distance learning network (outgoing audio).

Power amplifiers provide for the ability to drive room speakers, locally amplifying the audio from the remote site, and any locally required audio included as part of a distance learning presentation (VCRs, audio tapes, etc.).

In addition to basic transmitting and receiving of voice signals, points to consider when selecting audio equipment for a distance learning facility include the need for auxiliary inputs and outputs, such as video cassette recorders to record the meeting for future reference and audio recording equipment to record the audio portion of meetings.

The placement of loudspeakers and microphones in each room, and acoustic treatment of the room's surfaces, needs to be controlled in such a way as to diminish, not magnify, any acoustic problems in that room.

Acoustic Feedback

Each room has unique acoustic properties. The acoustic response of a room is determined by the room's physical properties (size, shape, construction materials used), and background audio noise present. The acoustic response of a room determines the room's natural frequency, which is that portion of the audio frequency spectrum that the room will amplify without any help from microphones and amplifiers. It is this self-amplification of the room's natural frequency that is the cause of most acoustic feedback. Determination of the room's natural frequency can provide a big help in reducing feedback in the audio system. In extremely difficult cases, notch filters, or parametric equalizers can be used to filter out the room's natural frequency, helping to eliminate acoustic feedback problems.

The installation of acoustic panels or drapes helps to reduce reflected sound, and should be strategically placed based on the locations of sound sources (loudspeakers) and sound regenerators (microphones). Floor carpeting, and acoustic ceiling tiles can provide a significant help in reducing acoustic feedback. These floor and ceiling treatments can even be applied to walls, providing economic solutions to the problem of acoustic feedback.

Acoustic feedback can also be reduced by "de-sensitizing" the feedback generators, or sources and generators of sound. In each distance learning classroom, these are simply the microphones and speakers. Because of the large number of participant microphones present in the distance learning classroom, the number of feedback generators is large. Because of the large number of generators, it is best to reduce the system gain in the microphone audio system and compensate or increase the system gain in the outgoing audio gain controls. Since local audio is not amplified locally, this can help reduce the possibility of acoustic feedback. Similarly, speaker volume (incoming volume) should be kept at low, but comfortable levels. All adjustments in the audio system should provide maximum range of control, without introducing feedback. This can be accomplished with an audio system that provides maximum flexibility on all inputs (audio sources) with regard to gain, attenuation, and frequency response, allowing the room's natural frequency to be "filtered" out. The elimination or reduction of acoustic feedback greatly simplifies instructor adjustment of volume controls by allowing greater range of adjustment.

Loudspeaker Placement

Loudspeakers, used for the incoming audio only, should be placed close to the incoming video monitor. This produces a natural effect, since participants look at the monitor and expect to hear the sound in the vicinity of the image they see. The loudspeakers should be aimed away from the microphones, and toward acoustically treated surfaces that will reduce reflections back into the microphones.

Background Noise

The distance learning classroom must have acceptable low levels of background noise (street noise, HVAC, adjacent classroom noise, corridor noise, etc.) that will not interfere with distance learning sessions. Noise from HVAC systems can be compensated for by fitting the room with large, low velocity registers to eliminate some of the noise. HVAC ducts should preferably be round, to eliminate wall vibrations. High levels of background noise may be difficult to cancel, amplifying the noise to the network, and requiring high levels of audio in the classroom. These conditions will contribute to acoustic feedback problems. Mix-minus audio systems, microphone mixers, and gated microphone systems can compensate for some background noise.

Lighting

The distance learning classroom should provide the minimum level of light required for the camera to provide a picture with adequate depth of focus. A classroom that uses bright lights and obtrusive cameras, can make the users feel uneasy and tense. The lighting system should provide the most natural environment possible, and avoid unnecessary seating restrictions due to inadequate light.

Consideration should be given to direction, color temperature, and shielding of lighting equipment. The lighting should not cause shadows on the subjects, and should not cause discomfort due to glare or heat. Lighting direction should be controlled, with light sources facing forward of the participants and above the eye's normal included angle of view, while still maintaining a low enough angle to eliminate facial shadows. Light sources placed directly overhead, without adequate diffusers, can cause facial shadows such as dark eye sockets. Most existing classroom lighting fixtures, with adequate diffusers, will produce acceptable levels of lighting. In some cases, additional lighting such as backlights and fill lights can be used to improve the classroom's lighting quality.

In all cases, care should be used to provide suitable and consistent lighting color temperature for optimal video camera performance. Normal fluorescent lamps found in most classrooms have a color temperature shifted into the blue spectrum. This contributes to a blue shift in the video image as recorded by the video camera. A replacement fluorescent lamp—a typical lamp is a GE Chroma 50 fluorescent lamp—can be used to economically compensate for this, and improve the color temperature of the classroom lighting. This can provide a low cost solution to improving the color temperature of the distance learning classroom, by simply re-lamping existing fixtures.

Lightly colored desk tops should be provided. This will reflect the overhead light up into the participant's faces, reducing facial shadows. The participant's video monitors should be shielded from the overhead lighting, so no reflections appear on the screen. Shrouding, or tilting the monitors down, can help reduce screen glare from the overhead lighting. Also, selective fixtures can be dimmed, disabled, or lamps removed/reduced to help reduce video monitor glare.

Video cameras should be positioned to prevent the camera from viewing the ceiling lights, causing the automatic iris to close and making the broadcast image appear dark.

Outside windows must be covered with adjustable blinds or drapes. Panning the video camera to uncovered outside windows will cause the automatic iris to close, making the broadcast image appear dark. Interior rooms without windows offer the best and least expensive solution.

In addition to providing adequate lighting for the participants, other lighting needs such as white boards, demonstration or lab areas, lecterns, or areas where observers may be seated must be determined and provided for.

Excerpted with permission from ''Guidelines for Designing an Interactive Distance Learning System'' presented at USTA (US Telephone Association) Operations and Planning Conference June, 1995.

I-TV TRANSMISSION NETWORKS

I-TV networks use either private or public transmission facilities, or a combination of the two. Examples of public transmission providers are the local telephone company, long distance telephone company, local cellular telephone provider, and local cable television companies. All can provide various capacity and quality of transmission facilities. Examples of private transmission facilities include lines leased or purchased from one of the above public transmission providers, or dedicated transmission facilities installed by the school district.

The three common means for transmitting I-TV signals today are analog fiber optic cable, DS-3 (digital service three—also a fiber optic cable), and compressed video via copper wires. This section introduces several key characteristics of I-TV transmission networks, and then considers each type as it relates to these criteria.

(Note: There are several alternative means of transmitting I-TV signals, including microwave, instructional television fixed service, cable television, closed-circuit television and satellite.)

Network Characteristics

Multipoint Capability

Unless a network is to be used only for connecting two sites at a time, it will need the ability to conduct multipoint classes and conferences. There are two major types of multipoint viewing: (1) sequential, and (2) continuous.

Sequential viewing is usually handled by a centralized switcher (through a device called a multiconferencing unit, or MCU) that switches the signal between sites. Sequencing can be based on either teacher command (the teacher can choose which site is being seen), a timer (usually 7 to 9 seconds per site), or voice activation (which switches to the site that is talking). This is a less than ideal situation in an educational setting for several reasons. Regardless of the type of switching used, sequential viewing leaves students visually unsupervised for periods of time. In addition, a time-based viewing rotation can cause an illogical sequence of sites being viewed, while voice-activated sequencing excludes from view those sites which are not actively engaged in the current discussion.

Continuous viewing allows all sites to see all other sites simultaneously. This is also sometimes referred to as full-presence videoconferencing. Simultaneous viewing is achieved by viewing remote sites in multiple monitors or by viewing remote classrooms in quadrants on a single monitor.

Video Quality

An I-TV video image is transmitted either as broadcast quality, near broadcast quality, or compressed video. Broadcast quality video is synonymous with the output of a commercial grade VCR. In technical terms this means a signal of equal clarity and resolution to a 6 Mhz NTSC composite video signal (580 scan lines and 30 frames per second). When converted to a digital form, a 6 Mhz analog video signal requires approximately 90 mbps (megabits per second) of bandwidth. Therefore almost all digital video must be compressed to some degree.

Near broadcast-quality video, while technically a compressed digital signal (e.g., 3 to 1 compression) shows no significant difference from a broadcast-quality signal. Highly compressed video, typically transmitted at bandwidths of 1.54 mbps or lower, is of less clarity and resolution. This degradation of the video signal is caused by the high degree of compression that is required to transmit the signal through such a low-bandwidth medium. The main concerns with regard to compressed video are fluidity of motion and resolution of the image. These characteristics determine the ability to easily discern one person from another and to see facial expressions clearly.

Remote Camera Control

The ability of a teacher to control the pan, tilt, zoom and focus of cameras at remote sites requires the ability to transmit computer commands from one I-TV site to another over the network. During multipoint classes this requires additional control options (and additional equipment) for selecting which site's cameras to adjust.

Analog Fiber Optic

Analog fiber optic technology uses a thin strand of glass fiber as a transmission medium for video, audio, data, and telephone signals, which have been translated into beams of light. An analog network is capable of transmitting multiple video and audio signals over one fiber line—typically a maximum of sixteen channels of NTSC video. Maximum channel capacity is increased to thirty-two when Wave Division Multiplexing (WDM) is used. Analog technology provides the highest quality video and audio signals available today. The sixteen- (or thirty-two-) channel capacity allows for many sites to be involved in one class or conference. For practical purposes relating to supervision and inter-activity, classes do not routinely involve more than four or five sites. This educational consideration does not limit the number of multipoint classes occurring simultaneously. For example, in a twelve-school cluster, four schools might be involved in one class, while four additional schools were involved in another, and the remaining four schools were paired in two separate classes. In addition, the sixteen channels are not limited to carrying video. Network data can be placed on analog fiber systems at rates up to 10 megabits per second (mbps).

Analog fiber optic technology uses a similar method of transmitting information over one fiber (actually a pair of fiber cables) that cable television uses to bring dozens of channels to your home on one cable, i.e., frequency division. The signals for one site are broadcast at a unique frequency that can be "tuned in" by other sites on the network. A good analogy for describing frequency division is to think of a piano. Each of the eighty-eight keys on a piano represents a unique frequency. Imagine

Table 2.1. Advantages and Disadvantages of Analog Fiber Optic Transmission Networks.

Advantages	Disadvantages
No need for sequential viewing; all sites see each other at all times.	Sometimes expensive; limited availability.
Highest quality video and audio. No compression or CODEC required; no need for echo cancellation.	Often disliked by phone companies— has limited utility for their future purposes. A pair of fibers must be dedicated to the network.
The fiber can carry multiple signals; no requirement for computer scheduling of classes.	Quality of analog signal degrades over distance. A repeater or amplifier is required every twenty to thirty miles to boost the signal.
Network is easily expanded to a maximum of sixteen or thirty-two sites.	Lack of privacy; anyone at any of the network sites can view any broadcast by simply tuning the TV monitor to the same channel.
Several multipoint classes can occur concurrently.	Not available in some parts of the country. Cable and telephone companies may not wish to lease or sell analog fiber optic cable access.

a person using one key (frequency) to type a message in Morse code. Now imagine eighty-eight people typing out Morse code signals, each using a different key. All of the signals would be transmitted through the medium — air. The problem is in isolating (tuning in) the signal of interest; in television or I-TV, a tuner does the job for us. (An alternative method for sending multiple signals over the same fiber is sequence division; see the section, ''Asynchronous Transfer Mode'' which appears later in this chapter.)

Digital Service Three — DS-3

Digital Service Three, or DS-3, uses a strand of glass fiber and light to transmit information, as does analog fiber technology, but with DS-3 the signal is digital and slightly compressed.

A DS-3 system works by taking the NTSC analog video signal from the classroom and converting it into digital form, while at the same time compressing the signal by a factor of three to one. This is done by a piece of equipment called a CODEC, or *COder DECoder*. A CODEC compresses the analog NTSC signal by eliminating redundancies and unnecessary information in the video. The compressed signal is then sent through the DS-3 line at approximately 45 mbps. The result is a very high-quality video signal with such a small reduction in resolution that it is considered to be nearly equal to broadcast quality; national television networks often use DS-3 video to transmit from coast-to-coast.

The main difference between analog and DS-3 networks is that DS-3 cannot usually carry multiple signals over the line. Instead, a DS-3 circuit provides for one video/audio channel coming in and one video/audio channel going out. This works fine for point-to-point classes. For multipoint classes, one of the following special arrangements must be made in a DS-3 network:

- A switching unit that allows for sequential viewing can be used (see above).
- A group of quad-splitters — additional pieces of equipment — at a central location combines the video from multiple sites and then relays the combined signals to the sites involved in the course. A quad-splitter will allow up to four remote sites to be viewed simultaneously on one monitor, see Sidebar 2.2.

Table 2.2. *Advantages and Disadvantages of Digital Service Three (DS-3)*
Transmission Networks.

Advantages	Disadvantages

Virtual broadcast quality video
Long-distance transmission capability
Capacity for simultaneous voice,
   data, and video transmission over
   the same lines
	Sometimes prohibitively expensive
	Computer scheduling is required
	Lack of equipment standards,
	   especially in CODECs, makes it
	   difficult to interconnect systems

- A third alternative is to provide multiple DS-3 lines to each school. Currently, this option is almost always cost-prohibitive.
- A final option, currently available from only one vendor (Grass Valley), involves the use of a "J Series" CODEC which allows the splitting of a single DS-3 into multiple (up to four) separate signals. This allows for a near broadcast-quality signal to be sent to multiple classroom monitors, thereby emulating an analog fiber environment.

A major disadvantage from the perspective of the educator is that every class or conference on a DS-3 network must be scheduled by a computer (see Network Control below). The user cannot simply walk into the room and tune in a remote site on the monitor as is possible in an analog fiber network.

Sidebar 2.2. Multipoint Classes via Quad-Split

A quad-split system works by converting the digital signal from each site back to NTSC video, passing that video through a series of distribution amplifiers and quad-splitters and back to the sites. This allows multipoint classes to be full-presence, that is, able to see each other at all times. In addition to the video, the audio is also converted to an analog signal and combined in a device called an audio bridge. The combined audio is then passed back through the CODECs to the classrooms.

The system diagrammed below allows up to five sites to participate fully in one multipoint class. Note that participants at a particular site do not see themselves on the screen. By using a data channel in the transmission line, the quad splitters can be controlled to allow one site to be seen at full screen size at all sites. This technology adds to system cost as additional codecs, distribution amplifiers and quad-splitters must be purchased.

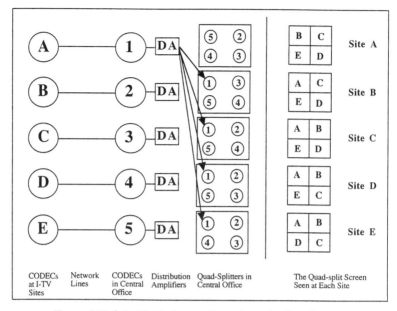

Figure SB2.2.1. Multi-class configuration using "quad-split."

Compressed Video

A compressed video network is very similar to a DS-3 network, except that the transmission medium is not fiber optic cable, but rather copper wire, and the video is of noticeably lesser quality. As in a DS-3 network, a CODEC is used to digitize and compress the video and audio signal. However, the signal is more highly compressed than in a DS-3 network. The video signal of a highly compressed network typically has noticeably reduced resolution and fluidity of motion.

Compressed networks can be designed to work over a variety of telecommunications lines. Lines are specified by the maximum number of bits per second (bps) they can transmit; the quality measured by bps is called bandwidth. For example, a 64k line can transmit 64,000 bps, whereas a 256k line can transmit four times that amount—256,000 bps. The larger the line, the more data can be transmitted; this translates into less need for compression and, therefore, improved audio and video.

Note: Certain digital transmission lines are usually referred to by a short-hand term instead of the bps transmitted. For example, a 1.54 mbps line is usually referred to as a T1 line. A quarter-T1 is a line that

Table 2.3. Standard Terms for Bandwidths.

Term	Bandwidth	Standard
T1 or DS-1	1.5 mbps	North America Digital Hierarchy
T2 or DS-2	6.18 mbps	North America Digital Hierarchy
T3 or DS-3	44.73 mbps	North America Digital Hierarchy
OC-1	51.84 mbps	Synchronous Optical NETwork (SONET)
DS-4	139.2 mbps	North America Digital Hierarchy
OC-3	155.52 mbps	Synchronous Optical NETwork (SONET)
OC-9	466.56 mbps	Synchronous Optical NETwork (SONET)

transmits 1/4 of that bandwidth or 386 kbps. (See Table 2.3 for more information on terms and bandwidths.)

Audio and video signals are compressed by means of various standard or vendor-specific (proprietary) algorithms. These algorithms are mathematical formulas that work by either eliminating redundant information, transmitting only changed data, or averaging pixels. (See Sidebar 2.1 for more information on compression standards.)

Note: Usually the transmission lines in a compressed network are dedicated, meaning that they are priced on the basis of 24-hour availability. However, it is now possible to use low bandwidth lines (e.g., 56 kbps) on a dial-up or as-needed basis—making it very easy to link with other networks over long distances. While video quality may be unsatisfactory in the K−12 educational environment, low bandwidth dial-up capability makes it possible for schools in an analog, compressed, or DS-3 network to link, on an occasional basis, with class-

Table 2.4. Advantages and Disadvantages of Compressed Video Networks.

Advantages	Disadvantages
Can cost-effectively span long distances	Lower picture quality
Utilizes standard interfaces, making interconnectivity between clusters easier	Computer scheduling of the network is required
Uses widely available, copper telephone wire	No capacity to add other services in the classroom, such as data, telephone, or fax without sacrificing video and audio quality
Network costs can be less than analog fiber or DS-3	Possible compatibility and upgrade problems between network sites

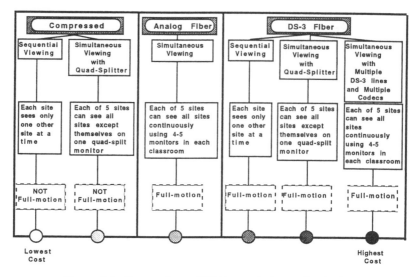

Figure 2.3. Comparison of I-TV transmission technologies.

rooms around the world. (Note: AT&T and MCI are currently deploying dial-up T-1 capabilities, which should be readily available, and potentially cost-effective.)

NETWORK CONTROL

Each class in a DS-3 or compressed video network must be scheduled by a computer. This is done through software that interfaces with transmission company equipment, and/or MCUs (multi-conference units). Such network control requires a daily schedule of class times to be entered on the computer, along with the locations of each class site and the originating site. The software then connects the proper sites at the specified times and shifts control of some functions to the teaching site. This information can be entered for a semester or year at a time, or it can be entered sporadically or intermittently to accommodate non-routine network activities such as student-teacher conferences, teacher professional development workshops, etc. Figure 2.4 shows an example of one such scheduling program.

Network scheduling software should be capable of checking for conflicts such as scheduling two multipoint classes at the same time or scheduling the same room for two different classes simultaneously.

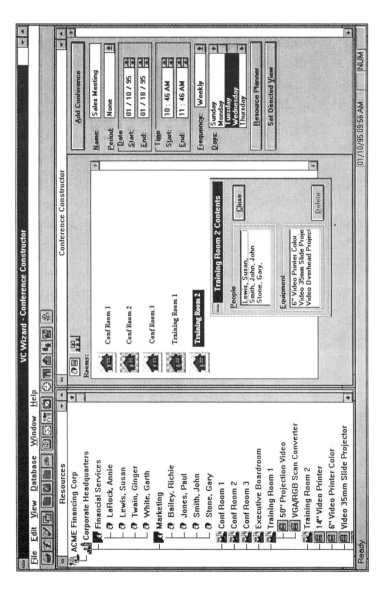

Figure 2.4. Scheduling program. Scheduling software is required for digital networks. This particular software package also tracks audiovisual resources at each site. The basic function of network scheduling software allows events to be scheduled at various frequencies (daily, weekly, monthly) over several months or years (figure courtesy of AC&E, Ltd.).

Another vital function of a good scheduling program is to set off an alarm when the MCU or phone company switches have failed. While it is possible to remotely schedule the network from any site, it is logistically better to have one person control all scheduling functions. This eliminates the possibility of scheduling conflicts.

DESKTOP VIDEOCONFERENCING

As personal computers become more and more powerful, videoconferencing technology is rapidly moving from dedicated networks to the desktop. Desktop videoconferencing is a far cry from the full-motion and full-resolution video of an analog fiber network; most systems are lucky to achieve five to twenty frames per second of low-resolution black and white video. However, the development of better compression methods and faster computer networks will bring an acceptable quality of videoconferencing to personal computers within the next few years.

Desktop videoconferencing is not, nor is it likely to be, a viable alternative to two-way interactive television. However, its does offer some interesting possibilities for combination with I-TV networks; the potential for integrating this technology into I-TV networks should not be ignored.

Several desktop videoconferencing packages are currently available (see Sidebar 2.3 and Photograph 2.4). These systems operate over a variety of mediums, including dedicated telecommunications lines (56K, ISDN, etc.), local area networks, wide area networks, analog telephone lines, or the Internet.

CU-SeeMe is public-domain desktop videoconferencing program for Macintosh and IBM computers developed at Cornell University (CU) which uses the Internet as a transmission network. Hardware requirements include a TCP/IP Internet connection, a video camera and a video input card for the computer.

Desktop videoconferencing sessions can be either point-to-point or multipoint. CU-SeeMe uses a program called a reflector to host multipoint sessions. Photograph 2.4(b) shows a CU-SeeMe multipoint session reflector; note that all participants can see themselves and each other. The video quality is poor and the audio is often spotty, but the potential for this technology is exciting.

An effective use of this technology might be to expand opportunities

Photograph 2.4. Two examples of desktop videoconferencing. Desktop videoconferencing is becoming increasingly sophisticated and more widespread in business and industry. In addition to exchanging video and audio, most systems allow the users to share documents and data files over dial-up lines or over local or wide area networks, such as Intel's Proshare system (a) (photograph courtesy of Intel Corporation).

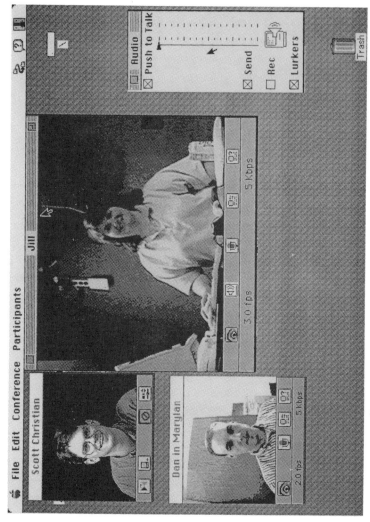

Photograph 2.4 (continued). Two examples of desktop videoconferencing. The Internet is also becoming a medium for desktop videoconferencing (b) (photograph by J. Scott Christianson). While this technology currently suffers from limited resolution and small screen size, it is adequate for some applications.

for home-based students. For example, a student could use a desktop videoconferencing system to "dial in" to an I-TV class, provided the I-TV classroom had a computer with the appropriate video and audio connections. The student would be able to see and hear the instructor as well as be seen and heard. While a little cumbersome, this scenario would allow the home-bound student to fully participate in a class with his or her peers.

Outside the traditional I-TV network, desktop videoconferencing can be used for small multipoint classes as well as point-to-point classes. In fact, many audiographic tele-learning systems (see Chapter 1) are switching to desktop videoconferencing systems.

Sidebar 2.3. Desktop Videoconferencing Products Index, by Leigh Anne Rettinger

This is an abridged version of an index of desktop videoconferencing products compiled by Leigh Anne Rettinger (email: larettin@eos.ncsu.edu) to aid in comparing systems based on several key features. Reproduced with permission.

AT&T TeleMedia Connection
Version: 1.01.01
Provider: AT&T Global Information Solutions
Description: Video/Audio/Tools over ISDN.
Platforms: PC
Contact Info: AT&T Global Information Solutions
      1700 S. Patterson Blvd.
      Dayton OH, 45479-0001 USA
      phone: 1-513-445-5000
      toll free: 1-800-225-5627

BVCS (Bitfield Video Conferencing System)
Version: 2.1
Provider: Bitfield Oy
Description: Video/Audio over ISDN (single/multi BRI, PRI), LAN (TCP/IP, NetBIOS), T1/E1 and other networks.
Platforms: PC
Contact Info: Bitfield Oy
      Ukonvaaja 2
      02130 Espoo
      Finland
      phone: +358-0-5024 220
      fax: +358-0-455 2240
      email: info@bitfield.fi

Cameo Personal Video System
Provider: Compression Labs Inc.
Description: Video over Switched 56, ISDN, and Ethernet. Audio re-
quires ISDN or Analog phone line.
Platforms: Macintosh
Contact Info: Compression Labs Inc.
    2860 Junction Ave.
    San Jose CA, 95134 USA
    phone: 1-408-435-3000
    toll free: 1-800-CALL-CLI

CommunicatorIII
Provider: EyeTel Communications Inc.
Description: Video/Audio/Tools over Switched 56, ISDN, T1, Ethernet, or
Token Ring.
Contact Info: EyeTel Communications Inc.
    #206–267 W. Esplanade
    N. Vancouver
    B.C., Canada, V7M1A5
    phone: 1-604-984-2522
    toll free: 1-800-736-3236
    fax:1-604-984-3566

Communique!
Version: 3.2
Provider: InSoft
Description: Video/Audio/Tools over ISDN, Frame relay, FDDI, SMDS,
Ethernet, ATM.
Contact Info: InSoft
    4718 Old Gettysburg Rd. #307
    Mechanicsburg PA, 17055, USA
    phone: 1-717-730-9501
    email: info@insoft.com

Connect 918
Provider: Nuts Technologies
Description: Video/Audio/Tools over Analog, Switched 56, ISDN, or
Ethernet.
Platforms: Macintosh, PC.
Contact Info: Nuts Technologies
    101 Metro Dr., Suite 750
    San Jose CA, 95110,USA
    phone: 1-408-441-2166
    Applelink: NUTS.USA

CU-SeeMe
Provider: Cornell University

Description: Video/Audio over the Internet. (PC version is video only).
Platforms: Macintosh, PC. Free, by anonymous ftp from ftp://gated.cornell.edu/pub/video/
Contact Info: Dick Cogger
   email: R.Cogger@cornell.edu
   phone: 1-607-255-7566

DECspin (DEC Sound Picture Information Network)
Version: 1.0
Provider: Digital Equipment Corporation
Description: Video/Audio using standard network protocols.
Contact Info: Diana Lapointe
   phone: 1-508-493-1327

ES + F2F (Electronic Studio's Face 2 Face)
Version: 1.0
Provider: Electronic Studio
Description: Video/Tools over ISDN, Analog, Ethernet. Audio requires ISDN or Analog phone line.
Platforms: Macintosh
Contact Info: The Electronic Studio
   7 Fitzroy Square
   London, W1P 6HJ, Great Britain
   phone: 1-408-974-0784
   toll free: 1-800-377-8681

InPerson
Provider: Silicon Graphics
Description: Video/Audio/Tools over Analog, Ethernet. A conference includes a shared whiteboard and a ''shared shelf'' for visual file transfer.
Platforms: InPerson runs on any SGI platform with graphics.
Contact Info: toll free: 1-800-800-7441
   email: inperson@sgi.com

INTERVu
Provider: Zydacron, Inc.
Description: Video/Audio/Data over IsoEthernet (802.9), ISDN, Switched 56, or V.35/RS366.
Platforms: PC
Requirements: 386 or higher, Microsoft Windows 3.1 or higher.
Contact Info: Zydacron, Inc.
   670 Commercial St.
   Manchester NH, 03101 USA
   phone: 1-603-647-1000

InVision
Version: 3.0

Provider: InVision Systems Corp.
Description: Video/Audio/Tools over LAN/WAN (including Ethernet,
Token Ring, FDDI, Frame Relay, ATM, ISDN, etc.)
Platforms: PC
Contact Info: InVision Systems Corp.
       317 S. Main Mall, Suite 310
       Tulsa OK,74103 USA
       toll free: 1-800-847-1662
       phone: 1-918-584-7772
       fax: 1-918-584-7775
       email: info@invision.com
       Compuserve: 72002,1677

IRIS
Provider: SAT
Description: Video over ISDN.
Platforms: Macintosh
Contact Info: SAT
       Division Communications d'Enterprise
       Centre Tolbiac Massena
       25 Quai Panhard et Levassor
       75624 Paris CEDEX 13
       France, (Lionel Bonnot)
       phone: + 33 1 40 77 11 27
       fax: + 33 1 40 77 11 50

IVS (Inria Videoconference System)
Provider: RODEO Project, INRIA Sophia Antipolis, France.
Description: Video/Audio over the Internet.
Platforms: Sun SPARCstation, HP9000, DECstation 5000, SGI Indigo.
Free, by anonymous ftp from ftp://zenon.inria.fr/rodeo/ivs
Contact Info: email: Thierry.Turletti@sophia.inria.fr

MacMICA
Provider: Group Technologies
Description: Video/Audio over Appletalk networks.
Platforms: Macintosh
Contact Info: Group Technologies
       phone: 1-703-528-1555

Ntv
Provider: Peregrine Systems
Description: Video/Audio/Tools over Ethernet and Token Ring.
Platforms: PC
Contact Info: Peregrine Systems, Inc.
       1959 Palomar Oaks Way
       Carlsbad CA, 92009, USA

phone: 1-619-431-2400
toll free: 1-800-638-5231
fax: 1-619-431-0696
email: info@www.peregrine.com

NV (Network Video)
Provider: Xerox/PARC
Description: NV provides video over the Internet. It is commonly supple-
mented with VAT (Visual Audio Tool) and WB (Whiteboard) for full-fea-
tured video/audio conferencing and collaboration.
Platforms: Sun SPARCstation, DECstation 5000 and Alpha, SGI,
HP9000, IBM RS6000.
Contact Info: Ron Frederick
frederick@parc.xerox.com

Person To Person
Provider: IBM
Description: Video/Tools over Analog, ISDN, Ethernet, or Token Ring.
Audio requires separate ISDN or Analog phone line.
Platforms: PC
Contact Info: phone: 1-404-238-6726
fax (in US): 1-800-IBM-4FAX
fax (outside US): 1-415-855-4329
email: p2p@vnet.ibm.com

Personal Viewpoint
Provider: ViewPoint Systems
Description: Video/Audio/Tools over Analog, Switched 56, ISDN, Ether-
net, Token Ring.
Platforms: PC
Contact Info: ViewPoint Systems Inc.
2247 Wisconsin St., Suite 110
Dallas TX, 75229, USA
phone: 1-214-243-0634

PICFON
Provider: Specom Technologies
Description: Video/Audio over Analog and ISDN phone lines.
Platforms: PC
Contact Info: Specom Technologies Corp.
2322 Walsh Ave.
Santa Clara CA, 95051, USA
phone: 1-408-982-1880
fax: 1-408-982-1883

PictureTel Live PCS 100
Provider: PictureTel

Description: Video/Audio/Tools over Switched 56, ISDN.
Platforms: PC
Contact Info: PictureTel Corp.
The Tower at Northwoods
222 Rosewood Dr.
Danvers MA, 01923, USA
phone: 1-508-762-5000
toll free: 1-800-716-6000
fax: 1-508-762-5245

PictureWindow
Provider: BBN
Description: Video/Audio over the Internet.
Platforms: Sun SPARCstation.
Contact Info: BBN
150 Cambridge Park Drive
Cambridge MA, 02140, USA
phone: 1-617-873-2000
toll free: 1-800-422-2359
fax: 1-617-873-5011
email: picwin-sales@bbn.com

ProShare
Provider: Intel
Description: Video/Audio/Tools over LAN/WAN.
Platforms: PC
Contact Info: Intel Corp.
2200 Mission College Blvd.
P.O. Box 58199
Santa Clara CA, 95052-8119, USA
phone: 1-503-629-7354
toll free: 1-800-538-3373
fax: 1-800-525-3019

PSVC (Paradise Software Video Conferencing)
Provider: Paradise Software, Inc.
Description: Audio/Video/Tools over ISDN, Ethernet, ATM.
Platforms: Sun SPARCstation
Contact Info: Paradise Software, Inc.
7 Centre Drive, Suite 9
Jamesburg NJ, 08831, USA
phone: 1-609-655-0016
fax: 1-609-655-0045
email: support@paradise.com

ShareView 3000
Provider: Creative Labs

Description: Audio/Video/Tools over Analog phone line.
Platforms: Macintosh
Contact Info: Creative Labs, Inc.
            1901 McCarthy Boulevard
            Milpitas CA, 95035, USA
            phone: 1-408-428-6600
            toll-free: 1-800-998-1000
            fax: 1-408-428-6611
            AppleLink: SHAREVIS.MKT

ShareVision PC 3000
Provider: Creative Labs
Description: Audio/Video/Tools over Analog phone line.
Platforms: PC
Contact Info: Creative Labs, Inc.
            1901 McCarthy Boulevard
            Milpitas CA, 95035, USA
            phone: 1-408-428-6600
            toll-free: 1-800-998-1000
            fax: 1-408-428-6611

ShowMe
Version: 2.0
Provider: Sun Microsystems
Description: Video/Audio/Tools over the Internet.
Platforms: Sun SPARCstation
Contact Info: toll free: 1-800-873-7869
            email: sunsol-www@sunsolutions.eng.sun.com

TelePro with VisionTime
Provider: Specom Technologies Corp.
Description: Video/Audio/Tools over WAN (Analog phone lines and ISDN).
Platforms: PC
Contact Info: Specom Technologies Corp.
            2322 Walsh Ave.
            Santa Clara CA, 95051, USA
            phone: 1-408-982-1880
            fax: 1-408-982-1883

TeleView 1000C
Provider: VCC (Video Conferencing Communications, Inc.)
Description: Video over Analog phone lines.
Platforms: PC
Contact Info: Video Conferencing Communications, Robert Medrano
            phone: 1-714-452-0800

VC7000
Provider: British Telecom

Description: Video/Audio.
Platforms: Stand-alone unit (does not require a PC).
Contact Info: phone: + 44 171 777 7725
(Visual Services Sales Support)

VicPhone
Provider: VIC Hi-Tech Corporation
Description: Video/Tools over Analog, ISDN phone lines or Ethernet. Audio can be sent over the same analog line with a voice-modem. No additional line required for voice over ISDN.
Platforms: PC
Contact Info: VIC Hi-Tech Corporation
2221 Rosecrans Avenue, Suite 237
El Segundo CA, 90245, USA
phone: 1-310-643-5193
fax: 1-310-643-7572
Compuserve: 70544,2472

VidCall
Provider: MRA Associates Inc.
Description: Video/Tools over Analog, ISDN, Ethernet, Token Ring. Audio requires separate phone line or voice/data modem to send voice and video over one telephone line.
Platforms: PC
Contact Info: MRA Associates Inc.
2102B Gallows Rd.
Vienna VA, 22182, USA
phone: 1-703-448-5373
fax: 1-703-734-9825

VISIT Video
Provider: Northern Telecom Inc.
Description: Video/Tools over ISDN or Switched 56. Audio requires separate ISDN or Analog phone line.
Platforms: PC, Macintosh.
Contact Info: Northern Telecom Inc.
2221 Lakeside Blvd.
Richardson TX, 75082 USA
toll free: 1-800-667-8437
fax: 1-214-684-3866

Vivo320
Provider: Vivo Software, Inc.
Description: Video/Audio/Tools over ISDN.
Platforms: PC
Contact Info: Vivo Software, Inc.
phone: 1-617-899-8900

toll-free: 1-800-848-6411
fax: 1-617-899-1400
email: info@vivo.com

VS1000
Provider: Mentec International Ltd.
Description: Video/Audio
Platforms: PC
Contact Info: Mentec International Ltd.
      Mentec House
      520 Birchwood Boulevard
      Birchwood, Warrington, WA3 7QX
      Great Britain
      phone: 44 925 830000

ASYNCHRONOUS TRANSFER MODE

Asynchronous Transfer Mode, or ATM, is an emerging transmission technology which provides a powerful means of transferring video, audio, and computer data. This technology is also known as cell-relay because the digital data transmitted along an ATM network is broken up into digital ''cells,'' or packets, of a fixed length, with headers (digital address labels) containing information about where the cells are from and where they are going.

The advantage of packaging data into standardized compartments is similar to that afforded by standardized shipping containers for transporting products and materials. In the shipping industry, a product can be packaged into a standard shipping container to be carried by boat, truck, or train—put the appropriate information on the box about its destination and shipping charges and off it goes.

ATM works the same way. The difference, as Nicholas Negroponte, pointed out in *Being Digital,* is that bits (information) are shipped instead of matter (products). Once data is put in a cell and onto an ATM network, it will be faithfully carried along the ATM network to its destination, independent of whether the cell travels over fiber optic lines, copper lines, satellite, or microwave radio. Moreover, multiple types of packets can be sent along the same ATM line using a form of sequence division.

Sequence or time division is a digital method of combining multiple types of data in one communications path. Figure 2.5 is a diagram of how ATM networks ship different types of packets. Instead of separating

Table 2.5. Advantages and Disadvantages of ATM Networks.

Advantages	Disadvantages
Virtual broadcast quality video and CD quality audio Long-distance transmission capability Capacity for simultaneous video, audio, and data transmission with no loss of video quality Remote testing and maintenance capabilities	Cost—ATM may be the most expensive of all I-TV technologies—check locally applicable tariffs Cannot always interconnect with other technologies cost-effectively Maximum of four sites involved in any one class Computer scheduling of the network is required

data by frequency, it is separated by time. Because ATM networks work extremely fast, some in the gigabit per second range, ATM networks can simultaneously transmit video, audio, voice, and data in such a way that the communication appears instantaneous to the user. Due to the small delay associated with delivery of packets, however, ATM-based I-TV networks require echo cancellation capabilities.

ATM was developed originally for broadband fiber transmission at an

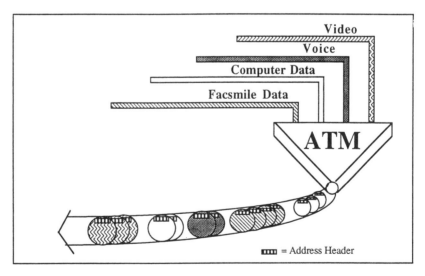

Figure 2.5. ATM diagram. ATM uses sequence division to transmit multiple types of data cells over the same fiber optic line. Each cell is identified by a unique header that facilitates routing.

OC3 rate (155 mbps or the equivalent of three DS-3's), but can be used at slower rates. This tremendous capacity can provide broadcast-quality video and has the capacity to provide other services over the same fiber as well. ATM can be used in either a multicast mode (with multiple monitors) or utilizing quad-split capability (where remote sites are seen in quadrants on one TV screen); however, computer scheduling of the network must still be done.

ATM is still very new. The practical problem at this point is one of inter-connectability to other types of networks. For example, ATM-based networks in Texas and North Carolina work well within their respective networks, but the ability to connect with other technologies in a cost-effective manner is still not available. In order to be able to provide a stable platform for I-TV networks, ATM must be able to interface, i.e., interconnect, with other I-TV technologies in a seamless, affordable way.

PART TWO

BRICKS, MORTAR, AND IMAGINATION: BUILDING AN I-TV NETWORK

Establishing a School-Based
I-TV Network

THIS chapter attempts to place in semi-chronological order the steps necessary to implement a school-based, two-way interactive television network. Each section of the chapter corresponds to one of the nine recommended steps for establishing the school-based I-TV network presented in Figure 3.1.

(Note: The document, ''A Consortium Planning Guide for Establishing a Two-Way Interactive Television Network,'' is available on the Internet via WWW at ''http://cmc2.cmc.edu/mite.html''. This guide helps groups of schools chart their progress through the I-TV planning and implementation process.)

STEP ONE: NEEDS ASSESSMENT

While this step is most often glossed over or taken for granted in the implementation of technology projects, I-TV is too important a step and too costly a venture to find out only after implementation that the usage of the network was not as extensive as thought or that the need for the technology was only transient.

A needs assessment does not need to be externally conducted or extremely time-intensive, but it should take all stakeholders into account. Potential adopters may choose to use a written survey process or a more informal process of talking with different groups of people potentially affected by the technology. Table 3.1 shows the basic steps for both a formal and an informal method of assessing needs. While the formal process may be slightly more time-intensive, it is also much more

Portions of this chapter were first published in ''An Adopters' Manual for Two-Way Interactive Television: A Guide to Researching, Planning and Implementing Distance Learning in your School and Community,'' MIT-E, WeMET and EPN networks, March, 1995. Available from the Missouri Alliance for Interactive Television, K-12 Users' Group. Contact: Missouri Rural Opportunities Council, P.O. Box 118, 301 W. High Street, Room 720, Jefferson City, MO 65102 (573-751-1238).

STEP ONE: NEEDS ASSESSMENT
    Formal Method of Needs Assessment
    Informal Method of Needs Assessment
    Take State Curriculum Mandates/Guidelines into Account
    Decide What You Want to Accomplish
        Expanded Course Offerings.
        Dual-Credit Course Offerings.
        Joint Teacher In-Service Training.
        Community Education.
        Community/Economic Development.
    Coordination with Telemedicine or Other I-TV Initiatives
    Secure School Board and Staff Support

STEP TWO: BACKGROUND RESEARCH
    Learn About the I-TV Technologies Available
    Other Sources of Information
    Visit I-TV Network Sites
    Decide on the Technology Characteristics Which Best Meet Your Needs

STEP THREE: CLUSTER DEVELOPMENT
    Determine Common Needs of Area Schools
    Secure School Board Approval to Proceed
    Meet to Discuss Cooperation
        Identify the Cluster Size Desired.
        Identify Member Districts of I-TV Cluster.
        Identify College or University Partners.
        Secure Commitment to Develop a Common School Calendar.
        Secure Commitment to Develop a Common Bell Schedule.
        Secure Commitment to Share Work in Preparation and Planning.
        Identify an Acting Director or Hire a Director for the Consortium.
        Establish a "Network Development Fund."
    Conduct Economic Cost-Benefit Analysis and Establish Funding Capacity

STEP FOUR: IDENTIFY TRANSMISSION LINE PROVIDERS
    Initiate Discussion with Phone Companies
    Initiate Discussion with Cable TV Companies
    Determine the Technology to Be Implemented
    Cost Estimates for Chosen Technology
    Make Sure That the Technology Chosen Allows for Full Interconnectivity

Figure 3.1. Suggested steps for establishing a school-based I-TV network.

STEP FIVE: IDENTIFY SOURCES OF I-TV CLASSROOM EQUIPMENT
   Determine Phone or Cable Company Capacity to Provide Classroom
      Equipment
   Assess Advantages/Disadvantages of Acting as Your Own Subcontractor

STEP SIX: DETERMINING NEED FOR/HIRE A CONSULTANT
   Can You Provide Your Own Leadership?
   Will the Transmission Line Provider Supply Technical Assistance?
   Is There Sufficient (and Reliable) Technical Expertise Available?
   Hiring an I-TV Consultant

STEP SEVEN: PLAN OF OPERATION
   Final Commitment from Cooperating Districts
      Develop a Joint Powers Agreement or Form a Corporation.
      Develop Bylaws and/or Network Policies.
      Identify a Fiscal Agent for the Consortium.
      Determine Basis for Achieving Sending/Receiving Equity.
      Determine Responsibility for Day-to-Day Program Operation.
      Develop a Common Calendar and Bell Schedule.
   Identify Courses to Be Taught—Develop I-TV Course Schedule
   Secure Staff Commitment to Teach Over the Network
   Teacher Training
   Develop Community Usage Programs
      Make Preliminary Contact with Community Organizations/
         Agencies/Businesses.
      Work with Local/Regional Community and/or Economic
         Development Commissions.
   Prepare Classroom and Install Equipment
      Classroom Preparation.
      Teacher Podium and Riser.
      Equipment Installation.
   Identify a Facilitator(s) in Each District
   Develop a Maintenance Plan/Budget
   Determine Who Will Serve as Network Scheduler

STEP EIGHT: IDENTIFY COMMUNITY USERS OF THE NETWORK
   Schedule a Community Open House to Showcase the Network
   Make Presentations to Community Organizations to Spur Interest in
      Using the Network
   Construct a List of Potential Community Users
   Recouping I-TV Line Lease Costs

STEP NINE: EVALUATION

Figure 3.1 (continued). Suggested steps for establishing a school-based I-TV network.

Table 3.1. Methods of Conducting a Needs Assessment.

Formal Methods	Informal Methods
Prepare a checklist for school administrators	Conduct a joint meeting of school administrators
Survey school board members	Talk to school board members
Survey teaching staff	Talk with teaching staff
Survey community patrons	Meet with community patrons

reliable. With verbal feedback, it is always easy for the person conducting the interviews to ask only those who will have a favorable opinion or to only hear what they want to hear. The method of needs assessment should be selected with this in mind.

Formal Method of Needs Assessment

The first step in the formal needs assessment is to complete the "School Administrator Needs Assessment Checklist." A sample checklist is presented in Figure 3.2. If the answer to question #1 is "yes," the justification for pursuing I-TV is probably not present and the process should likely be discontinued. If the general response to questions 2 – 13 is "yes" for half or more of the questions, the district probably meets the primary criteria for pursuing I-TV.

The next step in formally assessing need for development of an I-TV network will likely involve a survey of school board members (see sample survey in Figure 3.3). Board member responses to the sample survey questions should be weighed very carefully. A more objective assessment may be possible if the survey is given to the board members with no explanation; if the board knows that a needs assessment for I-TV is being conducted, their responses might be affected by any predispositions regarding educational technology. Surveys can be mailed to board members or completed during a regular meeting. Results will be most informative if the members do not collaborate on their responses as the survey is completed.

Discussion of the tabulated results of the board survey and the administrator's checklist should be put on the agenda for the next board meeting; the discussion alone will be a very instructive process for the board. If preliminary survey results are positive, the next step would be to plan a broader I-TV needs assessment, including faculty and community.

Administrator Checklist		
Yes	No	
___	___	1. Do you feel this district currently provides all courses needed by its students?
___	___	2. Are there areas of the curriculum that are deficient in number of course offerings? If so, what are they?_____
___	___	3. Is it difficult or impossible for students to take dual credit or college courses while in high school?
___	___	4. Do you often have trouble hiring quality teachers with the combination of multiple certifications to meet your needs? If so, in what areas?_____
___	___	5. Do students often have difficulty working needed classes into a tight four-year schedule?
___	___	6. Is teacher turnover and rehiring a significant problem in some curriculum areas? if so, in which areas?_____
___	___	7. Are students limited to single section course offerings in some high demand classes? If so, in which classes?_____
___	___	8. Has there been any recent talk within the school or community regarding the need to consolidate with another district?
___	___	9. Do you currently offer classes in which enrollment often falls below five students?
___	___	10. Do you feel students with specific academic interests in such areas as music theory or composition, pre-law, pre-medicine, graphic arts, etc. have difficulty acquiring relevant high school courses?
___	___	11. Does the district often have a problem matching existing certification of teaching staff with changing course demands?
___	___	12. Does the district routinely drop and add high school classes from year to year based on student enrollment?
___	___	13. Are there classes in your curriculum which are only offered in alternating years?

Figure 3.2. Sample school administrator needs assessment checklist.

Needs Assessment Survey
(For use with School Board Members, Faculty, and Community)

1. Do you think the (district name) school district currently meets the academic needs of all of its students? __ Yes __ No

2. Do you think that students graduating from the (district name) school district have:

    a) any trouble meeting increased college entry requirements?
    __ Yes __ No

    b) any disadvantage in college when competing with students from larger high schools? __ Yes __ No

    c) as much opportunity to take advanced courses in high school as students from larger high schools? __ Yes __ No

3. Do you believe that the (district name) school district should expand its high school course offerings, especially in the areas of advanced math, science, and foreign language? __ Yes __ No

4. Do you think the (district name) school district should provide its students an opportunity to receive college credit while enrolled in high school, through the provision of dual credit course offerings? __ Yes __ No

5. Do you think (district name) students have a sufficient course selection to allow them to investigate areas in which they might have an interest in college or in the work place? __ Yes __ No

6. Do you think the school district should provide additional community education, adult education, or access to college course offerings for community residents? __ Yes __ No

7. Would you like to see additional professional development opportunities offered for teachers within the district? __ Yes __ No

8. What, in your opinion, are the three most important curriculum goals the (district name) school district should be working toward?

    1)

    2)

    3)

Please return this questionnaire to the Superintendent's Office.

Figure 3.3. Sample needs assessment survey.

The same survey completed by board members can also be used with the faculty. Faculty should be provided with feedback on their collective responses, along with those of administrators, board members, and community.

The same survey can likewise be used with parents and community patrons. Options for distribution include:

(1) Sending a survey home with the oldest child in each family
(2) Printing a blank questionnaire in the local newspaper
(3) Making copies of the questionnaire available to all local service or business organizations for distribution to their members, e.g., Chamber of Commerce, Kiwanis, Lions Club, County Commission, senior citizens' groups, etc.

Return instructions should be clearly written on the bottom of the survey and the results should be tabulated and reported back to the community in a widely read format, such as the local newspaper.

Informal Method of Needs Assessment

If the informal method of needs assessment is utilized, it is crucial to include all stakeholder groups. Informal needs assessment can be done in isolation, that is, within a single school district, or it can be done in concert with other districts who might be likely partners in the development of an I-TV network. The advantages of the latter approach would be the joint timing of information collection and the development of a point-in-time "snapshot" of public opinion across multiple communities.

School administrator opinions regarding the needs of the local district should be sought from the superintendent, principal(s), and counselor(s). This could be done independently in each district or it could occur in the context of a joint administrator meeting of cooperating districts. An individual should be appointed as secretary to accurately document the scope of attitudes, opinions, and stated needs. This step will mean little if there is no documentation of the attitudes expressed.

Opinions of school board members could be sought through a similar informal process, again with the assurance that attitudes, opinions, and needs were at least summarized in a written format.

Opinions of teaching staffs could be solicited informally in the context of a regular teachers' meeting. Community patron response to school district needs could be obtained by asking the major service organizations in the community to discuss the topic at their next meeting and to report back to the school superintendent either verbally or in writing. Not involving staff and community from the beginning will be a missed opportunity for them to "buy into" distance learning and I-TV.

Take State Curriculum Mandates/Guidelines into Account

All states have suggested or mandated curriculum requirements which impact local district curriculum decisions. Many colleges and universities have curricular entry requirements. These requirements are continuing to escalate as the perceived need for academic rigor increases; it is important to review district needs in this context. The need for advanced math courses or multiple years of foreign language instruction can serve as the impetus for I-TV network development. While such needs may serve as the only rationale for I-TV development, other opportunities afforded by the technology should be investigated as well.

Decide What You Want to Accomplish

Based on the needs assessment information that was collected and compiled, a listing of goals for a two-way I-TV network can be assembled. Such a list might include the following categories.

Expanded Course Offerings

List those high school courses for which there is a need, but which are not currently offered in the school. This list is likely to include advanced courses in math, science, and foreign language, as well as limited demand courses such as music theory, graphic arts, computer multimedia applications, etc.

Dual-Credit Course Offerings

List those areas in which students could most benefit from dual-credit offerings, i.e., those classes most often required for college freshmen. The length of this list will likely be influenced by the level of flexibility in the course schedules for upperclassmen.

Joint Teacher Inservice Training

List major areas in which district teachers currently do not have access to professional development opportunities – opportunities which might be provided jointly across several districts through I-TV. Estimate the number of hours of training that could be productively utilized.

Community Education

Depending on the level of local interest during the needs assessment, list community education, adult education, and college course offerings which might be provided through I-TV.

Community/Economic Development

The sample assessment survey in Figure 3.3 doesn't address community or economic development applications of I-TV. While opportunities for community and economic development occur as by-products of the school-based I-TV network, they are usually not the primary impetus for its development. However, any economic or industrial development boards in the community should be contacted to gain their feedback on the usefulness of the technology in the following areas:

(1) Coordinated job training and re-training programs between vocational schools, private industry councils, and local businesses or industries
(2) Provision of continuing education courses, e.g., medical, legal, para-legal, insurance, etc.
(3) Local access to university extension and community development activities and workshops
(4) Small business development training seminars
(5) Intercommunity business/agency/organization meetings
(6) Community drug and alcohol abuse awareness/prevention activities
(7) Intercommunity club activities, e.g., Boy and Girl Scouts, 4-H, Campfire, etc.
(8) Access to continuing education for emergency response personnel, e.g., EMT, fire fighters, police, etc.

(9) Local access to pesticide use workshops, hunter safety training, etc.
(10) Intercommunity cooperative meetings, e.g., MFA, RUS (formerly REA), Pork Producers, Cattlemen's Association, etc.

Coordination with Telemedicine or Other I-TV Initiatives

Hospitals and medical clinics in the community should also be contacted as planning for an I-TV network begins. Uses of I-TV technology for purposes of teleradiology, telepathology, and remote diagnostics and consultation are becoming increasingly widespread. The potential for sharing infrastructure costs with other community users as well, e.g., major employers, vocational schools, etc., should not be overlooked.

Secure School Board and Staff Support

After the results of the needs assessment are compiled, it is time to present the findings to the board of education. The Board presentation should be as clear and concise as possible. It is important that the breadth of opportunities made available through I-TV technology be conveyed. There will undoubtedly be discussions of cost at this time; discussions of estimated costs should be straightforward, but it should be emphasized that what is sought at this point is support for continued investigation of the feasibility of developing a network.

If the board endorses a continued investigation of the technology, faculty and staff should be kept abreast of all decisions and their input should be continually sought. It is vitally important that faculty not be left out in the process of technology development. It is important to continually broaden the knowledge base of each stakeholder by providing an opportunity to view videotapes and/or participate in site visits to operating networks as planning progresses.

STEP TWO: CONDUCT BACKGROUND RESEARCH

Learn about the I-TV Technologies Available

Although a number of technologies have been utilized for distance learning, this book focuses on only those technologies that are capable of full, two-way interactive and simultaneous viewing. The four major transmission technologies discussed (see Chapter 2) are:

(1) Analog fiber optic cable
(2) DS-3, a fiber-based digital system
(3) Compressed video using copper lines
(4) ATM, which is also a digital fiber technology

It is important to assess the advantages, disadvantages, capabilities, limitations, accessibility, and costs of each technology in the context of local needs. The fit between technology and need can easily be over-shadowed at this point by any number of ''authoritative opinions.'' Following are a few of the myths regarding two-way I-TV that Hobbs, Pellant, and Chastain (1990) have identified.

(1) ''Forget analog—it's an old technology and everything is going digital.'' To the extent that computers have digitized the world, this is true, but do not immediately discount the ability of an analog I-TV system to meet your needs.
(2) ''Only the telephone company can provide the transmission lines.'' Anyone who owns copper or fiber optic lines can provide the means for transmission of an I-TV network. In addition to telephone companies, this could include cable companies, competitive access providers, and utility companies. Alternatively, a group of school districts may choose to lay their own fiber optic lines, negating the need for ongoing monthly line leases.
(3) ''All compressed video networks look alike.'' The issue is not whether video is compressed, but the extent of compression and the algorithms used in displaying it. There is a very noticeable dif-ference in video quality between a 56K line and a full T-1 line. Video quality is further defined by the codecs used and whether the algorithms are proprietary or standard. Currently, it is believed that use of compressed networks for educational two-way I-TV at the K-12 level should not go below a bandwidth approximating a full T-1 (1.54 mbps), or the video quality equivalent of current T-1 technology.
(4) ''I-TV prices are fixed—like buying a computer off the showroom floor.'' The I-TV adopter should be cautious of ''first round'' cost estimates supplied by transmission line providers. Telephone com-

pany tariffs — the structure by which prices are set — will usually vary between telephone companies, and, in many cases, on a case-by-case basis. Unlike the computer off the showroom floor, pricing standards often bear no resemblance to the cost of supplying the service.

Other Sources of Information

There are really no periodicals currently available which are devoted exclusively to educational two-way interactive television. Most technology-related magazines, however, do include some coverage of two-way interactive television. It is important, however, to sort out the teleconferencing articles from those covering true, two-way interactive technologies. In addition, one must differentiate between the articles discussing menu-driven entertainment (e.g., movies on demand) that is also known as interactive television and educational I-TV. Appendix 3 lists resources, both hardcopy and electronic, for two-way interactive television. An ERIC search on interactive television and distance learning can also yield informative articles.

Visit I-TV Network Sites

The best way to gain an understanding of two-way interactive television is to visit an existing network. Appendix 2 lists several networks in the United States that are willing to receive visitors or talk to potential adopters; information about I-TV networks in your state can be obtained by calling your state department(s) of education. Visits to existing networks should involve as many of the stakeholders as possible: teachers, principals, telecommunications providers, a representative from a parents' organization, school board members, etc.

Before conducting a visit, it is helpful to prepare a list of questions regarding network operations. Figure 3.4 lists several areas to explore. In addition, some helpful questions might include:

(1) What capabilities of your network do you think are most important?
(2) What capabilities would you add if you had the opportunity?
(3) What has been the reaction of your teaching staff to the I-TV network? (Ask to meet with one or two I-TV teachers if possible.)
(4) What has been the reaction of your students? (Ask to talk with several I-TV students, if possible.)

Site Visit Questions

1. Name of network
2. Number of schools involved in network
3. Number and type of other sites involved in network
4. Technology utilized
5. Date of network start-up
6. Transmission line provider; transmission line fees and other annual costs
7. Number and size of monitors in classroom and purpose of each
8. Number and type (e.g., 3-chip or 1-chip) of cameras in classroom and purpose of each
9. Sketch (or photographs) of I-TV classroom
10. Number of students accommodated in I-TV classroom
11. Height of teacher riser and design of teacher console
12. Auxiliary equipment available, e.g., computer, laserdisk player, audio cassette player, VCR, etc.
13. Use and location of FAX machine
14. Existence of monitor/VCR in principals' office
15. Number and type of courses taught over the network
16. Other uses made of the network
17. Annual maintenance budget allocated/type of maintenance agreement (if any)
18. Network staff hired, e.g., network director, technical coordinator, etc.
19. Procedure for resolving technical problems
20. Copy of joint calendar and course/bell schedule
21. Number of students enrolled in I-TV courses

Figure 3.4. Areas of investigation for I-TV site visits.

(5) What were the mistakes you made in planning/implementing your I-TV network?

Decide on the Technology Characteristics Which Best Meet Your Needs

There are basically two considerations when choosing an I-TV technology. One is which technology best fits identified needs; the other is the availability and cost of transmission lines. It is always best to identify the most suitable technology and then determine if it is available and affordable. A reversal in this process will unduly limit the scope of the options investigated. (See Chapter 9 for assistance in assessing costs.)

The matrix in Figure 3.5 will help in determining what technology

	Copper Lines	Analog Fiber	DS-3 Fiber	ATM Fiber
1. Teacher and students can see and hear all sites simultaneously	Yes	Yes	Yes	Yes
2. Network can transmit data	Yes	Yes	Yes	Yes
3. Interconnectivity between different clusters is possible	Yes	Yes	Yes	Yes
4. Full-motion video (at or near broadcast quality)	No	Yes	Yes	Yes
5. "Quad-split" technology allows the viewing of up to four remote sites on a single monitor	Yes	No	Yes	Yes
6. Separate TVs are used to view other participating sites	No	Yes	No*	Yes
7. Requires no computer to schedule events; unrestricted viewing	No	Yes	No	No
8. Scheduling is handled by a computer; privacy more easily maintained due to restricted viewing	Yes	No	Yes	Yes
9. System allows multiple video inputs, e.g., computer, VCR, etc.	Yes	Yes	Yes	Yes
10. System allows control of cameras at remote sites (in point-to-point broadcasts only)	Yes	Yes	Yes	Yes
11. More than one multi-point broadcast possible at one time	Yes	Yes	No	In multi-cast mode only
12. Capacity for simultaneous voice, data, and video transmission exists (may be additional cost)	Yes	Yes	Yes	Yes
13. Number of sites that can participate in one class	5	Limited only by # of monitors	4	4

*This limitation may be overcome in some instances.

Figure 3.5. Matrix of educational capabilities associated with I-TV technologies.

attributes will be most beneficial. The matrix should be used by choosing those capabilities which should be included in the network and then identifying which technology meets most of the selected criteria.

STEP THREE: CLUSTER DEVELOPMENT

Determine Common Needs of Area Schools

It is important for area schools to get together for a common discussion of needs and goals relative to distance learning. Ideally, this discussion should occur after each school has completed a needs assessment.

An I-TV consortium works best with schools of similar size and needs. The impulse for smaller surrounding schools to band together with one large district will not likely yield an ongoing viable arrangement. It is much better to create a symbiotic relationship among schools where each is dependent upon the other. In addition, the organizational dynamics of a consortium are enhanced when the ability to make decisions and wield power is equally distributed among partner schools.

Secure School Board Approval to Proceed

While final board approval is not necessary at this point, it is wise to bring the school boards up to speed on the discussions among area schools and to ask for their approval to proceed in discussions regarding I-TV network development.

At this point, there is a danger that board members will tend to focus on the potential cost of an I-TV system, to the exclusion of other considerations. The needs assessment and background research on the network will be invaluable in helping keep attention focused on the benefits of continuing to investigate and plan for the network. It is often the case that if the need for a network is profound and the potential community benefits of the technology are substantial, a way can be found to finance it. It is also likely that prices initially quoted will be higher than costs that are subsequently negotiated.

Meet to Discuss Cooperation

Area districts should come together as a cooperative group to discuss the initial considerations for I-TV cluster development.

Identify the Cluster Size Desired

The number of schools participating in an I-TV cluster can theoretically number between two and sixteen, or even more. However, there are several practical limitations which should be considered:

(1) A cluster of two to three schools will only allow for one class per period to be broadcast since at least two schools participate in each class; a third school would have no one with which to share classes if its needs were different from the other two.

(2) A cluster of four to five schools is usually able to meet the curriculum needs of all members and has the advantage of ease of decision making due to the small number of parties involved.

(3) A cluster of six to eight schools is considered ideal, since it is possible to have multiple classes occurring simultaneously, thereby increasing the network's capacity to meet the needs of each participant school.

(4) A cluster of nine to twelve schools can yield an I-TV schedule with multiple, simultaneous course offerings, but the decision making process is made cumbersome by the sheer number of schools involved.

(5) A cluster of more than twelve schools is not recommended. At that point, it is preferable to divide the interested schools into two clusters and then to interconnect the clusters. This will achieve the benefit of potential linkage between many sites, but maintain manageable cluster size for most decision-making purposes.

Identify Member Districts of I-TV Cluster

Network partners are chosen based on common needs and similar size. Until such time that inter-LATA restrictions are lifted, all I-TV partners should reside within the same LATA or telephone area code if phone lines are likely to be the means of transmission. There is currently no means of affordably crossing LATA boundaries as it would require the payment of long-distance carrier charges. It should not be assumed that this is a definitive barrier, however. As the prevalence of I-TV networks increases and as the telephone industry moves toward increased competition, inter-LATA operation will become more feasible.

It is also advantageous—although not essential—to select schools within a common local exchange carrier, e.g., telephone company, if phone lines are likely to be the means of transmission. When schools

from within a single telephone service area band together, the amount
of time saved by eliminating the need to coordinate multiple telephone
companies can be substantial.

Identify College or University Partners

If given the opportunity, most K – 12 clusters will want to link with a
higher education institution to take advantage of the dual-credit courses,
teacher inservice training, etc. Do not overlook the possibility for
linkage with a junior college, community college, or any two- or
four-year, public or private institution. The likelihood of linking with a
higher education institution on an "equal partner" basis is increased by
affiliating with a small institution, rather than a major university. In fact,
an ideal situation might be linkage with a small institution for provision
of dual-credit courses, one-on-one teacher mentoring, etc., and with a
major university for other selective purposes, such as periodic access to
content specialists, e.g., an internationally known professor of physics,
or specific professional development programming.

Secure Commitment to Develop a Common School Calendar

It will not be possible for each school to maintain its own calendar. A
network calendar which is interrupted by different beginning and ending
dates, different holidays, spring breaks, and Christmas vacations, and
different teacher professional development and work days is not viable.
Not only will instruction be seriously impaired, but any state mandate
on minimum number of instructional hours or days will be impossible
to meet. While it is not necessary to decide on a common calendar at this
point, it is wise to determine if there are any vacation days, etc., which
are "non-negotiable" among the partner schools.

The information collected at this point may be valuable in determining
the final partners to be involved in the network. If, for instance, there is
one school that refuses to budge from a particular position, it is always
possible to eliminate that school from the cluster and replace it with
another more "willing" partner. It is better to identify such recalcitrance
at this point rather than later in the adoption process.

Secure Commitment to Develop a Common Bell Schedule

Although a common school calendar is necessary, a common bell
schedule is absolutely critical. Without a common bell schedule, par-

ticipating schools will never be able to take full advantage of the network. However, there are three exceptions to this hard and fast rule:

(1) Where one or more schools, because of long bus routes, cannot accommodate an early start time, it is possible to leave out those schools for the first period of the day, while making sure that all subsequent periods coincide.

(2) Multiple lunch periods of varying duration may prove to be a formidable problem. One can build morning and afternoon I-TV class schedules, leaving a "lunch block" during the middle of the day during which I-TV classes are not held or are held only among some partners. This has an advantage in that other activities, e.g., student-teacher conferences, administrator meetings, etc., can occur over the network during this time block.

(3) Some schools may have a "block scheduling" format. Where all schools cannot agree on either a common block schedule or conventional 50 or 55 minute class periods, it is possible to operate a joint I-TV schedule if "block" periods are in multiples of 50 or 55 minutes + passing time. In this way, students in block schools can take two 50- or 55-minute I-TV classes during that time without affecting the rest of their schedules.

Secure Commitment to Share Work in Preparation and Planning

A commitment should be secured from the tentative network partners to share in the work of developing a plan for implementing I-TV. This can be formalized by assigning duties to each superintendent, or districts can informally agree to have different persons or committees work on different aspects of the plan. Most clusters work well when one superintendent assumes a leadership role for the planning and implementation of the I-TV network. However, when one person takes sole responsibility for all aspects of I-TV planning and implementation, it is likely that the other partners will neither become as well informed or as committed to implementation.

Identify an Acting Director or Hire a Director for the Consortium

It is important that the consortium appoint an acting director at this point or, if possible, hire a director to help the consortium through the network development process. The acting director may be a lead superintendent or a technology-wise teacher released for a portion of the school day.

Establish a "Network Development Fund"

Pooling a small amount of resources from each district involved into a "Network Development Fund" and identifying a fiscal agent for the consortium will provide the means for hiring a consultant, paying incorporation fees, or covering the other start-up costs associated with network development. It is important to keep an exact account of the start-up costs to which all schools contribute. This running tab will help determine the cost at which new members can enter the consortium. Any member district of the consortium can serve as the fiscal agent for the group.

Conduct an Economic Cost-Benefit Analysis and Establish Funding Capacity

To assist districts in determining the balance between costs and benefits, a cost-benefit analysis should be completed. Chapter 9 identifies the issues involved and provides a "walk through" of a publicly available computerized cost-benefit analysis. This analysis will help schools to identify the factors related to both costs and benefits and will enable them to determine the "break-even point," that is, the minimum number of students involved in I-TV courses for costs to equal benefits.

While establishing the costs (and benefits) of the I-TV network, it is also essential to begin determining the capacity of the local district to absorb the costs associated with I-TV implementation. It can generally be said, however, that if sufficient local need exists for the technology, reallocated dollars can be found to cover the ongoing costs of I-TV operation. Funds for initial I-TV costs can often be identified from state or other sources.

STEP FOUR: IDENTIFY TRANSMISSION LINE PROVIDERS

Initiate Discussion with Phone Companies

Contact the local telephone company to determine the preliminary availability of I-TV transmission capabilities in the area. There are several questions that can be asked to gauge their level of knowledge, capability, and cooperation regarding I-TV implementation. The following questions should be asked of all likely I-TV providers, e.g., telephone company, cable company, rural electric cooperative, or power/utility association, in your area.

(1) To what extent is fiber optic cable available in your area? Does it exist only between one telephone company central office and another? What part of the local telephone network is copper-based?

(2) Which I-TV technologies will they support? Full T-1? Analog fiber? Digital fiber? ATM?

(3) Has the company filed a distance learning tariff with the state public service or utilities commission? What are the rates for each technology included in the tariff? Is there an educational discount which applies?

(4) If the company has not filed a tariff, what customer-specific pricing would they apply to a request? (Note: In order to get an answer to this question, the phone company will most likely need a list of all schools to be included in the network.)

(5) Does the company have a list of classroom equipment specifications and/or costs?

While it may not be possible to determine the exact cost of a transmission line lease at this point, the relative availability and affordability of I-TV in your area can be determined. T-1 copper is widely available as a transmission medium across the United States. Some phone companies, however, may choose to make T-1-based systems unavailable by charging prohibitively high monthly rates; theoretically, T-1 should be the least costly of all networks since the lines are already installed.

**Sidebar 3.1. Our Only Limitation Is Our Own Imagination
by James Chadwick, Superintendent of
Haven Public Schools, Kansas**

The original statement was more like, "Our only limitation is the collective imagination of all those involved." Perhaps a bit wordy but the intention, at the time, was to get the attention of those involved in the development of an I-TV system. It started as a "sales pitch" but it soon became a rallying cry, for me at least, in my attempt to generate the enthusiasm I believed necessary to bring a dream into the realm of reality.

In the beginning weeks and months of the development of the A+ network we knew what the basic applications of an I-TV network could be and that the network would meet identified needs. These applications were not enough for the naysayers. It was a way of putting the impetus for development on the shoulders of the participants. It was my way of attempting to get others to become risk takers. Somewhat like, ''Build it and they will come,'' an unheard of approach in rural Kansas.

''Build it'' we did and the applications are still presenting themselves. Things we never dreamed are now everyday occurrences. The system currently offers approximately forty (40) units of credit just for high school students and adults. The evening schedule has expanded each year with college credit courses and extension offerings. Most of the bus driver training, first aid, defensive driving and required safety meetings are conducted via the network.

The list of meetings, special offerings, and special education applications is endless. The A+ Network has just recently connected with a second network, a community college, and a University. Through network interconnections, the A+ Network now has the capability of reaching anywhere in the world with interactive television.

The A+ Network has certainly surpassed our early imagination. It has provided expanded educational offerings for small, rural schools. It has provided a certain amount of economic development to the area, though that aspect is grossly underdeveloped at this time.

Looking back on those early days of I-TV in rural Kansas I can see my approach was definitely a win-win situation. The potential of Interactive Television in educational settings is truly unlimited if one is creative and willing to explore any and all possible applications. It is essential to have creative, innovative teachers and to give them the latitude to fail with continued support and succeed with full credit for their efforts.

The statement has since become a philosophy that I believe applies to most areas of education and specifically to areas of advancing technology.

I am currently in a new position in an area with no I-TV system. We are working toward the development of a system but the earlier question, ''How will we ever use the system?'' has been answered many times over. The statement ''our only limitation is our collective imagination'' is still applicable.

Note: James Chadwick was formerly Superintendent of Schools in Comanche County, Kansas and was a pioneer in the development of the Kansas A+ Network.

Initiate Discussion with Cable TV Companies

Do not overlook the possibility for a progressive local cable company to either include the schools in their plans for fiber deployment or contract with the schools for use of their existing fiber. This possibility may, in some circumstances, be markedly less expensive than working with a telephone company. As deregulation of the telecommunications industry is carried out, greater interconnectivity among telecommunications providers will be possible.

Determine the Technology to Be Implemented

Based on the accumulated information—preferred technology, technologies available, and cost—a decision should be made as to which technology will be implemented. Some clusters may not have the luxury of adopting a common technology for every school. For example, one school—because of its location within a particular phone company service area—may be forced to adopt a technology which is either not possible or prohibitively expensive for schools in another telephone company service area. Connectivity is still possible between the technologies, but remember that shared broadcasts will always be viewed at the lowest common denominator. For example, a school receiving a course via a T-1 copper line in an otherwise DS-3 fiber network will appear to other schools at a lower video quality; broadcasts transmitted by other DS-3 sites on the network will likewise be seen at lower video quality at the T-1 site. Such cross-technology broadcasts will also require additional central office equipment to transfer the signals between technologies.

Cost Estimates for Chosen Technology

After all transmission line providers for the cluster have been determined, one telephone company (or other provider) should be identified as the primary point of contact. Pricing requests for other providers should be handled through this single point of contact. In this way it can be assured that routing, hub determination, and network architecture will be worked out among line providers without the school or cluster having to play that role.

Insure that cost estimates are developed for several lease periods, e.g., 3-year, 5-year, 7-year, or 10-year periods, and ask that a separate line item be included for lease/purchase of classroom equipment. One-time costs should be listed separately from ongoing monthly costs. Be sure that pricing options are requested for all of the following, and that it is made clear whether each cost is a per site or a per cluster cost: quad-split video, far-end camera control, freeze-frame (still) video, gateway access (to other clusters), Ethernet option, and Internet access.

Also the request for pricing should include a combined cluster amount which is then divided by the number of schools/sites in the cluster. In this way, both the distance-sensitive rates as they apply to each school and the equally divided cost for the entire cluster will be available.

A word of warning: It may be tempting, especially for those schools who happen to be located in close proximity to the telephone company central office (CO), to want each school to pay their actual calculated monthly cost. Avoid the temptation. The cluster will work much better organizationally, and there will be much less cause for later conflict, if all sites equally divide the entire cluster cost among themselves.

Make Sure That the Technology Chosen Allows for Full Interconnectivity

In discussions with line lease providers, demand that the equipment they are advocating has the potential to interconnect with other networks. The immediate concern will be focused on the connectivity of schools within the cluster, but eventually the cluster may want to connect with other clusters or with other higher education institutions.

STEP FIVE: IDENTIFY SOURCES OF I-TV CLASSROOM EQUIPMENT

Determine Phone or Cable Company Capacity to Provide Classroom Equipment

You will have far fewer headaches and equipment compatibility problems if the transmission line lease provider (telephone company or cable company) provides or subcontracts for I-TV classroom equipment and installation. No doubt, there are equipment vendors who will claim to—and probably will—be able to equip an I-TV room for $15,000 or less. However, cost-cutting measures are paid for many times over in repair and replacement, not to mention inferior audio and/or video quality and problems with compatibility of classroom and transmission equipment.

It is imperative that corners not be cut, especially on audio equipment. Ninety percent of the technical problems encountered will be audio problems. Money spent up front on high quality audio equipment will be worthwhile. Current experience places the range of classroom equipment costs at between $25,000—$35,000. Costs will undoubtedly come down somewhat over time, but these figures are good ballpark estimates of typical equipment costs, including installation charges.

Assess Advantages/Disadvantages of Acting as Your Own Subcontractor

If there is no phone company or other line lease provider willing or able to subcontract the classroom equipment and installation, a cluster will be faced with acting as its own subcontractor. Be aware of the challenges involved: finding a reputable dealer knowledgeable about I-TV installations; insuring compatibility of equipment; accurately assessing equipment quality; and having to negotiate between transmission line and classroom equipment specifications.

STEP SIX: DETERMINE NEED FOR/HIRE A CONSULTANT

Can You Provide Your Own Leadership?

Many clusters manage to provide their own leadership during the discussion, planning, and I-TV implementation process, but decide to hire a director or coordinator to actually run the network. Other clusters simply cannot allocate the time necessary to handle all the leadership responsibilities for planning and implementation and choose to hire a consultant to take responsibility for managing the entire process. Still other clusters — usually small ones — are able to handle planning and implementation as well as network operation by relying on a division of labor among network superintendents.

Each cluster needs to assess its capabilities in each area — network planning, implementation, and operation.

Will the Transmission Line Provider Supply Technical Assistance?

Determine the extent to which the line lease provider can supply all needed technical assistance. Are they willing to hire a consulting firm to design the network, including classroom equipment?

Is There Sufficient (and Reliable) Technical Expertise Available?

There are three areas in which expertise is particularly needed:

(1) Network design, including the network configuration, hub site selection, fiber deployment plans (if necessary), and negotiations among

phone companies. This is most appropriately handled by a lead telephone company with the assistance of an engineering firm hired by the telephone company(ies). These costs should not be borne by the school districts.

(2) Classroom design, including recommendations for room modifications, room orientation (e.g., front, back, etc.), monitor, microphone, and speaker placement, and specifications for location of teacher podium and riser. This can also be handled by the lead telephone company, however, it will most often be done by a sub-contractor. If the engineering company with whom the line lease provider is working cannot adequately provide this service, a list of experienced consultants may also be available from existing I-TV clusters. The cost of this service may be covered by the line lease provider(s); however, it will most usually fall to the school district cluster.

(3) Educational and organizational planning, including assisting in development of a joint calendar and bell schedule, working out an I-TV class schedule, working out negotiations with higher education institutions for dual-credit classes, conducting student course interest surveys, etc. This aspect of I-TV development, while often considered to be less important than the technical aspects, is one area in which I-TV networks can easily falter. Unless constant attention is given to the educational planning for I-TV — which is, after all, the motive for doing all of this — clusters can end up with a technically operative network with few users.

A lead superintendent can take responsibility for this component, a consultant can be hired to help with this process, or a network director or coordinator can be hired at this point, on a full- or part-time basis, to make sure that the educational planning is adequately and comprehensively handled.

Hiring an I-TV Consultant

If the decision is made to hire an I-TV consultant, it is advisable to seek references from experienced I-TV clusters. Identify two or three consultants or consulting firms. Make sure that the consultants' experience includes involvement in networks similar to the one being planned. A broad-based "technology consultant" will not suffice. Secure cost estimates from two or three consultants along with the scope of activities to be performed by each. Be sure that the consultant is not requiring payment for services which are already reliably provided by the telephone company. Determine the cost basis upon which the consulting firm is operating, e.g., per hour, per day, or per contract period. If consultant fees are based on the preparation of cluster documents, make sure that the documents provided are individually prepared for your cluster, not simply a copy of a document prepared for other clusters.

It is suggested that the decision to hire a consultant be based on (in order of priority):

(1) Reputation of consulting firm
(2) Experience with other K-12 two-way interactive TV networks
(3) References given by other K-12 clients
(4) Cost

STEP SEVEN: PLAN OF OPERATION

Final Commitment from Cooperating Districts

Up to now, operations have been with an informal cluster of schools loosely organized around a common goal. The cluster should be formalized as the implementation of the network becomes certain; action should be taken in the following six areas.

Develop a Joint Powers Agreement or Form a Corporation

This method of I-TV network formation may be undertaken less formally through a joint powers agreement or enacted more formally through the formation of a not-for-profit corporation. (See Chapter 4 for details on Network Organization and Administration.)

Develop Bylaws and/or Network Policies

Regardless of the method of organization, it will be necessary to develop written policies and procedures covering a large number of issues. Bylaws typically address issues such as consortium agreement, governing authority, meetings of the corporation, negotiable instruments, bylaw ratification and amendment, financial issues, and issues of withdrawal, expulsion, dissolution, and expansion of membership. Other network policies, such as employee duties and responsibilities, instructional delivery and classroom management, curriculum account-ability, student policies, visitation, monitoring, network privacy issues, scheduling, and community access are usually spelled out in a policies and procedures manual.

Identify a Fiscal Agent for the Consortium

Regardless of the organizational structure chosen, one school should be identified as the fiscal agent for the consortium. Under a joint powers agreement the district serving as fiscal agent will handle all money through the existing district accounting system. In a not-for-profit cor-poration, the treasurer can be a person unaffiliated with any school district or may be the bookkeeper in one of the participating districts. In either case, the fiscal agent should maintain a separate set of accounting books for the cluster.

Determine Basis for Achieving Sending/Receiving Equity

There are several ways that equity can be achieved between sending and receiving schools. A preferable method, which insures that all participating schools play a major role in the provision of courses as well as in their reception, requires that each school originate a minimum of one course per year over the network. In this way financial equity will be realized over time, without the need for money to change hands based on class enrollments and number of courses taught.

Determine Responsibility for Day-to-Day Program Operation

While the governing board or board of directors will assume overall responsibility for network decision making, day-to-day decisions still must be made. One alternative for handling such decision making is the formation of three councils (see Chapter 4 for detailed information):

(1) I-TV superintendents' council—which handles major decisions and places recommendations for action on the Board agenda
(2) I-TV principals' council—which handles decisions regarding class and teacher selection, as well as the bulk of day-to-day decisions
(3) I-TV teachers' council—which serves as a problem-solving and peer support group. Recommendations for action to the principals' or superintendents' council may originate here.

Develop a Common Calendar and Bell Schedule

At this point it is necessary that a common calendar and bell schedule be decided upon. (Chapter 4 provides detailed information on this matter.) A good rule of thumb is that a compromise be reached by allowing no school to maintain its existing calendar or bell schedule exactly. In this way, with all schools similarly compromising, the beneficial effect of having all schools starting out on an equal footing can be achieved.

If the need of the participating schools for I-TV is great enough, a way can be found to reach a common calendar and bell schedule. This statement implies, of course, that where opportunity, rather than need, is driving the decision to implement I-TV among one or more members, joint decisions involving districts will be more difficult.

The make-up of an I-TV consortium may change during the early discussion and planning stages. It is likely that a larger group will be involved during the early stages than at the point of actual implementation. Districts unwilling to give up their autonomy in scheduling may fall by the wayside during the process of developing a common calendar and bell schedule. It is best that such reluctance to compromise be discovered at this point, rather than after I-TV implementation. Allow such districts the option to bow out. After the right combination of cooperating schools are found, a decision on common calendar and bell schedule can be reached in a short period of time.

Identify Courses to Be Taught—Develop I-TV Course Schedule

Up to now the cluster has been operating on the assumption that certain courses were needed as additions to the curricula of individual districts. A joint I-TV course schedule should now be developed. Chapter 4 describes how the pertinent information can be collected and assembled into a course schedule.

Secure Staff Commitment to Teach over the Network

As the I-TV Joint Course Schedule is being developed—or immediately prior to it—staff commitment to teach over the network should be secured. Assuming that each I-TV teacher is a current employee of one of the cluster districts, no special arrangements need to be made with respect to teaching contracts. Each teacher will remain the employee of the "home" or "originating" school district from which the class is taught. If additional staff are hired to teach an I-TV course, the cooperating schools will need to decide whether that person becomes the employee of one school or of the consortium.

Teacher Training

While learning to use the I-TV technology takes very little time, providing for teacher training – and more importantly practice time – is imperative. Two components should be included in any I-TV teacher training workshop. The first covers the technical aspects, i.e., what buttons to push and what camera to look at. The second involves the process of adaptation to and incorporation of all of the instructional technology tools available in the I-TV classroom (see Chapter 7). The curriculum need not change from that employed in the traditional classroom and, for that matter, neither do the teaching techniques. However, teachers will very quickly see the advantage of using the graphics camera instead of the blackboard, or of incorporating a videotape segment into a lesson at the press of a button, or of demonstrating dissection techniques over the video monitor so that all students can see as if they are standing over the specimen, or showing an entire class outline directly from the teacher's computer screen. These are only a few of the capabilities which will undoubtedly impact teaching techniques and styles. Adequate teacher training time allows teachers to learn to take advantage of the many instructional opportunities available in the I-TV classroom.

The "technical" portion of the workshop can be separated from the "curriculum development" or "instructional techniques" section and may be done by separate workshop instructors. In this, case, however, be sure to include the "instructional techniques" instructor in the "technical workshop," so that he or she will be able to operate the I-TV equipment.

Develop Community Usage Programs

Make Preliminary Contact with Community Organizations/ Agencies/Businesses

Now is the time to make potential community users more aware of the capabilities of the I-TV network. Any entity – community organizations, agencies, businesses, or governmental offices—which may have a need for intercommunity linkage is a potential user. Meet with such groups to show videotapes of similar networks and instigate discussion on the potential uses that could be made of the I-TV network outside the school day.

Work with Local/Regional Community and/or Economic Development Commissions

An application of I-TV that is often overlooked is the potential of the technology to facilitate community or economic development. The notion of a "telecommunity center"—made possible by the availability of an I-TV classroom for community residents for after-school use— should be explored. Tying the plans of economic development commissions or industrial development authorities with the planning for an I-TV network is a wise step.

Prepare Classroom and Install Equipment

Classroom Preparation

Assuming that an existing classroom will be used, the amount of preparation required for the I-TV classroom is dependent upon the age, structure, and location of the classroom chosen. A modern, recently constructed classroom will likely require very little in the way of room modifications; an older classroom may require more extensive work. If no classroom is available and additional space must be remodeled within the school for the I-TV classroom, costs will obviously be greater than if a few room modifications are all that is required.

If no space is available within the school building and additional space must be purchased or leased, consider the possibility of moving a traditional class to a temporary classroom rather than using a temporary or mobile classroom as the I-TV room. It will be virtually impossible to sufficiently make acoustic treatments in a mobile classroom and the audio quality will suffer.

Requirements for the I-TV classroom can generally be grouped into the following categories:

(1) Air conditioning: Because of the temperature requirements of the equipment, air conditioning is recommended. Some transmission

line providers require that their network equipment be located in an air conditioned environment.

(2) Carpeting: Because of the decrease in audio quality caused by bare floors, carpeting is usually recommended.

(3) Acoustic wall treatment: Recommendations vary, but a good rule of thumb is that a minimum of two adjacent walls should be covered in some sort of sound-soak material. This can be either acoustical paneling or carpeting. Some equipment vendors suggest that no wall treatment be done until the audio is tested under current conditions. Generally speaking, concrete block or masonry walls are more problematic than other wall surfaces because of audio reflection.

(4) Window treatment: A general recommendation is that all windows in the I-TV room be either covered or eliminated so the video cameras can be correctly balanced. (If windows are eliminated, take care that fire safety codes are taken into account.) In some situations, covering of windows with blinds and heavy draperies will suffice. The springtime temptation to raise the blinds, pull back the curtains, and open the windows, however, is likely to reduce I-TV video quality.

(5) Lighting: Modern fluorescent panels typically provide sufficient lighting in the I-TV classroom. Placement of the panels, however, may be a consideration in orienting the I-TV room, e.g., determining the front and back of the room. Addition or removal of panels—for instance, directly above the teacher—may be necessary. ''Egg crate diffusers'' placed under the fluorescent lighting panels will provide for much more even lighting.

The above recommendations are general in nature and should be specifically determined for each individual classroom. Assistance in this area may be provided by the transmission line provider, e.g., telephone company, or by a consultant.

Teacher Podium and Riser

It is generally agreed that an elevated teacher platform enables both students and teacher a better view in the I-TV classroom. This riser is usually 6−8″ high and can be built directly under the teacher desk or podium or may extend across the entire front of the classroom. An added advantage of using a riser is the ability to conceal beneath the floor the wiring associated with equipment located in the teacher podium.

The design of the teacher podium will depend on the equipment to be included in it. (The design of the podium may be done through a vendor or consultant service.) Generally speaking, either a rectangular or L-shaped design is most serviceable. Considerations in the design include:

(1) Cutout for preview monitor in top of podium/desk
(2) Mounting for graphics camera or placement of document camera on top of the podium
(3) Kneehole in which the preview monitor is mounted
(4) Desktop location for computer monitor and keyboard
(5) Desktop location for video microscope (if used)
(6) Desktop location for system keypad controller
(7) Inside shelf space for any combination of VCR, CODEC, CPU, echo canceller, video switcher, audio/video controller, etc. (Exact equipment is dependent upon the specific technology chosen. Some equipment may be located in a separate fan-cooled cabinet.)

Equipment Installation

Once the room is modified, the riser built, and the teacher podium installed, the room is ready for equipment installation. This will be done by the transmission line provider or by a classroom equipment vendor. In those cases where the transmission line provider does not take responsibility for both purchase of classroom equipment and its installation, it is vitally important that the line provider work in concert with the classroom equipment provider in order to avoid problems in equipment compatibility. It is wise to avoid placing the schools in the position of mediating between the transmission line provider and the classroom equipment provider.

Equipment should be installed in time to allow teacher training to occur over the completed I-TV network and to allow for additional teacher practice time prior to the first day of the semester.

Identify Facilitators in Each District

Even though there is no need for a supervisor in each remote classroom, there are some duties which must be handled by an adult facilitator at each remote site. Chapter 4 presents a complete listing of facilitator duties. The major activities for which a local facilitator is required include:

(1) Faxing/mailing materials, such as tests and homework between sites
(2) Delivering test materials to an I-TV classroom or proctoring tests upon request by the I-TV teacher
(3) Assisting community I-TV users with use of the network

Develop a Maintenance Plan/Budget

At some point equipment maintenance will be required. There are basically two options for dealing with maintenance: 1) negotiate an ongoing maintenance contract with the transmission line provider (or classroom equipment provider); or 2) pay as you go.

In reality the best recommendation is probably a combination of the two, that is, to negotiate a maintenance contract based on time plus materials, while also maintaining a separate maintenance fund to which all schools contribute. In this way, accumulated funds can be drawing interest until they are needed.

Current recommendations, until such time that greater experience exists in I-TV maintenance requirements, are to have each site contribute $1500 to $2000 toward a joint maintenance fund in the first year after warranties are exhausted (or five to seven percent of the classroom equipment costs). The contribution per site in subsequent years will depend on the extent to which the maintenance funds were depleted during the previous year, the number of sites in the network, and the extent to which the maintenance fund will also be used as an equipment update fund. A maintenance/equipment update fund of $15,000 – $20,000 should be adequate for a cluster of six to eight schools.

Determine Who Will Serve as Network Scheduler

In T-1, DS-3, and ATM networks a person must be designated as "network scheduler." This person enters the times and dates of regular and one-time events into the computer scheduling program that controls the system (see Chapter 2). While it may be possible for each site to remotely dial in and schedule classes, one person should serve as the central point of scheduling to avoid scheduling conflicts. This is usually done by the network director or technical coordinator.

STEP EIGHT: IDENTIFY COMMUNITY USERS OF THE NETWORK

The foundations for this step should have been laid during the initial network development. If the community has been brought along in the planning process, a list of potential community users will have been developed prior to the network coming online. Upon implementation of the I-TV network, however, it will be necessary to make sure that the community has a chance to see the network in action.

Schedule a Community Open House to Showcase the Network

A community open house, perhaps held in conjunction with a PTO meeting, can serve to make a large number of people aware of the capabilities of the network. An I-TV Parents Night, in which parents of I-TV students are invited to talk with their student's teacher over the network, can also serve as a source of community information.

Make Presentations to Community Organizations to Spur Interest in Using the Network

A superintendent or a network director can make presentations to various community organizations, agencies, and other groups. Additionally, a meeting can be held over the network, to engage similar groups across two communities in a discussion of how the network might be used to further their goals.

Construct a List of Potential Community Users

Based on contact with various community groups, compile a list of potential community I-TV users in your network's geographic area. Depending on the extent to which the network wishes to market after-hours use of the network, contact with potential community users can be maintained through mailings or periodic contact.

Recouping I-TV Line Lease Costs

Depending upon the arrangements that have been worked out with the community, the network may be in a position to recoup some I-TV costs by charging community users for use of the network. In some states, however, legal authority to resell telecommunications services resides only with telecommunications providers. Depending on the state, this authority may be transferred at the discretion of the telephone company, or legislation may be enacted which would allow an exception in the statute for school districts. Networks will want to investigate this potential means of offsetting I-TV costs with the telephone company or other transmission line provider.

STEP NINE: EVALUATION

Evaluation is a vital component of a school-based I-TV network. Networks need to have a plan for determining whether they are achieving the goals set forth in the needs assessment stage. Chapter 5 provides detailed information on network evaluation.

Network Organization and Administration

CHAPTER 3 outlined a model for creating a school-based I-TV network. This chapter provides a model for network organization and administration. The authors believe that this is an effective means of bringing together all parties with an interest in the success of the network, along with the necessary technical and educational expertise. Chapter 4 also provides tips on developing an I-TV course schedule, creating a classroom management plan, and eliminating administrative hassles.

NETWORK ORGANIZATION

A formal organization needs to be established in order for a network to function as a consortium of districts. The two commonly used methods of organization for local networks are the creation of a joint powers agreement and the formation of a not-for-profit corporation.

Joint Powers Agreement

A joint powers agreement is a contractual arrangement that defines the privileges, power, and authority of each signer in such areas as equipment ownership, fiscal responsibilities, and network expansion and disbandment; this legally binding contract distributes the decision making and responsibility for the network among all signers. Networks in the process of forming a joint powers agreement can either modify an

Portions of this chapter were first published in "An Adopters' Manual for Two-Way Interactive Television: A Guide to Researching, Planning and Implementing Distance Learning in your School and Community," MIT-E, WeMET and EPN networks, March, 1995. Available from the Missouri Alliance for Interactive Television, K−12 Users' Group. Contact: Missouri Rural Opportunities Council, P.O. Box 118, 301 W. High Street, Room 720, Jefferson City, MO 65102 (573-751-1238).

agreement obtained from an existing I-TV network or hire a consulting firm to assist in the *pro forma* development of an agreement.

Not-for-Profit Corporation

A not-for-profit corporation is a legal entity composed of member districts or institutions. This is usually a preferable method of organization because it allows for tax-deductible contributions to the network. There are several costs involved in establishing a not-for-profit corporation, including:

(1) A fee for registering the articles of incorporation and bylaws with the Secretary of State
(2) A $465 fee to the Internal Revenue Service for processing an Application for Recognition of Exemption as described in Section 501(c)(3) of the Internal Revenue Code
(3) A $200 – $400 attorney fee for preparing and reviewing the articles of incorporation and bylaws (Note: A network may choose to avoid this cost by writing its own bylaws. The ''Small Business Incorporation Series'' provides state-specific manuals on forming corporations; contact P. Gaines Company, P.O. Box 2253, Oak Park, IL 60303.)

If a not-for-profit corporation is formed, bylaws will be required. Bylaws will generally cover the areas of consortium agreement, governing authority, meetings of governing authorities, negotiable instruments, bylaw amendment, financial issues, withdrawal of members, and expansion of membership.

NETWORK ADMINISTRATION

A formal administrative structure for the network will ensure effective communication between the parties involved. Figure 4.1 shows a diagram of the administrative model for I-TV consortiums described in this chapter.

In this model, a facilitator at each site is responsible for coordinating day-to-day activities on the local level (turning the system on and off, distributing tests and quizzes, returning homework, etc.). Beyond this level, there are four administrative bodies which are responsible for different aspects of the network: the board of directors or governing

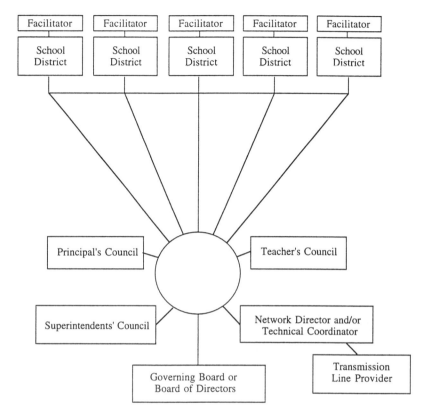

Figure 4.1. An administrative model for school-based I-TV clusters.

board, the superintendents' council, the principals' council and the teachers' council. In addition, a network director and/or technical coordinator is involved in the day-to-day troubleshooting and long-term administration of the network. The roles, duties, and authority of each of these groups are described below.

Board of Directors or Governing Board

The board of directors or governing board is the primary decision-making body of the network. In a school-based network, the board may consist of the president of each school board. Post-secondary institutions in a K − 12 consortium can be represented by a member of the board of curators or regents. In addition, each district superintendent usually sits on this board as a non-voting member. (In the event of the absence of a district's school board representative, the superintendent may vote in that person's place.) This board meets occasionally – for example, every quarter – and is responsible for determining network policy and budget. In addition, the board of directors acts as the final authority on all issues of network expansion and in assessing network fees from its members.

Superintendents' Council

The superintendents of each of the secondary institutions and the chief administrative officer or designee of each of the post-secondary member institutions serve on the superintendents' council. The network director also serves on this council as convenor, facilitator, and non-voting member. The superintendents' council meets as needed, dealing with issues such as:

(1) Development of policy and procedural recommendations for action by the board of directors
(2) Administration of contractual agreements for network staff
(3) Consideration of network growth and expansion
(4) Arranging for the use of the network outside the regular school day for private or public community purposes

Principals' Council

The principals' council consists of the principals of each K-12 educational institution and the curriculum director or designee of each post-secondary member institution. Again, the network director serves on this council as convenor, facilitator, and non-voting member. It is the responsibility of the principals' council to make decisions regarding day-to-day operation of the network, including:

(1) Arranging for common scheduling in all participating schools
(2) Determining student curricular needs for meeting secondary and post-secondary goals
(3) Identifying courses and instructors
(4) Facilitating maintenance of the system and equipment at the building level
(5) Maintaining curriculum accountability and coordination between network schools

(6) Making recommendations to the superintendents' council and board of directors

Teachers' Council

The teachers' council is composed of the current I-TV teachers. This council provides an open forum for discussion of concerns and needs. The network director is responsible for making sure that issues raised and recommendations made by the teachers' council are referred to the appropriate administrative council for action. Meetings of the teachers' council can also be used to provide additional technical training.

NETWORK EMPLOYEES

As mentioned earlier, facilitators are responsible for the day-to-day care and coordination of local I-TV sites, while the network director is responsible for the overall administration of the network.

Local Network Facilitators

The duties of the local network facilitators may be tended to by a single employee within each district or the duties can be distributed among several people at the site. For instance, a school secretary may be responsible for facsimile transmission and mailing, a study hall teacher may be responsible for proctoring a test, and an activities director may be designated to unlock the school and assist with after-hours events.

Schools may choose to pay each of their facilitators an extra stipend for the duties covered during school hours or these duties can be added to those of existing personnel with no extra compensation. Duties carried out after school hours will usually require additional compensation. Facilitator fees for community use may be covered by charging an hourly rate, e.g., $10/hour, from those using the system.

Commonly, local network facilitator duties include:

(1) Distribution and collection of tests, assessments, and evaluations at the request of the remote instructor
(2) Distribution of mailed materials to the I-TV classroom "in boxes" and mailing of materials left in "out boxes" to remote instructors

(3) Daily assistance in initial camera adjustment and audio balancing of equipment

(4) Contacting the network director regarding malfunctioning equipment, technical troubleshooting, and equipment replacement

(5) Sending and receiving daily messages arriving on facsimile or electronic mail systems

(6) Assisting visitors and observers in the interactive classroom

(7) Relaying information on schedule modifications or other potential disruptions identified by the network director to the local instructor(s) and vice versa

(8) Turning on and shutting off the I-TV classroom on a daily basis

Network Director

The network director is responsible for overseeing the quality and operation of the network. The network director works closely with the superintendents, principals, and faculty in each network school. The optimum qualifications for a network director include successful teaching and/or administrative experience; strong leadership and human relations skills; demonstrated organizational and program development skills; experience in community and adult education, gifted education, or other alternative education programming; experience in program evaluation; and interest and demonstrated competence in use of audio/video equipment and computers.

The network director can be a full time employee of the network, or a teacher who has been released for a portion of the school day. Alternatively, the duties can be divided into two positions. A part-time network director can assume responsibility for the organizational administration and educational planning of the network while a part-time technical coordinator can take responsibility for the technical aspects of the network, including equipment troubleshooting, technical adjustments, and minor repair.

Responsibilities of a network director may include:

(1) Working with the superintendent's council, principals' council, and board of directors to develop, implement and coordinate the educational services of the network

(2) Coordinating, facilitating, and promoting after-hours use of the network

(3) Organizing and coordinating I-TV teacher training*

(4) Providing technical and curriculum development support to I-TV teachers

(5) Assisting in the development of a joint calendar, bell schedule, and I-TV class schedule

(6) Coordinating activities and interconnections with other networks

(7) Initiating public relations efforts

(8) Developing network publications and documents

(9) Preparing meeting agendas and documents for the board of directors, superintendents' council, and principals' council

(10) Maintaining the day-to-day scheduling for the network*

(11) Acting as first point of contact for equipment malfunction

(12) Troubleshooting faulty I-TV transmission and classroom equipment*

(13) Serving as a liaison with telecommunications line providers and equipment vendors*

(14) Coordinating, scheduling, and developing itineraries for visitors

(15) Conducting evaluation studies as directed by the superintendents' council

(16) Making presentations to local civic, governmental, agency, and business groups on behalf of the network

[Note: Items with an asterisk (*) can be assigned to a separate technical coordinator position.]

POLICIES

Regardless of the method of organization, it is necessary for I-TV networks to develop written policies and procedures. Written policies are important since issues which were easy for districts to deal with on their own may become a source of conflict when districts are joined together via I-TV. For example, differences between districts in student attendance policies will likely result in confusion or lack of control unless such policies are coordinated across network schools. Anticipating and resolving potential conflicts before they arise will diminish the amount of tension and interruption in the teaching-learning process.

Some of the issues and questions that networks will want to resolve before going online include:

(1) What are the fees for non-member usage of the network? Can the network re-sell use of the network? What community groups will have access to I-TV facilities and equipment?

(2) What will be the standards for teacher evaluation? Who will be responsible for conducting performance-based evaluation of I-TV teachers?

(3) How will student conduct be monitored? What disciplinary actions will be available to I-TV teachers and on what basis?

(4) What will be the policies covering site visitation? Will students be electronically monitored? How will student and teacher privacy issues be safeguarded?

(5) What standards will cover the operation and care of equipment and furnishings?

(6) Will extracurricular meetings or events be held during I-TV class times? How will the I-TV teacher be informed of legitimate excuses for remote school activities in advance? How will tardiness be handled?

(7) What will be the admission and grading policies in I-TV classes? Will course prerequisites be agreed upon by all participating districts?

(8) What will be the notification procedures of other districts in the event of early school dismissal or cancellation due to inclement weather?

(9) How will scheduling of zero or eighth hour classes be handled?

(10) How will parent-teacher conferences be scheduled over the network?

SAMPLE POLICIES

Listed below are examples of policies used by I-TV clusters to deal with some of the most essential I-TV issues. These examples are intended to provide the reader with ideas for resolving local issues, rather than to provide prescriptive recommendations for policy development.

Provision for Student Texts and Resources

The transmitting teacher is responsible for selecting the textbooks and additional resources to be used in I-TV classes. Selections can be subject to review by the principals' council. Texts and resources (including materials and equipment) should be included in the course description/syllabus (see Classroom Management below).

Each remote school should be responsible for acquisition of text and other resource materials. However, at the discretion of the originating school, the originating teacher may take responsibility for text and material disbursement, either retaining ownership of the texts or requesting payment for them from each remote site.

Student Code of Conduct

The I-TV classroom will be unfamiliar for many students; students must demonstrate considerable self-discipline to function effectively in the I-TV classroom. Each school district participating in the I-TV network is offering a valuable service to its students by providing secondary and dual-credit courses to which they would not otherwise have access. Student participation is a privilege that can be limited or revoked.

Class attendance, participation in inter-school discussions, completion and transmission of assignments, and attentiveness are the primary responsibilities of the student. Network standards of behavior are expected to be met by all students, whether teachers are present in the classroom or instructing from a remote site. As in any classroom, defacing or abusing furnishings and equipment is considered a major disciplinary infraction.

Instructors will expect and require the student to assume responsibility for his/her learning. All students are required to complete a Student Enrollment Contract (see Figure 4.2) which clearly defines student responsibility and the expected code of behavior. In the event of violation of the behavior code, responsibility for imposition of penalties will remain with the student's school of official enrollment.

Student Operation of Equipment

Students will not operate I-TV equipment without the authorization of the I-TV teacher or network employee(s). Such authorization will only occur after the student exhibits an understanding of the value of the equipment and its operation. Two students will be identified as student aides in each class. These aides will be trained in equipment operation and will be responsible for making camera and sound adjustments at the beginning of class.

I-TV Student Contract

Two-way interactive television allows schools to provide low-incidence courses or dual-credit college courses to students who would not otherwise have access to them. Because of the uniqueness of two-way interactive television, certain standards are expected of students enrolling in these courses. This contract is intended to make both the students and parents aware of the standards expected of enrolled students.

As the undersigned student of record in a two-way interactive television course, I understand and accept the Student Code of Conduct Policy and agree to abide by the policies and procedures established by the _____ Network. *I agree that:*

1. Insubordination of any kind (behaviors or incidents that disrupt or interfere with teaching or learning) will not be tolerated in the I-TV classroom;
2. Inappropriate language or gestures will not be tolerated;
3. I can be recorded (visual or audio) at any time without specific warning;
4. I will position myself in the classroom to be in camera view at all times;
5. I will not manipulate equipment in the classroom without expressed direction or permission from supervisors or instructors;
6. I will not be involved in any academically dishonest activity; I will not cheat nor will I assist others in cheating;
7. I will conform to any additional rules as specified orally or in writing by the instructor.

Further, I understand that if I am found to be in violation of any of the policies listed above, I will be subject to the following disciplinary action.

First Offense: Verbal or written warning from instructor followed by parental notification of the infraction through written letter. The warning will be delivered to the student using procedures that assure student privacy. A copy of the letter will also be sent to the students' principal.

Second Offense: The student will be removed from the class until such time that a conference of parents, student, instructor, and principal offers assurance that the misconduct will not reoccur.

SEVERE MISCONDUCT, including damage or defacing I-TV equipment or facilities, threats, violent behavior or intent, drug or alcohol use, or repeated policy violation may result in permanent removal from the class. The student may be subject to loss of full or partial credit for coursework.

This Student Contract does not supercede policies or provisions
for student conduct recognized by the student's home school.

_____	_____	_____
Student Signature	Parent/Guardian Signature	Principal Signature
_____	_____	_____
I-TV Course(s)	Address	Home School
_____	_____	_____
Date	Phone Number	School Year

Figure 4.2. Sample student enrollment contract.

Student Grievance Processes

Students who are unable to resolve a grievance regarding I-TV instruction, coursework, discipline, or other issues may seek resolution through the principal at the school of enrollment. The principal may engage the instructor, transmitting site administrators, or other appropriate persons in seeking a positive resolution to the conflict.

Visitation and Observation of Network Sites

Visitors may be scheduled to observe interactive instruction in any or all I-TV classrooms at the discretion of the network director, instructors, and principals. Such visitations will be scheduled so as to ensure the least disruptive atmosphere for students and instructors. The network director and/or principals will provide advance notice of planned observations to instructors. Individual I-TV teachers may request that visitors not be allowed in their classrooms. Visitation will be limited to two visits per week in any one I-TV classroom.

Grading and Reporting

Students in I-TV classrooms will encounter grading scales and systems with which they are not familiar. Grading scales in I-TV classes will be based on the standards announced by the I-TV instructor. This scale may differ from the standards of the remote sites and should be clearly communicated both orally and in writing to all students, e.g., some teachers may set a standard of 95% or above for an "A," as opposed to 90% or 93% or above.

(Note: Schools that adopt grading standards based on outcomes or I-TV instructors who rely on various forms of authentic assessment will collaborate to provide students with grades and/or assessment information that reflects the system on which their transcript is based. In other words, students in I-TV classes will be graded based on the standards of the originating school, but translation to an alternative reporting system may be necessary and, if so, will be accommodated.)

Instructor and Student Privacy Provisions

Individuals who instruct or enroll in I-TV courses do so with the full knowledge that video and audio transmission, monitoring, and/or taping may be undertaken at any time without advance notice. Information regarding student grades, assessment, or disciplinary actions will be transmitted by private telephone conversation, courier, or mail to ensure student privacy.

Administrative Monitoring of Instruction

Members of the superintendents' council, principals' council, and the network director may periodically monitor network transmissions without prior notice given to staff or students. The goal of such monitoring is to:

(1) Provide administrators with the means for student disciplinary review
(2) Assist the network director in identifying needed technical improvements and needed teacher training
(3) Assess educational strengths and weaknesses of the technology

Neither the network nor videotaped segments from the network will be used for purposes of teacher evaluation. Performance-based teacher evaluation remains the responsibility of the home school principal.

Archival Provisions/Copyright Protection

It is the responsibility of the transmitting instructor/school site to arrange for daily taping and archiving of courses. It is recommended that daily taping occur at each remote site to assist absent students in makeup work. Cataloging and short-term storage (approximately seven days) of video recordings of classes is recommended. Recordings of students, class proceedings, or presentations, whether directly authorized by the network or not, remain the property of the network and are not for dissemination, sale, or other unauthorized use.

DEVELOPING A COURSE SCHEDULE

Perhaps the most daunting—and most important—annual network task is developing the course schedule. The following process is designed to help principals in designing a course schedule that will meet the needs of the member districts.

Conduct a Student Course Interest Survey

Survey the sophomores and juniors regarding their potential interest in various courses if those courses were available. The list of possible courses should include dual-credit as well as high school courses. Figure 4.3 is a sample I-TV course interest survey.

Identify Those Areas in Which the District Curriculum Is Weak

Each high school principal, in conjunction with the counselor, should determine the areas in which the district's course offerings are insufficient. Information such as findings of any state reviews and difficulties experienced by graduates in meeting college entry requirements should be taken into account. This information should be compiled at a joint meeting of principals and should include both differences and commonalities among schools. Figure 4.4 shows a matrix that can be used for this purpose.

Identify Areas in Which Districts Have a Master Teacher

Each high school principal should identify the subjects in which a "master" teacher is already on staff. This does not mean only teachers with a master's degree, but rather those teachers who possess an exceptional ability to inspire learning among their students. A list of these teachers should be compiled for each district and a composite list developed by subject area.

Design a List of Possible I-TV Courses

It will be possible to generate a list of potential I-TV courses by carefully and systematically matching student interests, areas of curriculum weakness, and availability of exceptional teachers. For example, a class in which a large number of students indicated an interest, which was identified as a need by two or more principals, and for which a master teacher was available on staff would receive highest priority as an I-TV class. An entire prioritized list of course offerings can be constructed in this manner.

Student Course Interest Survey

High School You Attend: _____

Current Grade Level: ____9th ____10th ____11th

The list of course offerings below includes classes that may not be currently offered in your high school. Through interactive television technology you may now be able to take many courses which you would not otherwise be able to take in a small school, while still being able to see and hear your instructor and other students at all times and to ask questions as spontaneously as in your regular classroom.

Please check the courses below in which you are **fairly certain** you would enroll, if they were offered in your high school NEXT YEAR.

___ Anatomy and Physiology		___ Physics	
___ Ecological and Environmental Science		___ Calculus	
___ Biology II (Advanced Biology)		___ Trigonometry	
___ Marine Biology		___ Math Analysis	
___ Indiv. Science Investigations		___ Data Processing	
___ Chemistry I ___ Chemistry II		___ Advanced Computer Applications	
___ Astronomy		___ Advanced Computer Programming	
___ Geology			

___ Music Theory		___ Literature of the World	
___ Humanities		___ Journalism	
___ Art History		___ Broadcast Journalism (Radio and TV)	
___ Drawing		___ Creative Writing	
___ Photography		___ Advanced Composition	
		___ Debate/Drama	

___ World Geography		___ World Marketing & Investment	
___ Missouri History		___ Business Economics	
___ Sociology		___ Small Business Management/	
___ Economics		Entrepreneurship	
___ Family and Society		___ Introduction to American Law	
___ Global Issues in Contemporary Society		___ Child Development	

___ Spanish	Level I___	Level II___	Level III___
___ French	Level I___	Level II___	Level III___
___ Latin	Level I___	Level II___	Level III___
___ German	Level I___	Level II___	Level III___
___ Russian	Level I___	Level II___	Level III___
___ Japanese	Level I___	Level II___	Level III___

___ Other: _____

___ Other: _____

Figure 4.3. Sample I-TV student course interest survey.

Do you plan on going to college ? ___ Yes ___ No

If courses were offered that could provide both high school and college credit, would you be interested in paying the college tuition fees to enroll? ___ Yes ___ No

Taking advanced placement courses in high school could allow you to have the equivalent college freshman course waived. If your academic achievement qualified you for enrollment in an advanced placement course, would you be interested in enrolling? ___Yes ___ No

It is likely that dual credit courses will be available for you to take next year within your high school. In which of the following interactive TV classes would you be interested in enrolling next year for both high school and college credit?
___ Beginning Speech
___ Art Appreciation
___ College Algebra
___ World Literature I
___ Composition & Rhetoric (College Freshman English)
___ US History
___ Civics & Government
___ Spanish I (College Spanish)
___ German I (College German)
___ Japanese I

Are there other dual credit or college courses in which you would be interested in enrolling?_____

_____

_____

_____

Figure 4.3 (continued). Sample I-TV student course interest survey.

Develop an I-TV Course Schedule

After a prioritized list of I-TV course offerings is constructed, the process of constructing a joint I-TV course schedule can begin. Each principal should come to the planning meeting with a copy of his or her school's existing course schedule. Some schools may choose to use this opportunity for revamping their entire schedule.

Start by placing the highest priority classes in the time periods in which master teachers are potentially available and in time periods which do not conflict with the existing class schedule. This should be continued until the schedule is complete (see Figure 4.5). Keep in mind that multiple classes can occur during the same class period. (Note: In T-1, DS-3, and ATM systems usually only one multipoint class can occur simultaneously, but any number of point-to-point classes can be held.)

I-TV Course Scheduling Worksheet

School: _____

Principals' Priorities:				
What Classes Do You Need?	1 ___ 2 ___ 3 ___ 4 ___ 5 ___ 6 ___ 7 ___	1 ___ 2 ___ 3 ___ 4 ___ 5 ___ 6 ___ 7 ___	1 ___ 2 ___ 3 ___ 4 ___ 5 ___ 6 ___ 7 ___	1 ___ 2 ___ 3 ___ 4 ___ 5 ___ 6 ___ 7 ___
Subject Area of Master Teachers:				
What Classes Can You Offer?	1 ___ 2 ___ 3 ___ 4 ___ 5 ___ 6 ___ 7 ___	1 ___ 2 ___ 3 ___ 4 ___ 5 ___ 6 ___ 7 ___	1 ___ 2 ___ 3 ___ 4 ___ 5 ___ 6 ___ 7 ___	1 ___ 2 ___ 3 ___ 4 ___ 5 ___ 6 ___ 7 ___
Student Interests:				
What Classes Do Students Want?	1 ___ 2 ___ 3 ___ 4 ___ 5 ___ 6 ___ 7 ___ 8 ___ 9 ___ 10 ___	1 ___ 2 ___ 3 ___ 4 ___ 5 ___ 6 ___ 7 ___ 8 ___ 9 ___ 10 ___	1 ___ 2 ___ 3 ___ 4 ___ 5 ___ 6 ___ 7 ___ 8 ___ 9 ___ 10 ___	1 ___ 2 ___ 3 ___ 4 ___ 5 ___ 6 ___ 7 ___ 8 ___ 9 ___ 10 ___
Needed Classes For Which a Master Teacher Does Not Exist:				

Figure 4.4. *Worksheet for scheduling I-TV courses.*

I-TV CLASS SCHEDULE

DRAFT DATE: ____

| 19 __ - __ __ |
| 19 __ - __ __ |

	School 1	School 2	School 3	School 4	School 5	School 6
1st Hour MP Time:						
1st Hour PTP						
2nd Hour MP Time:						
2nd Hour PTP						
3rd Hour MP Time:						
3rd Hour PTP						
4th Hour MP Time:						
4th Hour PTP						
5th Hour MP Time:						
5th Hour PTP						
6th Hour MP Time:						
6th Hour PTP						
7th Hour MP Time:						
7th Hour PTP						

NOTES: MP = Multipoint classes; PTP = Point-to-Point classes.

Figure 4.5. Blank I-TV class schedule form.

117

Sidebar 4.1. Helpful Hints for Scheduling Courses

1. If possible, begin the process during January of the year preceding I-TV implementation.
2. It is unlikely that a final schedule can be worked out in a single sitting. After the first meeting a draft schedule can be distributed to all principals for review. Three to five versions of the schedule may be necessary before settling on a final copy. Be sure to date or number each version of the schedule.
3. Dual-credit classes may be either M-W-F or T-TH classes; try to align the scheduling of dual-credit classes to avoid the need for study hall or other supervision of students during non-class days.
4. In small schools, courses such as band may occupy most students during the class period in which it is offered. An obvious pairing of schools for a point-to-point class might arise from those which have common band times.
5. After a semi-final draft is worked out among the schools, each school should conduct a pre-enrollment to determine class numbers in each I-TV class. The pre-enrollment data may cause a final revision of the I-TV schedule; for example, a class may have no enrollment at one or more sites because of conflicts with required courses.

CLASSROOM MANAGEMENT

Interactive instruction requires detailed attention to daily, semester, and yearly planning. It is a good idea for teachers to prepare a course description/syllabus, a classroom management plan, and a unit- or theme-based study guide for each I-TV course they are instructing. This will provide all students with information about each course offering. In addition, these materials can be used by guidance counselors and principals when enrolling students.

Course Description/Syllabus

The purpose of a course description/syllabus is to provide both students and administrators with information on course content, student prerequisites, and textbooks and/or other materials and equipment needed. A sample course description/syllabus is provided in Figure 4.6.

Classroom Management Plan

By the first day of class, each I-TV teacher should have developed a

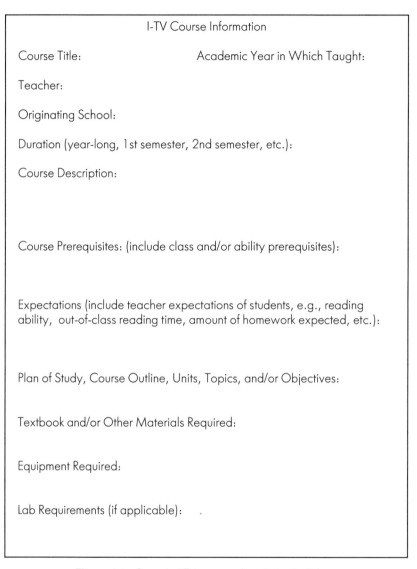

I-TV Course Information

Course Title: Academic Year in Which Taught:

Teacher:

Originating School:

Duration (year-long, 1st semester, 2nd semester, etc.):

Course Description:

Course Prerequisites: (include class and/or ability prerequisites):

Expectations (include teacher expectations of students, e.g., reading ability, out-of-class reading time, amount of homework expected, etc.):

Plan of Study, Course Outline, Units, Topics, and/or Objectives:

Textbook and/or Other Materials Required:

Equipment Required:

Lab Requirements (if applicable):

Figure 4.6. Sample I-TV course description/syllabus.

Classroom Management Plan

Classroom Goal: A classroom setting that promotes learning and personal growth in an environment that is clean, orderly, friendly, and comfortable for everyone.

Classroom Do's:
1. Help others in positive ways, not in ways that cause them to depend on you.
2. Ask questions in class—a question not asked is an opportunity for understanding not taken.
3. Participate in discussion. Share your learning with others.
4. Talk to the teacher about problems or concerns with class work. Do not tolerate failure or mediocrity. My goal is to help you succeed!
5. Offer suggestions to improve the class. No one person has all the answers—share your ideas.

Classroom Don'ts:
1. Private conversation during instruction time.
2. Profanity in words or in gestures.
3. Threatening or intimidating statements or actions.
4. Sleeping, eating, or drinking in class.
5. Copying another student's work.
6. Defacing furniture or equipment.

Class Expectations:
1. Turn homework in on time. Late homework will be accepted with a 10% penalty for every day it is late. Expect 20–30 minutes of homework nightly. Plan your time accordingly!
2. Be responsible for makeup work when you are absent for any reason.
3. Be in the classroom when the tardy bell rings or have an excuse from the office or another teacher.
4. Bring necessary materials to class every day. If you have to return to your locker for materials, you will be counted tardy to class. Required materials are: A blue or black ink pen, a notebook (preferably loose-leaf) and ruled notebook paper, and textbooks.

Make-up Work:
1. You have two (2) days from the day you return from an excused absence to make up missed work. I will try to remind you, but it is primarily your responsiblity to make up missed assignments.
2. Any work missed because of unexcused absences cannot be made up.

Grading Scale:

Grades will be based on a combination of homework assignments, special projects, and unit tests. The following grading scale will be used:

A 90–100%
B 80–89
C 70–79
D 60–69

Figure 4.7. Sample classroom management plan.

classroom management plan for distribution to local and remote students. The plan includes class goals, classroom do's and don'ts, class expectations, handling of make-up work and grading scale. A sample management plan is provided in Figure 4.7.

Teacher Absences

Realizing the possibility of teacher absence at some point, each I-TV teacher should prepare by:

(1) Maintaining at least two videotaped classes for purposes of course enrichment or extension. These lessons should not attempt to cover primary course content nor be tied to a specific unit or topic. The videotapes should capture the teacher in actual instruction, rather than relying on movies or other related programming. Prior videotaping of enrichment or extension topics will provide students with meaningful instruction in the short-term absence of the teacher.

(2) Providing advance notice of absences to remote site principals whenever possible

(3) Maintaining lesson plans to facilitate ongoing instruction in those cases where an I-TV trained substitute teacher is available

In cases of extended I-TV teacher absence (e.g., longer than three consecutive days) the originating site principal should confer with remote site principals regarding the best approach to be taken. In order of preference, the following contingencies can apply:

(1) Rapid technical training of a qualified substitute teacher

(2) Coverage of the class by the principal (or other faculty) based on lesson plans provided by the I-TV teacher

(3) Cancellation of the class

In the case of class cancellation for an extended period of time, decisions as to replacement classes should be made with the best interests of students in mind.

EASING ADMINISTRATIVE HASSLES

In/Out Boxes

Without a teacher or facilitator in the local I-TV room, paper transfer—getting the right papers to the right students at the right time—can be problematic. One way of easing this problem is through the use of in/out boxes (Figure 4.8), stackable file boxes, or wall-hung cubbyholes for papers to be delivered to students as well as papers to be returned to the distant teacher. Each class should have two file boxes. The "in box" should be used for all materials which students will need during that class period; the "out box" should be used for materials the students are sending back to the remote teacher.

Distribution Cover Sheet

The large number of papers moving between sites – by fax, by courier, and by mail – can be very confusing to the local facilitator. The use of a distribution cover sheet can alleviate this confusion. Distribution sheets are completed by the person sending the documents to let the local facilitator know where the materials should be directed, the means of transfer (e.g., fax, e-mail, courier, or posted mail) and the date needed. Any specific instructions, such as "Proctor requested for test on next Tuesday" or "Please make four copies before distributing to students," can be added to the distribution sheet (see Figure 4.9).

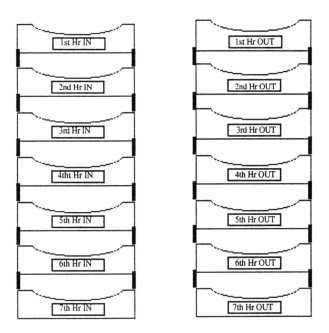

Figure 4.8. *In/out boxes for each class period aid teachers, facilitators, and students in keeping track of course materials.*

Distribution Sheet

Date Sent: ___ / ___ / ___   Total # of Pages Including Distribution Sheet: _____

TO:

<SITE>:	<SITE>:	<SITE>:	<SITE>:	<SITE>:
___ <Teacher>	___ <Teacher>	___ <Teacher>	___ <Teacher>	___ <Teacher>
___ <Teacher>	___ <Teacher>	___ <Teacher>	___ <Teacher>	___ <Teacher>
___ <Teacher>	___ <Teacher>	___ <Teacher>	___ <Teacher>	___ <Teacher>
___ <Facilitator>*	___ <Facilitator>*	___ <Facilitator>*	___ <Facilitator>*	___ <Facilitator>*

FROM:

<SITE>:	<SITE>:	<SITE>:	<SITE>:
___ <Teacher>	___ <Teacher>	___ <Teacher>	___ <Teacher>
___ <Teacher>	___ <Teacher>	___ <Teacher>	___ <Teacher>
___ <Teacher>	___ <Teacher>	___ <Teacher>	___ <Teacher>
___ <Facilitator>*	___ <Facilitator>*	___ <Facilitator>*	___ <Facilitator>*

SEND BY: ___ Fax   ___ Mail   ___ Courier   ___ Other

FOR:

<Course> @ <Time>	<Course> @ <Time>	<Course> @ <Time>	<Course> @ <Time>	<Course> @ <Time>
___ <Course> @ <Time>	___ <Course> @ <Time>	___ <Course> @ <Time>	___ <Course> @ <Time>	___ <Course> @ <Time>
___ <Course> @ <Time>	___ <Course> @ <Time>	___ <Course> @ <Time>	___ <Course> @ <Time>	___ <Course> @ <Time>

TEST: ___ Proctor Needed; Name: _____ (completed by facilitator)   **Test Tapes**

Date: ___ / ___ / ___ Time: _____ to _____   _Include Proctor instructions in Special Instructions below or on separate page_

Quizzes	Homework
Handouts	Practice Tapes
Worksheets	Other:

Make a copy for each student	**Distribute:** ___ upon receipt or	**Distribute by:** ___ In box	**Return by:** ___ Fax
___ in the class	date: ___ / ___ / ___ time: _____	Other:	Mail ___ Courier

Special Instructions:

Facilitator -- Date Completed: ___ / ___ / ___

Figure 4.9. Sample distribution sheet.

123

Figure 4.10. An effective means of insuring test security is for instructors to sign and seal test envelopes for students to open under the document camera.

Test Security

Most teachers will not require proctoring of tests in remote I-TV classrooms. Because I-TV teachers can see all remote sites simultaneously, there is little more opportunity for cheating than might be available within a traditional classroom. Providing security for the transfer of tests, however, may present more of a challenge, since tests are most often mailed ahead of time to the local facilitator. One good method is to place a sticker, piece of tape, or written message over the sealed envelope flap. Upon retrieving the sealed envelope from the "In Box," a local student can place the envelope under the document camera in order for the teacher to verify that the seal has not been broken (Figure 4.10). The student can then open the envelope on camera and distribute the quiz or test. Upon test completion, the same student can collect the tests, place them in an envelope, seal it, and put it in the "Out Box." Alternatively, the local facilitator may stop by the room at an appointed time to deliver or retrieve tests and quizzes.

Technical Training for Students

It is important that each student is familiar and comfortable with the

I-TV Student Hint List

Sound

- Look up and face forward while speaking, so that the ceiling microphones will pick up your voice. Speaking down (into the table top) will not allow your voice to be heard sufficiently at remote sites.
- Do not tap pencils/fingers or rustle papers. This creates an annoying sound at remote sites.
- Avoid private conversations during class as they just add noise and are not always private!
- Adjust the incoming audio so it is audible, but not too loud. Audio which is too loud will be picked up by the microphones in your room and cause feedback.
- If there is an audio problem at your site, check to make sure that all audio controls are positioned as per the audio diagram for your class and site; be sure that the MUTE button on the control pad is not lit.

Video

- Always sit in view of the camera.
- Adjust student camera at beginning of class (zooming in or out) so the picture is of students, not empty desks.

Faxing

- Use dark ink only—pencil or light ink is not always legible after faxing.
- Use white theme paper—no frayed edges, as they will jam the fax machine.
- Write well within the margins—always leave a minimum of 1 inch on all sides. Any writing too close to the edge will not show up after faxing.
- Write last name and page number on all pages—jams or problems in faxing may cause pages not to be received in order.
- Use only one side of the paper—back sides of pages may show through during faxing and two-sided pages have to be faxed in two separate calls.
- Write very legibly (type when possible).

General Hints

- Inform the teacher immediately when you can't see or hear any of the sites; if audio is lost, you can communicate that there is a problem by sending a note under the document camera or by telephoning the teacher.
- Act as though the microphone and camera are always on and any principal or teacher at any school may be watching—they certainly could be.
- If assigned to a seat, sit there.
- Videotape for absent students.

Figure 4.11. Sample student hint list [adapted from materials from the Minnesota Interactive Television Networks (MITN)].

I-TV classroom technology (Figure 4.11). A good way to achieve this is with ''get acquainted'' exercises over the first few days of school. For example, a teacher may ask that each student come to the front of the room, put on the instructor lapel microphone, change the student camera to teacher camera, optimize camera focus and zoom, introduce him/her-self, and show a picture (of his/her family, favorite pet, etc.) using the document camera. This simple exercise will acquaint the student with I-TV camera operation. Additional practice sessions and handouts on faxing operations and videotaping will round out each student's knowledge of equipment operations. These skills will be reinforced as the class progresses and students use the equipment in the classroom.

OTHER ORGANIZATIONAL AND ADMINISTRATIVE MODELS

There are many other ways to organize and administrate an I-TV network. For example, the Iowa Communications Network (ICN) is not organized in local clusters. Instead the ICN depends on the statewide connection of regional and community colleges, which in turn connects with interested K−12 districts. Elementary and secondary schools connect in a direct line to the state-owned network−both technically and organizationally−through their closest post-secondary institution (see Figure 4.12). This model was intended to provide a statewide network. Unfortunately, the ICN has suffered a great deal of criticism for its failure to take the needs of local K−12 institutions into account and not allowing the development of local clusters around which local schools could cooperate.

Several states are trying to create a hybrid system of statewide network(s) and local clusters. In Kansas and North Dakota, for example, the existence of independent, two-way I-TV networks preceded development of a statewide network. Both states are attempting to connect all I-TV clusters to a statewide compressed digital (T-1) backbone in order to preserve local autonomy while facilitating sporadic interconnections to distant sites and institutions. North Carolina has opted to create a statewide, but not a state-owned system, by establishing an ATM-based network through GTE, Sprint-Carolina, Southern Bell, and AT&T. The state plan is to integrate existing I-TV networks (using various technologies) into the statewide network.

Obviously, there are numerous examples of organizational models for

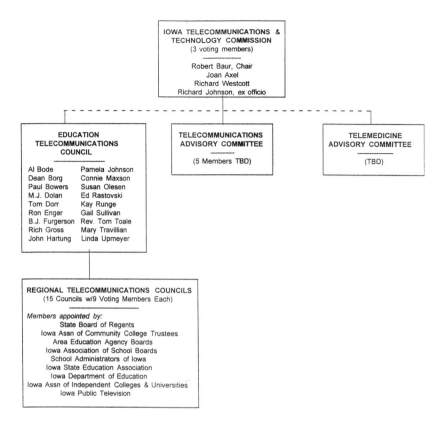

Figure 4.12. The Iowa Communications Network is just one of many alternative models for organizing school-based I-TV networks.

I-TV development around the country. Those networks that are most effective, however, allow for local autonomy and control. Problems will exist when statewide goals supersede those of local schools, as in Iowa, or when local cluster development is forced to occur without any means of statewide interconnectivity, as in Missouri. In summary, the most important factor in determining organizational and administrative structure is the appropriateness to the goals of the network.

We now turn to the subject of I-TV network evaluation—the process by which networks determine whether they are reaching their goals and objectives.

CHAPTER 5

I-TV Evaluation

THIS chapter focuses on the evaluation of ongoing I-TV programs by school districts and I-TV networks. This chapter is not intended to describe how to conduct a scientifically rigorous study of publishable quality. Rather, evaluation procedures described here allow networks to gain information on network success and detect needed programmatic and technical modifications.

Initially, the immediate need to make a new I-TV system work may take precedence over evaluation. However, evaluation of the effectiveness of the system should be an ongoing systematic process, beginning when the network starts up and continuing through subsequent years.

During the initial months of operation, I-TV evaluation should concentrate on short-term objectives and questions, for example, ''Do teachers feel that they are able to use the technology effectively?'' ''Are they receiving adequate and prompt technical support?'' and ''Are materials and homework being transported from one site to another on time?'' Network administrators will want to continually evaluate the network during the first few months, to answer these urgent questions, and modify the I-TV program accordingly. Over the long term, an evaluation of the network during each year of operation will help network members determine if network goals are being met and whether new goals need to be formulated. Yearly evaluations also serve as the impetus for the board of directors or governing board to make changes regarding network policy, addition or deletion of courses, and teaching assignments. Data from I-TV evaluations can also serve to provide

Portions of this chapter were first published in ''An Adopters' Manual for Two-Way Interactive Television: A Guide to Researching, Planning and Implementing Distance Learning in your School and Community,'' MIT-E, WeMET and EPN networks, March, 1995. Available from the Missouri Alliance for Interactive Television, K–12 Users' Group. Contact: Missouri Rural Opportunities Council, P.O. Box 118, 301 W. High Street, Room 720, Jefferson City, MO 65102 (573-751-1238).

valuable information for designing future I-TV teacher training workshops and modifying classroom equipment.

PERSPECTIVES ON I-TV EVALUATION

In nearly every state there has been a demand to know if distance learning instruction is ''as good as'' the traditional classroom and whether I-TV students learned ''as much as'' their peers in traditional classrooms. Preliminary and anecdotal studies suggest that there is no difference between I-TV and traditional student learning. However, no rigorous systematic comparison between students in a two-way I-TV classroom and traditionally taught students has been made. The large number of variables, which must be controlled or accommodated for among the characteristics of students and teachers is a barrier to conducting a precise scientific comparison. For example, student variables which must be controlled or accounted for include, among others, age, sex, intelligence level, level of prerequisite knowledge, level of motivation, number of students in the school/class, availability of courses (diversity of curriculum), type of school (rural or urban), and income level of parents. The teacher variables include teaching style, knowledge of content matter, and teaching experience. In addition, the low number of students that participate in I-TV courses makes a reliable research study difficult. In short, a reliable research study comparing the effectiveness of I-TV instruction to a traditional classroom would be extremely difficult to construct, given the number and difficulty of securing controls for all relevant variables.

Of course, such a research study comparing the effectiveness of I-TV instruction to that of a traditional classroom might not provide much relevant information anyway. Most students in I-TV courses would not have access to a particular class in a traditional format; the need for advanced math, science, and foreign language courses is typically what drives districts to initiate I-TV projects. In many situations, the comparison of traditional versus I-TV instructional effectiveness is moot. Practically speaking, the more relevant comparison may be what the value of an I-TV course is when compared to no course at all.

EVALUATION METHODS

Four methods of evaluation are discussed below. Evaluation methods should be selected according to their usefulness in answering the questions or concerns of network members. For instance, if the school board is concerned about student learning in I-TV classes, the network may choose to use standardized tests as a method of evaluating student learning. (Note: Tests chosen should adequately reflect the content of the course as taught locally.) However, attitudinal questionnaires will be more informative when dealing with questions of student, teacher, or community acceptance of I-TV as a teaching medium. A network evaluation plan will typically also include traditional benchmarks, such as student grades, to insure that I-TV courses are as rigorous as traditional classes.

Standardized Tests

Several subject-based standardized tests can be used for periodic or ongoing evaluation of student performance. Among them are the National Association of Teachers of German Level I Test, the National Spanish Examination, and the content area tests of the College Board's Scholastic Achievement One-Hour Test Series (English Composition, Math Level I, Math Level II, Biology, Chemistry, Physics, French, German, Spanish, and Latin).

The SAT Achievement Test Series is a set of subject-based tests which are used predominantly by post-secondary institutions for measuring student proficiency for placement purposes. For K − 12 networks choosing to use the SAT Achievement Test Series, there is some danger in making comparisons between high school and college students; average state and national scores are based on tests taken by college students. In addition, socio-economic variables must also be accounted for (see Sidebar 5.1). Despite the drawbacks, standardized tests can be very useful, especially for detecting learning differences between remote and local students.

Sidebar 5.1. 1993 − 1994 Missouri I-TV Evaluation Project

Three clusters of rural Missouri high schools formed two-way interactive television (I-TV) networks during the summer of 1993 and offered a total of twenty-three high school and dual-credit classes to approximately 300 students during the first year of operation—including twelve advanced science and math courses. These clusters jointly undertook an evaluation project that included a number of different qualitative and quantitative measurements for assessing the effectiveness of this distance learning technology (Christianson and Hobbs, 1995; University of Missouri, 1994).

Teacher Attitudinal Surveys

Attitudinal surveys were completed by teachers at the end of the first, second and fourth quarters. Among other areas of inquiry, teachers were asked to indicate how they perceived the difference between their role as a teacher in the I-TV class and their role as a teacher in a regular classroom—the results are presented in Table SB5.1.1.

Teacher surveys also indicated:

- Three-quarters of the teachers didn't perceive that the time involved in preparing for their I-TV class caused a decline in their teaching performance in other classes.
- Eighty-five percent of the teachers felt that there was no difference in "the amount learned" between home site and remote site students. (The fifteen percent that did feel there was a difference, perceived that the home site students learned more.)
- Ninety-eight percent of the teachers felt very comfortable with the I-TV technology (i.e. operating the classroom equipment).
- All I-TV teachers were glad they had the opportunity to teach over I-TV.
- All I-TV teachers would encourage other teachers to teach over I-TV.

Comments made by teachers were also compiled and used to address concerns throughout the school year.

Student Attitudinal Surveys

Attitudinal surveys were completed by students at the end of the first, second and fourth quarters. Students were asked to indicate their response to statements on a five-point Likert scale. Figure SB5.1.1 summarizes the data in the areas of technology and instructional issues.

Student SAT Achievement Series

SAT One-Hour Achievement tests, which are commonly used by some post-secondary institutions for placement purposes, were administered to

Table SB5.1.1. Teacher Responses.

Agree	Disagree	Statement
70%	30%	There is little difference between the two roles
53%	47%	Each requires a different teaching style
53%	47%	It is more difficult to know if your students in an I-TV class understand what you are teaching
30%	70%	There is less interaction between teacher and students in an I-TV class
8%	92%	Discipline is more of a problem in an I-TV class
15%	85%	Teaching is more rewarding in an I-TV class
47%	53%	Teaching is more exciting in an I-TV class
30%	70%	I feel I can teach "better" utilizing the educational tools available in the I-TV classroom

Technology Issues

SA	A	U	D	SD	Statement
26 %	51 %	10 %	12 %	1 %	I think the technology makes learning more exciting than in a traditional classroom.
5 %	20 %	17 %	43 %	15 %	I found the technology got in the way of learning.
23 %	57 %	13 %	7 %	—	The pad camera and the ability to view pictures or graphics is a real benefit to learning.
9 %	15 %	36 %	26 %	14 %	I prefer a regular classroom over an I-TV technology classroom.
31 %	49 %	16 %	4 %	—	I like having the opportunity to be in the same electronic classroom with students from other schools.
7 %	22 %	8 %	42 %	21 %	I have difficulty gaining the teacher's attention when I want to ask a question.
10 %	44 %	16 %	27 %	3 %	I feel like I am part of one big classroom; I often forget that some students are miles apart.

Instructional Issues

SA	A	U	D	SD	Statement
1 %	10 %	11 %	56 %	22%	I have difficulty understanding what is expected of me.
27 %	55 %	14 %	4 %	—	The teacher seems to be well organized.
8 %	31 %	11 %	40 %	10 %	The teaching methods used in this class are different than what I am used to.
19 %	54 %	16 %	8 %	3 %	The teacher conveys the subject matter in a way I understand.
5 %	24 %	40 %	27 %	4 %	The instruction in the I-TV class is better quality than many traditional courses which I have taken.
19 %	64 %	9 %	6 %	2 %	I have learned to adapt to the methods of the I-TV teacher.

Figure SB5.1.1. Student responses.

	SAT-V Mean	SAT-M Mean
Highest Level of Parental Education (HS diploma)	395	445
Income ($20,000-30,000)	404	453
Size of Senior Class (<100)	434	479
Type of High School (Public)	420	476
Location of High School (Rural)	441	498
		Mean=445

SAT V&M Mean for US	555	
Adjusted SAT V&M Mean for US	445	=1.25 Adjustment Factor for SAT V&M

Adjustment Factors (One-Hour Test Means/Adjusted SAT Verbal & Math)

Eng. Comp	=	558/445	= 1.25
Math I	=	536/445	= 1.20
Math II	=	603/445	= 1.36
Chemistry	=	600/445	= 1.35
Physics	=	609/445	= 1.37
German	=	574/384	= 1.49*
Spanish	=	530/445	= 1.19**

* Includes only one variable. Does not include adjustment for other five variables.
**Does not include adjustment for number of years of Spanish.

Figure SB5.1.2. Process for calculating SAT adjustment factor.

Table SB5.1.2.   Analysis of Adjusted SAT One-Hour Achievement Test Scores for I-TV Students.

Network	German*	Eng. Comp	Math I	Math II	Chemistry	Physics	Spanish
MIT-E	501(17)	606(12)	551(8)	–	595(15)	641(9)	–
EPN	–	573(5)	610(5)	826(3)	–	607(18)	463(12)
WeMet	–	–	527(28)	–	–	–	430(8)
MO I-TV	501(17)*	596(17)	541(41)	826(3)	595(15)	618(27)	452(20)**
US Average	571	523	554	663	582	504	556

*Includes only one variable. Does not include adjustment for other five variables.
**Does not include adjustment for number of years of Spanish.
Note: Number in parentheses is number of students taking that particular test.

students toward the end of the year in an attempt to assess the effectiveness of I-TV instruction. In order to be able to compare the MO I-TV data with national averages, it was necessary to control for several student variables including: Highest Level of Parental Education, Income, Size of Senior Class, Type of High School, and Location of High School. Student characteristic data on the SAT One-Hour Achievement tests was not available, therefore student data from the SAT Verbal and Math admissions test was used. Figure SB5.1.2 shows the process of calculating the adjustment factors.

These adjustment factors were then applied to the scores for comparison with national averages, see Table SB5.1.2.

Conclusions

While the data collected in this study is not robust enough to support broad generalizations about I-TV instruction, it revealed significant information about the attitudes, concerns and success of the teachers and students involved in this first year of operation.

For the teachers that used the network there were several important conclusions drawn:

- Discipline is a prime concern.
- Teaching in an I-TV classroom is not very different from teaching in a traditional classroom.
- Special accommodations must be made to coordinate communications between administrators and teachers at different locations. (Administrative failure to communicate is continually frustrating to teachers.)
- Small class size is optimal for I-TV.

Several important conclusions were also made about the student populations that participated in I-TV classes:

- Students expressed satisfaction with the technology.

- I-TV student responses on instructional issues mirror that of the traditional student.
- Students taking I-TV classes would be well positioned for college courses.
- Adjusted SAT Achievement Series scores show that I-TV students faired as well or better than the national average.

Attitude Surveys

Measurement of student and teacher attitudes at different points in time is instrumental for gauging acceptance of two-way interactive technology. Attitude surveys can, and should, be used prior to the first day of school and throughout the school year, e.g., each quarter. Information gained from attitudinal surveys will inform the school or cluster of needs and problem areas to be addressed.

It is important to collect baseline data prior to the beginning of school when conducting a study of attitudes over time. Figure 5.1 provides a sample of a "New I-TV Student Questionnaire" used for this purpose. Areas of inquiry in initial surveys might include student aspirations for the course, reasons for taking the class, expectations for course difficulty, and anticipated amount of homework.

Similarly, the foundation for subsequent studies of changes in teacher attitudes will be laid by conducting a teacher survey at the beginning of the year (perhaps during summer training). Figure 5.2 provides a sample "Beginning of the Year I-TV Teacher Questionnaire" which can be used to measure the expectations and attitudes of instructors prior to teaching over I-TV.

After school begins, student and teacher surveys should be administered on a regular basis; quarterly surveys work well. Quarterly student questionnaires provide data on changes in attitude over time and the level of student satisfaction with the technology. A sample quarterly student questionnaire is provided in Figure 5.3. Quarterly teacher questionnaires can measure changes in teacher attitude and detect continued technical, or other, problems with the I-TV network (see Figure 5.4). This information can be used to make adjustments to the network during the school year and also to make changes in the next year's I-TV teacher training workshops. As with student questionnaires, detecting the level of satisfaction with the technology is a major purpose of this evaluation instrument. This evaluation can also indicate the extent to which instructors feel that using I-TV has resulted in modifications in their teaching style.

New I-TV Student Questionnaire
Date: ____/____/____

COURSE: _____   I ATTEND: ☐ School from which course originates
                                        ☐ School at a remote site

1. Why did you decide to enroll in this distance learning course?

Yes   No
☐   ☐   a) I needed it for college
☐   ☐   b) I was interested in the subject
☐   ☐   c) It was the only way I could take the course
☐   ☐   d) I think I'll prefer distance learning over a regular class
☐   ☐   e) I like the idea of being able to get college credit while I'm still in high school
☐   ☐   f) I needed the college credit
☐   ☐   g) It sounded exciting
☐   ☐   h) It wasn't my idea; someone else persuaded me to enroll (Please check)
                __my parents __superintendent __principal __counselor __a teacher __a friend
☐   ☐   i) Other? _____

2. Would you have enrolled in the same course if it had been offered as a regular classroom course?
   ____ Yes   ____ No

3. Are you enrolled in more than one I-TV course this semester?   __ Yes   __ No
   a) If "Yes", in how many I-TV courses are you enrolled?   _____

4. What is your current grade level?   __9th   __10th   __11th   __12th
                                         __13th   __14th   __15th   __16th

5. Considering all of the classes you have taken in high school (or college), how would you categorize yourself?
   __ a) "A" student   __ c) "C" (average student)
   __ b) "A" or "B"(above average student) __ d) "D" (below average student)

6. [High school students only] Do you currently plan on going to college? __ Yes __ No

7. Do you feel that this distance learning course will be: (Check only one)
   ____ a) easier than a regular class in the same subject would be
   ____ b) harder than a regular class in the same subject would be
   ____ c) about the same difficulty level as a regular class in the same subject

8. How many hours per week do you expect to spend studying for this class outside of class time?
   __None   __1-2   __3-5   __ 6-10   __ more than 10

9. Do you think that this course will have: (Check only one)
   ____ a) more homework than a regular class in the same subject
   ____ b) less homework than a regular class in the same subject
   ____ c) about the same amount of homework as a regular class in the same subject

10. Is there anything about the I-TV course that concerns you at this point? (Please describe your concerns)

Figure 5.1. Example of a new I-TV student survey.

Beginning of the Year I-TV Teacher Questionnaire

Date: ___/___/___

HOME SCHOOL: _____

DISTANCE LEARNING COURSE(S) I WILL TEACH: _____

I am a: ☐ New I-TV Teacher   ☐ Returning I-TV Teacher

1. a) Number of years in the teaching profession? __ 1-2 __3-5   __6-10   __11+
    b) Number of years in current school or college? __ 1-2 __3-5   __6-10   __11+
    c) Degree(s) held: __ Bachelor __ Masters __ Ph.D __D.ED __Other? _____
    c) Age range?   __ 21-30   __ 31-40   __ 41-50   __ 51-60   __ 60+
    d) __ Male   __ Female

2. Please indicate your teaching schedule by class period for the coming school year:

	1st Sem Class	2nd Sem Class	Regular Class	I-TV Class	Planning Hr
0 Hour:	_____	_____	☐	☐	☐
1st Hour:	_____	_____	☐	☐	☐
2nd Hour:	_____	_____	☐	☐	☐
3rd Hour:	_____	_____	☐	☐	☐
4th Hour:	_____	_____	☐	☐	☐
5th Hour:	_____	_____	☐	☐	☐
6th Hour:	_____	_____	☐	☐	☐
7th Hour:	_____	_____	☐	☐	☐
8th Hour:	_____	_____	☐	☐	☐

3. New I-TV Teachers Only: At what point did you first hear about two-way interactive TV?
   (Check the appropriate response)

   __ before our school became involved in the project
   __ during the time that our school was planning to implement the I-TV network
   __ when I first came to teach at my present school
   __ not until I was asked to teach an I-TV class

4. At what stage did you first become involved in the two-way interactive TV project in your school?
(Check the appropriate response)
   __ in the early planning stages
   __ during the first year of operation
   __ this summer
   __ Other? _____

5. What caused you to become involved as an I-TV teacher? (Please check all that are appropriate)
   __ the principal or superintendent asked me   __ I enjoy a challenge
   __ I felt I had no choice   __ It offered an opportunity for professional growth
   __ I thought it would be interesting   __ I believe in technology-assisted education
   __ I feel strongly that all students should have   __ Other? _____
      access to advanced courses

6. Based on your current knowledge of I-TV, how well do you think your current course design will
   work over I-TV?
   __ Very well
   __ A few modifications may be necessary
   __ A fair number of modifications may be necessary
   __ The course may have to be extensively revised

Figure 5.2. Example of a beginning of year teacher survey.

7. How much time during the school year do you expect to devote to the I-TV course?

	Less than 2 hrs/wk	2-5 hrs/wk	6-10 hrs/wk	More than 10 hrs/wk
a) During the school day	___	___	___	___
b) After school hours	___	___	___	___

8. To whom would you turn for assistance if (when) technical problems arise? (Check all that are appropriate)
   ___ I don't know
   ___ The principal
   ___ The Network Director or Technical Coordinator
   ___ The telephone company
   ___ Other? _____

9. How would you rate your level of knowledge or experience with each of the following prior to becoming involved in the I-TV course?(Please circle)

	None	Very Little	Some	Moderate Amount	Great Deal
a) Use of computers	0	1	2	3	4
b) Modems	0	1	2	3	4
c) VCR's	0	1	2	3	4
d) Satellite receiving equiment	0	1	2	3	4
e) Computer software	0	1	2	3	4
f) Tape recorders	0	1	2	3	4
g) Speaker telephones	0	1	2	3	4
h) Videocameras	0	1	2	3	4
i) Fax machines	0	1	2	3	4

10. Do you use a written curriculum with learning objectives in your traditional classes?
    ___ Yes   ___ No

11. Do you anticipate using a written curriculum with learning objectives in your I-TV class(es)?
    ___ Yes   ___ No

12. In which of the following areas do you feel you need assistance or additional training? After indicating "yes" or "no" on each item, please **rank order** those items on which you checked "yes". (1=Highest Rank)

Yes	No	Rank		
☐	☐	___	a)	equipment operation
☐	☐	___	b)	equipment troubleshooting (knowing what to do if something doesn't work)
☐	☐	___	c)	understanding the basic elements of audio and video equipment design
☐	☐	___	d)	creating I-TV-appropriate student policies in the classroom
☐	☐	___	e)	organizing the curriculum
☐	☐	___	f)	adapting classroom presentation style to interactive TV
☐	☐	___	g)	tips on teacher position, movement, speaking, eye contact, etc.
☐	☐	___	h)	creating technology-appropriate teaching aides, e.g., graphics, overheads, videocassette tapes, computer presentations, etc.
☐	☐	___	i)	learning how to use the teaching tools available to best advantage, e.g., graphics camera, FAX, VCR, laserdisk, computer, etc.
☐	☐	___	j)	overcoming the barriers of geographic distance
☐	☐	___	k)	learning to relate to visual clues from remote site students

Figure 5.2 (continued). Example of a beginning of year teacher survey.

☐	☐	__	l)	learning techniques for controlling student discipline at remote sites
☐	☐	__	m)	experiencing what it is like to be located at a remote site away from the teacher
☐	☐	__	n)	learning techniques for incorporating remote site students into classroom discussions; questionning strategies; establishing interpersonal rapport
☐ ☐	☐ ☐	__	o)	practice teaching over the I-TV system
		__	p)	other? _____

13. What do you anticipate will be the difference between your role as a teacher in the I-TV class and your role as teacher in a regular classroom? (Please check "Yes" or "No" on each)

Yes   No

☐ ☐ a) There should be little difference between the two roles
☐ ☐ b) Each requires a different teaching style
☐ ☐ c) It is more difficult to know if your students understand in an I-TV class
☐ ☐ d) There is less interaction between teacher and students in an I-TV class
☐ ☐ e) Discipline is more of a problem in an I-TV class
☐ ☐ f) Teaching is more rewarding in an I-TV class
☐ ☐ g) Teaching is more exciting in an I-TV class
☐ ☐ h) I feel I can teach "better" utilizing the educational tools available in the I-TV classroom

14. What, in your opinion, are essential attributes for an I-TV teacher? How important are each of the following: (Please circle the appropriate response on each item)

	Very Important				Not Important
a) flexibility	4	3	2	1	0
b) superb organizational skills	4	3	2	1	0
c) an outgoing personality	4	3	2	1	0
d) an in-depth knowledge of the technology	4	3	2	1	0
e) an exceptional command of the subject matter	4	3	2	1	0
f) significant experience as a traditional teacher	4	3	2	1	0
g) a real interest in modern technology	4	3	2	1	0
g) other? _____	4	3	2	1	0

15. How do you anticipate the curriculum in your I-TV class will differ from that of the same class you have taught traditionally? (Check ☐ if you have not taught this course before)

Yes   No

☐ ☐ a) the curriculum will not differ; I plan on covering essentially the same material at the same pace
☐ ☐ b) the curriculum will not differ, but I may cover the same material at a slower pace
☐ ☐ c) I believe I can expose students to a wider array of information through the use of technology

d) I will likely cover ☐ less ☐ more ☐ the same   amount of material in the distance learning class.

e) I will likely rely ☐ less ☐ more ☐ to the same extent   on the textbook in the I-TV class.

f) I will probably lecture ☐ less ☐ more ☐ about the same amount   in the I-TV class.

Figure 5.2 (continued). Example of a beginning of year teacher survey.

g) I will likely rely ☐ less   ☐ more   ☐ about the same amount   on student projects or activities in an I-TV class.

h) There will likely be   ☐ less   ☐ more   ☐ about the same amount of   student discussion in an I-TV class

i) I will likely use   ☐ fewer   ☐ more   ☐ about the same amount of   worksheets or workbooks in the I-TV class

j) I will likely use   ☐ fewer   ☐ more   ☐ about the same number of   tests and/or quizzes in the I-TV class

k) (If appropriate)
    There will probably be   ☐ less   ☐ more   ☐ about the same   opportunity for lab work in the I-TV class

16. How do you anticipate: (Check all that are appropriate)

	Mail	Fax	Courier
a) sending tests/quizzes to remote students?	—	—	—
b) sending worksheets/notes to remote students?	—	—	—
c) having tests/quizzes returned to instructor?	—	—	—
d) having homework assignments returned to the instructor?	—	—	—

17. Do you anticipate any difference in the turnaround time for homework or tests to be returned to remote I-TV students as compared to students in your traditional classes?
    __ Yes   __ No

18. How much time delay do you anticipate in getting homework or tests returned to remote I-TV students?
    __ 1 day   __ 2-3 days   __ 4-5 days   __ 6-7 days   __ 8+ days

19. Do you anticipate a need for remote I-TV students to reach you outside class time?
    ___ Yes   ___ No

    a) If "Yes", please indicate the methods you would most like to have your students use:
        (Check all that apply)
            __ telephone
            __ the I-TV network during non-scheduled hours during the day
            __ the I-TV network before or after school
            __ FAX
            __ electronic mail
            __ regular mail

20. Do you anticipate a need for a "proctor" or supervisor at each remote site when you are testing?
    __ Yes   __ No

21. Do you expect any difference in "the amount learned" by remote vs. home site students?
    __ Yes   __ No

    a) If "Yes", whom do you expect to gain a better understanding of the subject matter?
            __ home site students
            __ remote site students

Figure 5.2 (continued).   Example of a beginning of year teacher survey.

22. Will you routinely videotape your I-TV classes? __ Yes   __ No

    a) If "Yes", for what purposes will the videotapes likely be used? (Check all that apply)
       ___ For students who are absent from class
       ___ For remote site students to view when their school is not is session, e.g.,
           snow days, etc.
       ___ For student review purposes
       ___ For student discipline purposes
       ___ To review my own presentation style
       ___ Other? _____

23. Do you feel that your school will be able to make the resources available to you to help make your
    course a successful I-TV course?   __ Yes   __ No

    a) What, if any, are your concerns as you begin this pilot I-TV project?
       (Please discuss below)

Figure 5.2 (continued). Example of a beginning of year teacher survey.

Observational Research

Observational research may be done in collaboration with a college or university. The purpose of such research is to identify specific instructional methods or accommodations to technology in the I-TV classroom. For instance, through observational research it is possible to determine the extent of interaction between the teacher and remote students. For I-TV clusters, this may be useful in determining if I-TV is the best approach, or whether a less interactive technology would suffice. However, it is unlikely that an I-TV network will disband based on the results of such an evaluation. More likely, such findings would be used to improve levels of interaction among teachers and students.

Observational research conducted either on site or through analysis of videotapes has a number of uses. For example, an I-TV board of directors that wants to investigate the perception that students located at the originating site have an advantage in the I-TV classroom may conduct a study involving the tallying of student-teacher interactions. The number and level of student-teacher or student-student interactions could be determined through observation of several I-TV classes or viewing class videotapes. This type of study would reveal whether student-teacher or student-student interaction differs between originating and remote sites.

Observational study is also appropriate for determining the degree of accommodation that I-TV teachers have made to the technology. The extent to which instructional tools (computer, overhead camera, VCR, laser disk use, etc.) are used can easily be determined. (Note: It is important that observations be conducted over a sufficient time period and in sufficient numbers to warrant the conclusions reached. One should not surmise, for instance, that multimedia tools are not being

I-TV Student Quarterly Questionnaire

Date: ___/___/___

ITV Course: _____ Home School: _____

Year in School (circle one):   9   10   11   12   13   14   15

1. During the first quarter, about how many <u>hours per week</u> did you spend studying for this class outside of class time? (Check only one)
    ___ None   ___ 1-2 hrs   ___ 3-5 hrs   ___ 6-10 hrs   ___ more than 10 hrs

2. Given your experiences during the first quarter, how would you compare this course with other high school courses you have taken? (Check only one)
    ___ a) it has been easier
    ___ b) it has been harder
    ___ c) it has been about the same difficulty level

3. During the first quarter, do you feel that this course had: (Check only one)
    ___ a) more homework than most other high school courses
    ___ b) less homework than other high school courses
    ___ c) about the same amount of homework compared to other high school courses

4. Which of the statements below best describes what you feel you have learned this quarter?
    (Check only one)
    ___ a) a great deal
    ___ b) an acceptable amount
    ___ c) not as much as I think I should have by now
    ___ d) not much at all

5. What <u>letter grade</u> did you receive (or would you have received, if not Pass/Fail) in this course this quarter?
    _____

6. Did you have the opportunity to take this class on a Pass/Fail basis? __ Yes __ No

7. Which grade is being recorded on your high school transcript for this course?
    __ Letter grade earned   __ Pass   __Fail

8. Would the actual <u>letter grade</u> you received (or would have received) in this course:

    ___ improved your GPA

    ___ resulted in no change in your GPA

    ___ lowered your GPA

Figure 5.3. Example of a student quarterly survey.

9. There are two separate issues with respect to I-TV courses this year. One is the technology by the which the course is delivered; the other is the teacher and the related instructional issues which may be new to you. Please respond to each item below as best you can with respect to your first quarter impressions. Circle 5 if you strongly agree with the statement; circle 1 if you strongly disagree with a statement. Circle 4 if you agree; circle 2 if you disagree ; circle 3 if you are unsure.

Technology Issues

SA A U D SD

a) 5 4 3 2 1   I think the technology makes learning more exciting than in a traditional classroom

b) 5 4 3 2 1   I found the technology got in the way of learning

c) 5 4 3 2 1   The pad camera and the ability to view pictures or graphics is a real benefit to learning

d) 5 4 3 2 1   I prefer a regular classroom over an I-TV technology classroom

e) 5 4 3 2 1   I like having the opportunity to be in the same electronic classroom with students from other schools

f) 5 4 3 2 1   I have difficulty gaining the teacher's attention when I want to ask a question

g) 5 4 3 2 1   I feel like I am a part of one big classroom; I often forget that some students are miles away

h) 5 4 3 2 1   I am often embarrassed or reluctant to ask questions of the teacher over the network

i) 5 4 3 2 1   I like having visitors come into the classroom to see the network in operation

Instructional Issues

SA A U D SD

j) 5 4 3 2 1   I have difficulty understanding what is expected of me in this class

k) 5 4 3 2 1   The teacher seems to be well organized

l) 5 4 3 2 1   The teaching methods used in this class are different than what I am used to

m) 5 4 3 2 1   The teacher conveys the subject matter in a way I can understand

n) 5 4 3 2 1   The grading is much tougher in this course than what I am used to

o) 5 4 3 2 1   The instruction in the I-TV class is better quality than many traditional courses which I have taken

p) 5 4 3 2 1   I have learned to adapt to the methods of the I-TV teacher in this course

q) 5 4 3 2 1   (Answer only if this is a dual credit class) I have had difficulty adjusting to a "college level" course

Figure 5.3 (continued). Example of a student quarterly survey.

r) 5 4 3 2 1 (HS students only) I think I will be better prepared to enter college after taking this course

s) 5 4 3 2 1 This course is much harder than I thought it would be

t) 5 4 3 2 1 The instructor seems to take a genuine interest in helping me succeed in the course

u) 5 4 3 2 1 I have difficulty with the instructor's method of teaching

v) 5 4 3 2 1 I feel that I am putting sufficient effort into this course

10. To what extent has the amount of technical difficulties experienced during this class impaired your learning this quarter?
___ A great deal
___ To some extent
___ Very little
___ Not at all

11. Please indicate the extent to which any of the following currently presents problems for you in the I-TV classroom. (Circle the appropriate number from 1 to 5) If a problem exists, **circle** "Intermittently" or "Continually" to indicate the frequency of the problem.

	Not a Problem			Serious Problem			If it is a problem, does it occur:	
a)	5	4	3	2	1	Hearing the teacher speak	Intermittently	Continually
b)	5	4	3	2	1	Hearing students from remote sites	Intermittently	Continually
c)	5	4	3	2	1	Being heard by the teacher	Intermittently	Continually
d)	5	4	3	2	1	Being heard by students at other sites	Intermittently	Continually
e)	5	4	3	2	1	Hearing echoes over the system	Intermittently	Continually
f)	5	4	3	2	1	Hearing noise or static over the system	Intermittently	Continually
g)	5	4	3	2	1	Audio volume	Intermittently	Continually
h)	5	4	3	2	1	Audio clarity (clearness)	Intermittently	Continually
i)	5	4	3	2	1	Seeing the teacher clearly	Intermittently	Continually
j)	5	4	3	2	1	Seeing students at other sites clearly	Intermittently	Continually
k)	5	4	3	2	1	Gaining the teacher's attention when trying to ask a question	Intermittently	Continually
l)	5	4	3	2	1	Glare from lights on the TV screens	Intermittently	Continually
m)	5	4	3	2	1	Seeing still graphics on the graphics monitor	Intermittently	Continually

Figure 5.3 (continued). Example of a student quarterly survey.

n)	5	4	3	2	1	Seeing live graphics on the student monitor	Intermittently	Continually
o)	5	4	3	2	1	Time delay in receiving still graphics	Intermittently	Continually
p)	5	4	3	2	1	Receiving materials by fax	Intermittently	Continually
q)	5	4	3	2	1	Sending faxes to the teacher	Intermittently	Continually
r)	5	4	3	2	1	Receiving materials by mail	Intermittently	Continually

12. Do you prefer (check one in each line):
a) ___ Seeing the teacher in a quad   or   ___ seeing the teacher full-screen
b) ___ Seeing the teacher full-screen   or   ___ being able to see students at remote sites
c) ___ Always seeing the teacher   or   ___ being able to see live motion graphics occasionally
d) ___ Seeing live motion graphics   or   ___ being able to see live and still motion graphics simultaneously on separate monitors

13. How important is it to you to be able to see students at remote sites most of the time?
___ Very Important
___ Somewhat important
___ Not important

14. Please try to assess how comfortably your I-TV teacher seems to be operating the system currently. (Circle the appropriate number) Give any suggestions for ways in which the operation of the system might be improved:

	Handles it well		Has Great Difficulty				Suggestions for improvement: (Use additional page if needed)
a)	5	4	3	2	1	Switching from teacher camera to student camera at appropriate times	
b)	5	4	3	2	1	Switching from teacher camera to graphics camera at appropriate times	
c)	5	4	3	2	1	Switching from quads to full-screen views at appropriate times	
d)	5	4	3	2	1	Use of the still graphics capability	
e)	5	4	3	2	1	Use of the live graphics capability	
f)	5	4	3	2	1	Focusing of the pad camera	
g)	5	4	3	2	1	Checking to see if everyone can hear	
h)	5	4	3	2	1	Adjusting audio volumes	
i)	5	4	3	2	1	Sending videotapes over the system	

Figure 5.3 (continued). Example of a student quarterly survey.

15. Do you routinely let the teacher know if:

Technical Problems

a) ___ Yes ___ No   There is no audio
b) ___ Yes ___ No   You cannot hear what is being said--the volume is too low
c) ___ Yes ___ No   You cannot hear what is being said--the audio is not clear
d) ___ Yes ___ No   You cannot hear what is being said--talking at other sites makes it difficult to hear the teacher
e) ___ Yes ___ No   There is no video
f) ___ Yes ___ No   You cannot see graphics clearly
g) ___ Yes ___ No   The teacher forgets to change to the appropriate camera
h) ___ Yes ___ No   You have not received a fax on time
i) ___ Yes ___ No   You have not received mailed materials on time

Instructional Problems

j) ___ Yes ___ No   You do not understand what is being taught
k) ___ Yes ___ No   You have questions about the subject area
l) ___ Yes ___ No   You are not sure what is expected from you
m) ___ Yes ___ No   You are having difficulty in the class

16. How would you assess network etiquette?

a) ___ Yes ___ No   Students at remote sites often talk among themselves while the teacher is trying to talk
b) ___ Yes ___ No   Students generally respond in class discussions or when asked questions
c) ___ Yes ___ No   Students are sometimes disrespectful to the teacher
d) ___ Yes ___ No   Students usually respond to teacher directions
e) ___ Yes ___ No   Students sometimes do homework from other classes instead of participating in the I-TV class

17. What additional improvements—either technical or instructional—would you like to see made in this course? (Please use an additional sheet, if necessary. Your comments are appreciated.)

_____

_____

_____

_____

_____

_____

Figure 5.3 (continued). Example of a student quarterly survey.

146

```
┌─────────────────────────────────────────────────────────────────────────┐
│                I-TV Teacher Quarterly Questionnaire                        │
│                                                                            │
│                         Date: ___/___/___                                  │
│                                                                            │
│ HOME SCHOOL: _____          │
│ DISTANCE LEARNING COURSE(s) I TEACH:                                       │
│                                                                            │
│ _____ is  ☐ a one-semester course  ☐ a two-semester course │
│ _____ is  ☐ a one-semester course  ☐ a two-semester course │
│                                                                            │
│ 1.  During the 1st quarter how much time did you devote to I-TV course planning and │
│ preparation?                Less than    2-5       6-10      More than      │
│                             2 hrs/wk     hrs/wk    hrs/wk    10 hrs/wk       │
│     a) During the school day   ___        ___       ___        ___          │
│                                                                            │
│     b) After school hours  .   ___        ___       ___        ___          │
│                                                                            │
│ 2.  During the first quarter how many hours per week did you expect students to spend on the I-TV class │
│ outside of class time?                                                     │
│ __ None      ___ 1-2 hrs.      ___ 3-5 hrs.      ___ 6-10 hrs ___ more than 10 hrs. │
│                                                                            │
│ 3.  Please rate the expedience with which you were able to get technical problems addressed: │
│          Very                                                              │
│     Good Good Fair Poor                                                    │
│     ___  ___  ___  ___  a) Procedure outlined for reporting a technical problem │
│     ___  ___  ___  ___  b) Ease of reaching someone to report a technical problem │
│     ___  ___  ___  ___  c) Amount of time delay from reporting a system failture to being back online │
│     ___  ___  ___  ___  d) Speed with which technical problems have been resolved │
│                                                                            │
│ 4.  How would you rate your current comfort level with the I-TV technology? (Check one) │
│             ___    Very comfortable                                        │
│             ___    Somewhat comfortable                                    │
│             ___    Still unsure of myself at times                         │
│             ___    Somewhat uncomfortable                                  │
│             ___    Very uncomfortable                                      │
│                                                                            │
│ 5.  Do you presently have a written curriculum with learning objectives for your I-TV class? │
│          __Yes      __ No                                                  │
│                                                                            │
│     a) If "Yes", to what extent is the curriculum completed? (Please check one) │
│             ___        day by day, as the year progresses                  │
│             ___        1-2 weeks ahead                                     │
│             ___        3-6 weeks ahead                                     │
│             ___        approximately 1 quarter ahead                       │
│             ___        the first semester is completed                     │
│             ___        more than half of the curriclum is complete         │
│             ___        the curriculum is complete for the entire year (Check here ___ if a semester course │
│                                                                            │
│ 6. Do you detect any difference in "the amount learned" by remote vs. home site students? │
│          __ Yes              __ No                                         │
│                                                                            │
│     a) If "Yes", whom do see gaining a better understanding of the subject matter? │
│                     __ home site students                                  │
│                     __ remote site students                               │
└─────────────────────────────────────────────────────────────────────────┘
```

Figure 5.4. *Example of a teacher quarterly survey. Note: "1st" quarter will need to be replaced with "2nd," "3rd," or "4th" depending upon the timing of the survey.*

7. In which of the following areas would you like additional training? After indicating "yes" or "no" on each item, please **rank order** those items checked, starting with "1".

Yes No Rank

☐ ☐ ___ a) equipment operation
☐ ☐ ___ b) equipment troubleshooting (knowing what to do if something doesn't work)
☐ ☐ ___ c) understanding the basic elements of audio and video equipment design
☐ ☐ ___ d) creating additional I-TV-appropriate student policies
☐ ☐ ___ e) organizing the curriculum
☐ ☐ ___ f) adapting classroom presentation style to interactive TV
☐ ☐ ___ g) tips on teacher position, movement, speaking, eye contact, clothing, eye glasses, jewelry, etc.
☐ ☐ ___ h) creating technology-appropriate teaching aides, e.g., graphics, overheads, filmclips, computer presentations, etc.
☐ ☐ ___ i) learning to use computerized multimedia presentation capabilities
☐ ☐ ___ j) learning how to use the teaching tools available to my advantage, e.g., graphics camera, FAX, VCR, etc.
☐ ☐ ___ k) overcoming the barriers of geographic distance
☐ ☐ ___ l) learning to relate to visual clues from remote site students
☐ ☐ ___ m) learning techniques for controlling student discipline at remote sites
☐ ☐ ___ n) experiencing what it is like to be located at a remote site away from the teacher
☐ ☐ ___ o) learning techniques for incorporating remote site students into classroom discussions; questionning strategies; establishing interpersonal rapport
☐ ☐ ___ p) other? _____

8. After one quarter's experience in the I-TV classroom, please indicate how you currently perceive the difference between your role as a teacher in the I-TV class and your role as teacher in a regular classroom? (Please check "Yes" or "No" on each)

Yes No

☐ ☐ a) There is little difference between the two roles
☐ ☐ b) Each requires a different teaching style
☐ ☐ c) It is more difficult to know if your students in an I-TV class understand what you are teaching
☐ ☐ d) There is less interaction between teacher and students in an I-TV class
☐ ☐ e) Discipline is more of a problem in an I-TV class
☐ ☐ f) Teaching is more rewarding in an I-TV class
☐ ☐ g) Teaching is more exciting in an I-TV class
☐ ☐ h) I feel I can teach "better" utilizing the educational tools available in the I-TV classroom

9. What, in your opinion, are essential attributes for an I-TV teacher? How important are each of the following: (Please circle the appropriate response on each item)

	Very Important				Not Important
a) flexibility	4	3	2	1	0
b) superb organizational skills	4	3	2	1	0
c) an outgoing personality	4	3	2	1	0
d) an in-depth knowledge of the technology	4	3	2	1	0
e) an exceptional command of the subject matter	4	3	2	1	0
f) significant experience as a traditional teacher	4	3	2	1	0
g) a real interest in modern technology	4	3	2	1	0
g) other? _____	4	3	2	1	0

Figure 5.4 (continued). Example of a teacher quarterly survey. Note: "!st" quarter will need to be replaced with "2nd," "3rd," or "4th" depending upon the timing of the survey.

10. Has the curriculum in your I-TV class differed substantially from how you would have taught the same class traditionally? (Please respond by checking "Yes" or "No" to the following statements.)

Yes No
☐ ☐ a) the curriculum has not differed; I am covering essentially the same material at the same pace
☐ ☐ b) the curriculum has not differed, but I am covering the same material at a slower pace
☐ ☐ c) I believe I am exposing students to a wider array of information through the use of technology

d) I am covering
☐ less
☐ more   material in the I-TV class.
☐ the same

e) I am relying
☐ less
☐ more   on the textbook in the I-TV class.
☐ to the same extent

f) I am lecturing
☐ less
☐ more   in the I-TV class.
☐ about the same amount

g) I am relying
☐ less
☐ more   on student projects or activities in the I-TV class.
☐ about the same amount

h) There is
☐ less
☐ more   student discussion in an I-TV class.
☐ about the same amount of

i) I am using
☐ fewer
☐ more   worksheets or workbooks in the I-TV class
☐ about the same amount of

j) I am using
☐ fewer
☐ more   tests and/or quizzes in the I-TV class
☐ about the same number of

k) The comprehension level in the I-TV class has been:
☐ greater than
☐ about the same as   that in a traditional class
☐ less than

l) (If appropriate) There is
☐ less
☐ more opportunity   for lab work in the I-TV class
☐ about the same

11. How do you: (Check all that are appropriate)

	Mail	Fax	Courier
a) send tests/quizzes to remote students?	—	—	—
b) send worksheets/notes to remote students?	—	—	—
c) have tests/quizzes returned to instructor?	—	—	—
d) have homework assignments returned to the instructor?	—	—	—

12. Is there any difference in the turnaround time for homework or tests returned to remote I-TV students as compared to students in your other traditional classes?   __ Yes __ No
a) If "Yes", Please explain the difference: _____

Figure 5.4 (continued). Example of a teacher quarterly survey. Note: "1st" quarter will need to be replaced with "2nd," "3rd," or "4th" depending upon the timing of the survey.

13. What is the current average time delay in getting homework or tests returned to remote I-TV students?

        __ 1 day   __ 2-3 days   __4-5 days   __6-7 days   __ 8+ days

14. What procedure(s) have you set up for remote students to reach you outside of class time? (Check all that apply)

        __ telephone
        __ the I-TV network during non-scheduled hours during the day
        __ the I-TV network before or after school
        __ FAX
        __ regular mail
        __ no procedures have been set up yet

15. Do you feel there is a need for a "proctor" or supervisor at each remote site when you are testing?   __ Yes   __ No

16. Please indicate to what extent each has presented a problem this quarter?

A great extent	Some extent	Seldom	Not at all	Technical Problems
__	__	__	__	a) scheduling malfunctions, e.g., classes not coming on line as scheduled
__	__	__	__	b) audio problems
__	__	__	__	c) video problems
__	__	__	__	d) problems with graphics camera output being seen at all sites
__	__	__	__	e) adjustment of instructor lapel mic volume
__	__	__	__	f) problems with playing videotapes over the system
__	__	__	__	g) adjustment of individual room speaker volumes
__	__	__	__	h) echo problems
				Instructional Problems
__	__	__	__	i) loss of instructional time in the course
__	__	__	__	j) variability in student prerequisite knowledge
__	__	__	__	k) student discipline
__	__	__	__	l) unwillingness of students to put in sufficient study time
__	__	__	__	m) lack of student interaction across sites
__	__	__	__	n) student inattentiveness
__	__	__	__	o) failure of students to turn in homework

17. Please estimate the number of class periods during the 1st quarter in which the following was true:

# of class periods

_____ a) the class was not held at all because of technical difficulties at:
        ☐ all sites   ☐ one or more sites

_____ b) 1-10 minutes of the class were missed due to technical difficulties at:
        ☐ all sites   ☐ one or more sites

_____ c) 11-20 minutes of the class were missed due to technical difficulties at:
        ☐ all sites   ☐ one or more sites

_____ d) 21-30 minutes of the class were missed due to technical difficulties at:
        ☐ all sites   ☐ one or more sites

_____ e) more than 30 minutes of the class were missed due to technical difficulties at:
        ☐ all sites   ☐ one or more sites

_____ f) significant audio portions of the class were lost at:
        ☐ all sites   ☐ one or more sites

_____ g) significant video portions of the class were lost at:
        ☐ all sites   ☐ one or more sites

Figure 5.4 (continued). Example of a teacher quarterly survey. Note: "1st" quarter will need to be replaced with "2nd," "3rd," or "4th" depending upon the timing of the survey.

18. Are you currently videotaping your I-TV classes? __ Yes   __ No

        a) If "Yes", for what purposes are the videotapes used? (Check all that apply)
             ___ (1) For students who are absent from class
             ___ (2) For remote site students to view when their school
                    is not is session
             ___ (3) For student review purposes
             ___ (4) For student discipline purposes
             ___ (5) To review my own presentation style
             ___ (6) Other? _____

19. Please list your students' 1st quarter grades by location: (Write in each site on the top lines)

Home Site   _____   _____   _____   _____

20. Are there additional resources (which you currently do not have) that you consider to be necessary
    for the I-TV course?   __ Yes   __ No

        a) If "Yes", what are they? Please explain: _____

        _____
        _____

21. What, if any, are your remaining concerns as you begin the 2nd quarter I-TV classes?
    (Please discuss below)

        _____
        _____
        _____
        _____

Figure 5.4 (continued).   *Example of a teacher quarterly survey. Note: "1st" quarter will need to be replaced with "2nd," "3rd," or "4th" depending upon the timing of the survey.*

adequately used by a particular teacher when based on observation of a single class period.)

This methodology is particularly relevant for determining the need for technological enhancements and for determining the agenda for future I-TV teacher workshops. Deficiencies not detected by questionnaires may be plainly evident to a classroom observer.

Although this form of research may be conducted by a post-secondary institution, it may also be conducted by the I-TV network director or some other party impartial to individual schools or teachers. If outside evaluators are used, it is important that they have a sufficient knowledge base regarding I-TV technology to extract useful data and draw meaningful conclusions.

Kathleen Collins Olivieri (1993) conducted an observational research study of the Mississippi FiberNet 2000 Project, a fiber optic, digital broadband I-TV network. In this study, Olivieri administered a preliminary "Classroom Environment Scale" to project participants. Dr. Olivieri then chose the two most varied courses—Automated Accounting and Broadcast Journalism—for a qualitative research phase involving observation of and interviews with teachers, facilitators, staff, and students. Her findings indicated the following:

- "Communication and interaction within and between sites was important, electronic mail increased the level of interaction, and there was more competition within than between sites."
- Adaptation to the technology occurred at a high level on the part of both teachers and students, although organizational and policy issues and physical and architectural concerns were present.
- Both students and teachers acknowledged the "rewards" of participating in the technology.

Self-Evaluation

Self-evaluation is the least rigorous evaluation method, but it can be valuable if done in an objective and comprehensive manner. Self-evaluation is not useful in comparing the I-TV program with other programs. Rather it is an effective way to answer locally relevant questions such as "What is I-TV doing for us?" "Is it worth it?" and "Does I-TV work?" Depending on the issues in question, the information collected may include number of students enrolled by course; number/percent of students who would not otherwise have had an opportunity to take each course; grades of students enrolled in I-TV courses; number of college hours earned by high school students; change in percent of post-secondary enrollment after graduation; number of courses added to the curriculum through I-TV; extent of community uses; and so on. Self-evaluation is mainly a systematic way of recording useful, potentially insightful, information.

A WHOLISTIC APPROACH TO EVALUATION

Mention was made above for the need for input, process, and outcome evaluation. The evaluation methods presented thus far, have largely focused on outcomes, with only some attention paid to process evaluation, e.g., instructional techniques utilized, extent of multimedia tools, etc. In order to place the findings of any evaluation into context, it is helpful to systematically record the "input variables," that is, those decisions made and approaches taken from the very beginning of the decision to build an I-TV network.

A key administrator, network director, or other significantly involved person should take responsibility during the planning stage to record all of the organizational and technical decisions made by the key decision makers for the network, the timing of those decisions, and how development of the I-TV network progresses (including problems and setbacks). This information will place other process and outcome evaluation data in a meaningful context.

PROBLEMS IN EVALUATION

It is often difficult to separate the evaluation of I-TV technology from the evaluation of the implementation of I-TV. Many schools have abandoned educational technologies because of problems in implementation rather than any inherent deficiencies in the technology. Evaluation plans should separate issues of technological limitations from issues of organizational policy and implementation. For instance, if it is found that little interaction occurs between teachers and students across sites, and as a result students' satisfaction with I-TV classes is low, an effort should be made to determine why interaction is not occurring rather than assuming that it is a problem inherent in the technology. Typically, efforts spent in teacher training and helping teachers adopt an interactive teaching style will eliminate this problem. On the other hand, if students report dissatisfaction at not being able to see all remote sites simultaneously—for example, in a switched digital system—the problem is a technological limitation of the system, rather than a deficiency in teaching technique; resolution of this problem would involve technical modifications rather than changes in organization.

Another challenge in evaluation is the temptation to evaluate an I-TV course in the same manner as a traditionally taught course. For example, administrators may use a measure of cost-per-student to economically justify I-TV. Comparing the cost per student of I-TV courses with that of the district's traditional classrooms is not a meaningful comparison. Most schools become involved in I-TV to provide advanced or low-enrollment courses to students who would not otherwise have access to those subjects in traditional classrooms. A more valid comparison is between the cost per student for I-TV students and the cost of hiring certified teachers for every school to teach all of the subjects available through I-TV.

Another consideration in I-TV evaluations is the need to take into account uses of the network beyond the provision of formal K−12 classes. It may be difficult to pinpoint dollar values associated with community use of the network, professional development opportunities for teachers, interdistrict teacher consultation and collaboration with post-secondary and other institutions, but these benefits are real nonetheless. It would be very short-sighted, indeed, to evaluate I-TV only in the context of course provision to high school students, without also studying the impact or potential impact of the technology on K−12 professional development opportunities for teachers, interdistrict teacher consultation, collaboration with post-secondary and other institutions, and community use in its many and varied forms.

SUBJECT-SPECIFIC EVALUATIONS

This chapter has thus far dealt with evaluation in a fairly broad sense. However, for some courses it will be valuable to assess how individual topics are adapted to the technology in order to determine whether similar courses should be offered in the future. For example, recording difficulties associated with laboratory courses such as chemistry or anatomy can be useful. Information on the manner in which laboratory experiments were handled – transporting students to a central facility, conducting experiments by computer simulation, or equipping students to perform them remotely – and any resulting problems will be helpful for determining whether the course can be successfully modified or should be discontinued. In concert with subject-specific evaluations, networks will want to consult with other I-TV networks that offer similar courses.

PROGRAM EVALUATION

Apart from the issues of student performance, is the assessment of the I-TV program itself, for example, data on technical problems encountered, rate of problem resolution, flexibility of the technology to meet school needs, ease of administration, parent satisfaction, extent of community use, degree to which the technology addresses community needs, etc.

Networks will want to collect the following data for each site and compile it across the network:

(1) Number of minutes of instruction lost due to technical difficulties
(2) Nature of technical difficulties encountered and method of resolution for each
(3) Level of teacher and student satisfaction with audio and video quality
(4) Number and duration of courses offered-high school and dual-credit
(5) Number of hours of course offerings by site
(6) Number of students enrolled by site – initial enrollments and percent completing courses
(7) I-TV student grades by quarter, site, and course
(8) Number, type, and attendance for after-hours use of the network. The person in charge of network scheduling should keep a log of all non-course I-TV uses, including community use, administrative use, teacher professional development workshops, non-certificated staff workshops, parent-teacher conferences, student-teacher conferences, adult education courses, etc.
(9) Monthly fax costs

(10) Amount of after-hours fees paid to I-TV facilitators

(11) Revenue generated from after-hours use of the network

(12) Equipment maintenance funds expended and detailed description log of expenditures

Annual Report

An important dissemination tool for both anecdotal and longitudinal evaluation data is the network annual report. This document can include items such as courses taught, enrollments, teaching staff, changes in network policies and procedures, network visitations, copies of all media coverage, copies of newsletters generated, annual network budget, network equipment updates implemented, I-TV teacher workshops held, and non-course use of the network. Data that is systematically recorded in an annual report serves as an important historical record that can be used in subsequent longitudinal evaluation efforts.

As a footnote to this chapter on I-TV evaluation, it should be pointed out that the evaluation of I-TV teachers is best done within the context of the performance-based teacher evaluation process conducted by the originating school. This process is most easily, fairly, and efficiently carried out by the home school principal, rather than holding I-TV teachers to separate standards or involving remote principals in the teacher evaluation process; each cluster needs to develop policies regarding how complaints involving teacher performance will be handled.

One interesting area of I-TV research is the degree to which modifications in teaching style are the result of using the technology. Differing schools of thought exist as to whether the technology forces accommodation or inspires change in teaching style. Chapter 6 provides a more in-depth discussion of these issues.

PART THREE

THE I-TV CLASSROOM: THEORY, PRACTICE, AND REALITY

Technology Tools in the Virtual Classroom

TEACHERS and students in an I-TV classroom have access to resources that are not normally available in traditional classrooms; most include a video cassette recorder, telephone, document camera, television(s), and a facsimile machine. Other resources such as a laserdisk player, computer, CD-ROM, remote camera, and audio tape player may also be available. These technology tools can assist teachers in expanding and enhancing their lessons beyond the capabilities of the traditional classroom, as well as in adapting their current lessons to the interactive television medium. (Note: See Chapter 4 for information on I-TV classroom management.)

I-TV INSTRUCTIONAL TECHNOLOGY

This section reviews a number of instructional technologies found in I-TV classrooms. Effective use of these instructional tools takes forethought, practice, and patience. Teachers need to develop a basic understanding of the capabilities of the technology in their I-TV classrooms before selecting the most appropriate technology for a particular lesson or task. Architects operate on the premise that "form follows function." In the I-TV classroom, instructional technology should follow content.

Overhead Graphics/Document Camera

The document camera is one of the most useful pieces of equipment in the I-TV classroom (see Photograph 2.1). Usually located on or above the teacher console, the document camera is primarily used to show

Figure 6.1.

written materials, either as live video or as still images—effectively replacing the traditional blackboard for the instructor and students. The document camera has the capability to reduce or enlarge images, thereby allowing the teacher to display documents of varying print sizes, as well as photographs, diagrams, or any other visual image.

The document camera can also be used to display a variety of three-dimensional objects. For example, the document camera can display the anatomical parts of a dissected cat, or the pistol and stamen of a flower, in outstanding detail and clarity to both local and remote students. The versatility of the document camera makes it a favorite among I-TV teachers. In fact, when I-TV teachers are asked about the one piece of technology they would like in their regular classroom, the document camera is most frequently mentioned. Even in the confines of a single classroom, an overhead or document camera can be a valuable instructional tool.

The document camera can be outfitted with auxiliary devices and lenses to allow it to display 35 mm slides, transparencies, and other visual graphics. The placement of a light box under the camera can facilitate the viewing of slides, photographs, and transparencies. Of course, a transparency can also be viewed by placing a white sheet of paper behind it or by simply making a photocopy of the transparency.

When preparing materials for display on the document camera, instructors should keep two things in mind.

(1) The ratio between the height and width of the television screen is different from that of a transparency or other presentation forms. In order to get maximum use of the screen, visuals will need to be in approximately the same proportions of the screen. The proportion of a screen, or other visual format, is defined by the aspect ratio (the ratio of height to width). For example, the aspect ratio of the video screen is 3 (height) to 4 (width). That is, the television screen is slightly wider than it is tall.

(2) The margin of the video image will be cropped slightly when transmitted to remote sites. Teachers will want to frame text and other images, including themselves, with a generous margin. Technically, there is an area inside the image area that is guaranteed of being transmitted. That area is known as the "NTSC safe area" (see Sidebar 6.1).

Many instructors prefer to write on either 5×8″ note cards or

---

Guidelines for Creating Visuals

- 5 to 6 lines per page

- 5 to 8 words per line

- San Serif fonts (24 Point)

- Wide Margin (Within Safe Area)

Figure 6.2. General guidelines for creating visuals.

8.5×11″ paper placed horizontally beneath the document camera; some instructors prefer to use pre-cut half-sheets of paper, e.g., 8.5×5.5″. An innovative twist is to place a ''markerboard,'' or dry erase board, under the document camera. This allows the teacher to use dry erase markers to write, quickly erase, and write again. When creating text specifically for display under the pad camera it is best to use about five to eight words per line and five to six lines per page (see Figure 6.2). Sanserif fonts that are 24-point or larger are the easiest for students to read. For more complex or dense material, it is best to distribute copies in advance by facsimile or mail, so they can follow along more easily.

In summary, the document camera can give the teacher the ability to provide a better view of any printed, graphic, or three-dimensional object to his or her students than could be produced using a blackboard or by having the students gather around a lab table in a traditional classroom.

Sidebar 6.1. Aspect Ratios and the NTSC Safe Area

Aspect Ratios

An aspect ratio describes the relationship of height to width in a visual field. The diagrams in Figure SB 6.1.1 show the aspect ratios for several visual formats, including video. I-TV instructors need to be aware that the aspect ratio of a video camera is 3 to 4 (height to width) and design materials accordingly. For example, a page created for a transparency is not best suited for projection through a video format such as a document

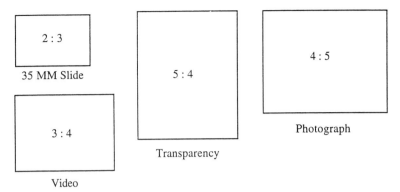

Figure SB6.1.1. *Aspect ratios.*

camera; the page will either be very small and have a large border or will have to be manually scrolled in order to view the entire length.

Safe Area

To ensure that the image transmitted to the audience is complete and not cropped off, position the camera so that text and other items of interest (graphics, you, etc.) are within the "Safe Area," the area of the screen that is transmitted. There are many methods for calculating the safe area. Figure SB6.1.2 shows two safe areas. Example A has margins encompassing 1/6 of the screen area and example B has margins of 10 percent of the screen. A 1/6 safe area is a standard for commercial TV productions, but for most I-TV applications, a safe area of 10 percent will work. To calculate the safe area for a document, divide the height and width into ten equal parts and then use a one-tenth margin along each side. Alternatively, one may create a template for routine use.

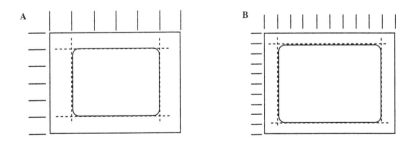

Figure SB6.1.2. *NTSC safe area.*

Remote/Mobile Camera

A remote or mobile camera greatly increases the ability of the instructor to display alternative classroom views to students. Photograph 6.1 shows how one physics teacher used a mobile camera to display an experiment in force and momentum. The view was better than could have been achieved by utilizing a stationary (wall-mounted) camera. Another example of where a portable camera may be useful is in conducting a mock trial as part of a literary analysis segment. In this case, the camera can be focused on an area of the I-TV room that has been temporarily converted to look like a jury box or witness stand.

Combined with a portable microphone and enough cable, a remote camera can also serve as a roving I-TV input, allowing video and audio to be included from other parts of the school. For example, an after-school program in the library or a community event in the gymnasium can be broadcast to other sites on the I-TV network. A mobile camera can also serve as a backup in case a stationary camera breaks down and

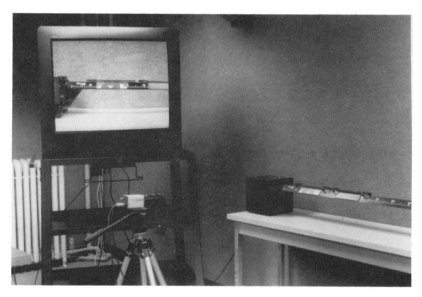

Photograph 6.1. Use of a mobile camera. A mobile camera is used by a physics teacher to show the image of a "zero-friction" table to both local and remote students as part of a unit on momentum. The view provided by the mobile camera is better than what could have been achieved with a stationary camera; the teacher can set the mobile camera up before class and then simply switch to that video input when appropriate (photograph by J. Scott Christianson).

has to be repaired – the mobile camera can simply be positioned to show the same view as the stationary camera.

Sidebar 6.2. Troubleshooting I-TV Problems

I-TV teachers should be prepared for technical problems; contact numbers for technical and support personnel should be readily available in the I-TV classroom. In addition, the administrators of the network should provide teachers with a guide or checklist for dealing with technical problems. Below are a few general guidelines for teachers to use when dealing with problems that are sure to arise.

Basic Guidelines

1. Don't panic. There are occasions when simply turning off the system and turning it back on can correct a problem. A written system "turn-on" procedure should be available. Review all system turn-on procedures and settings.
2. Check all on/off switches, volume controls and batteries. Commonly, a lack of instructor audio is caused by a dead battery in the teacher microphone. Extra batteries should always be available.
3. A diagram that shows the current intended settings of all microphones or other adjustments should be taped to the inside of the teacher console. When a problem occurs, the teacher can check the actual setting of all dials against the intended settings on the diagram and adjust accordingly.
4. Try to figure out what does work—which microphones, cameras, etc.— and use that to circumvent the problem.
5. Contact the Technical Coordinator or other technical personnel if help is needed in determining what is working, what can be fixed, and if class can continue.
6. Have an alternate plan prepared in case the problem cannot be solved. If audio is operative at all sites, verbally ask students to work on an assignment. If video is operative at all sites, use the document or overhead camera to write out the assignment to students.
7. If any site is without audio or video contact, immediately call the site(s) with the problem(s) and notify the principal or facilitator.
8. Record the problem on videotape, if possible. This can be extremely valuable for the diagnosis of system problems, especially intermittent ones.
9. Keep a written log of technical problems and solutions. When a problem is encountered and solved, keep a record of how it was remedied. Over time this will allow users to better diagnose and correct problems as they occur. Copies of all troubleshooting logs should be sent to the network director or technical coordinator so information from all sites can be compiled and updated. This can serve as the basis for an annual, technical, troubleshooting workshop prior to each school year.

Video Cassette Recorder

Every I-TV classroom should be equipped with at least one video cassette recorder (VCR). The VCR is used primarily for the following purposes:

(1) Playing videocassettes in class
(2) Recording classes for absent students
(3) Recording classes for the instructor's self-evaluation
(4) Maintaining a historical archive of videotaped classes for student review
(5) Recording remote classrooms in order to document a student discipline problem
(6) Pre-recording lessons in case of teacher absence

When playing a tape in class, there are several things that can be done to make it more effective (Sidebar 6.3 lists several). It is important to maintain interactivity in the classroom—instructors should avoid prolonged viewing of videotaped segments without periodically integrating dialogue or discussing the content.

Sidebar 6.3 VCR Tips, by Al Race

Reproduced with permission from *Cable in the Classroom*, March, 1991.

1. Do NOT turn out the lights—students can see the TV just fine with the lights on, and they will be less likely to drift off, get restless, or fall asleep.
2. Preview the tapes before you show them. You will want to know which parts of the program are relevant to your curriculum, where they are on the tape, and what kinds of activities you can generate from them.
3. Show only the best parts of the tape. You are NOT required to show an entire documentary, or even a 15 minute segment in its entirety. When previewing a tape, rewind it to the beginning of the section you want to use and then stop it. This is called "cueing up" a tape.
4. If there is more than one section you want to use on a tape, use the "tape counter" to assign a number to each section so you can fast forward to the next segment. Zero the counter at the beginning of the first segment and use that as a reference point for the remainder of the segments. Write down corresponding times to "search" to the next segment.
5. Use several tapes in one lesson. You can combine and contrast relevant material on different tapes by cueing up each tape to the segments you want to view and have them ready to pop in the VCR.
6. Use the "Pause" button. Stopping the tape in the middle of a segment

gives you time to explain a term or concept, ask a question, answer a question, point out an important part that is coming up, or make your students think about what they have just seen. With the picture stopped you won't be competing with it, and interrupting the flow will also keep students alert. (Note that these pauses will exist when you are cueing up and playing the segments.)

7. Show some segments twice. Discuss students' impressions in between. Analyze how they change after a repeat viewing. Turn off the sound the second or third time to focus on the visual impact of a segment.

8. Lead a pre-video discussion. Distribute a handout or a vocabulary list prior to watching the tape. Leave the students with something to look for, give them a purpose or a goal, make the video part of a larger exercise. Force them to take an active role in watching.

9. Lead a post-video discussion, prepared in advance. Answer your students' questions and ask new ones. Use the video as a springboard to other topics.

10. Be aware of the production techniques used in a video segment. What role did the music play, or the narrator, or the special effects, or the framing of the pictures? (Close-ups, wide shots, etc.) Editing? (Were there many shots edited or was the editing pace slow?) Was there a point of view expressed? Stop the tape before it ends and have the students guess the ending or create their own ending. Compare the different scenarios.

11. If the video is in a foreign language stop the tape and quiz the students either formally or informally.

Laserdisk Player

Although a laserdisk (or videodisk) player cannot be used affordably to record images, a laserdisk player has several advantages over a VCR in playing ability. A laserdisk never needs to be rewound. The information on the disk (either video or still images) can be accessed randomly and quickly. While VCR tapes must be played or visually searched from one end of the tape to the other, an interactive laserdisk can skip almost instantly to any part of the disk at the instructor's discretion. In addition, a laserdisk is not easily worn out and maintains superb video quality throughout its life.

Laserdisk technology is an ideal medium for illustrating concepts which are dynamic or otherwise difficult to teach through conventional means. Exploration or analysis of events that change quickly in space and time, such as muscle movement or hummingbird flight, are well suited to the technology. Laserdisks can also be used in lieu of complex physics or chemistry experiments that are too difficult, dangerous, or expensive to replicate in the classroom.

A laserdisk can be used to locate and isolate an individual image from among any of the thirty video frames viewed per second. This capability allows study of complex movement or action that is too fast for the unaided eye to follow. In contrast, when using a videotaped sequence of similar content, it is difficult to locate specific frames and the video resolution of an image on ''pause'' is very low.

Laserdisks and audio compact disks (CDs) are based on similar technology. Just as on a CD, the audio tracks on a laserdisk deliver extremely high quality stereo sound. Both technologies work by projecting a small laser beam onto the surface of the disk, measuring variations in the reflected light, and then converting these variations into ordinary video and audio signals.

There are two main formats for laserdisks: Constant Angular Velocity (CAV) and Constant Linear Velocity (CLV). The type of disk determines the amount of information (either still pictures or video) that can be stored. CAV disks, also known as standard play, can store about 30 minutes of video or 54,000 frames of still images per side. CAV disks have the advantage of high quality, freeze-frame capability. CLV disks can store approximately 60 minutes of video per side, but have lower quality freeze-frame capability. In the CAV laserdisk format, each video frame occupies one concentric track on the disk. Each of the tracks or frames has a unique number (1 − 54,000) assigned to it, any one of which can be accurately located in a few seconds.

There are three standard types of laserdisk players, each distinguished by a different level designation. Level one players are oriented mostly toward the consumer market and have limited interactivity. They are most useful for viewing movies linearly, i.e., from beginning to end. However, they have the capability, usually via remote control, to search for the beginning of video segments (called chapters), to freeze frames, and to move forward and backward.

Level two players are more advanced in that they contain an internal microcomputer that can interpret information encoded on the laserdisk about its contents and how different segments relate. A remote control unit is used for interaction with the player.

Level three players, are the most interactive and are controlled by an external computer. This allows computer presentations to be integrated with video segments and still images stored on the laserdisk. Many programs for independent learning and simulations are produced for use with a computer connected to a level three player.

Most modern players will play both CAV and CLV disks and can be equipped with a barcode reader that allows for accessing specific segments of the laserdisk. Players can also be used to play audio compact disks, if they are equipped with an adapter to hold the smaller disks. Laserdisk players are not, however, designed to play CD-ROMs (see below).

The tips offered in the previous section on maximizing the effectiveness of videotape in instruction (Sidebar 6.3) are also appropriate for use with laserdisks. Probably the biggest impediment to using laserdisk technology is the cost of disks; networks and schools that install laserdisk players should also insure that teachers will be allocated the necessary funds for purchasing laserdisk titles.

Auxiliary Inputs

Additional video and audio sources can also be wired into the I-TV

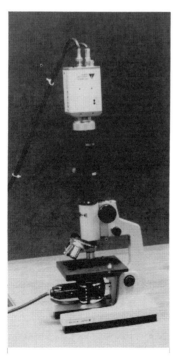

Photograph 6.2. Use of an auxiliary camera. An auxiliary camera has been mounted on a microscope to display specimens to local and remote students. Adapters for a number of different devices are available (photograph by J. Scott Christianson).

system. For example, the signals from a satellite dish or cable television connection can be added to the I-TV room. Additional cameras can be used as well. For example, an adapter can be used to mount an auxiliary camera on a microscope (see Photograph 6.2) allowing the instructor to display the image of a microscope slide on the graphics monitor. For I-TV students, this provides the same quality of image as if everyone had their own microscope focused on the specimen.

Additional audio inputs can be added without accompanying video. For example, a compact disk (CD) or audiotape player can be added for use in a foreign language class. The output of a short-wave radio or electronic keyboard can also be added to the I-TV audio selections; some systems also have the capability to patch telephone audio into the I-TV system.

Instructors with knowledge of some or all of the aforementioned technology tools may still have problems integrating these elements into their curriculum. What is often lacking is a way to combine the various elements of instruction into a cohesive whole, without the problems associated with switching between inputs and resources. For some I-TV instructors, computer multimedia can serve the purpose of unifying and presenting multiple forms of media in a controlled and integrated way.

COMPUTER MULTIMEDIA IN THE I-TV CLASSROOM

Multimedia has been defined in many ways. Vaughan (1994) describes multimedia as "any combination of text, graphic art, sound, animation, or video delivered to you by computer or other electronic means." By this definition, I-TV alone is multimedia. For many, multimedia in education has become synonymous with computer graphics and CD-ROMs. However, it is important to realize that there are several major types of computer-based multimedia applications, each with different capabilities and uses.

Presentation Software

Presentation software is a type of computer multimedia application that allows the user to display a series of pre-formatted screens. A good analogy is that of a slide projector, where each slide is viewed sequentially through either forward or backward movement. Unlike slide projectors, presentation software allows the presenter to add graphics, text, animations, videoclips, and audio to the show. Moreover, the content need not be static. Multimedia documents can easily be updated to reflect new content, new video examples, or new audio. For example, the background can be changed and the new version of the presentation can be saved and used immediately—no more going back to the darkroom or making new transparencies! Presentation programs are changing the way people create and think about presentations in much the same way that word processing programs transformed the way in which people view composition and editing tasks.

A number of powerful presentation programs exist; some examples are Astound, Harvard Graphics, Freelance Graphics, and Microsoft Powerpoint. Most of these use a "card" or "slide" as the basic unit for the presentation. Users design text and graphic elements on each slide or card and then display the series of cards linearly. Figure 6.3 shows one slide in a document created for a physics class. (Note: Many presentation programs also allow the user to move non-linearly in the presentation. For example, a button on a slide could move the presenta-

Figure 6.3. A slide from a multimedia presentation program. The slide contains both text, clip-art (rocket) and background graphics. In addition, three buttons in the lower left-hand corner allow the user to navigate forward or backward or end the presentation.

tion backward for review or ahead to more detailed information on a topic.)

Presentation software has several advantages for I-TV instructors:

(1) The presentation can be saved on computer disk and easily edited at any time.

(2) Material included in a presentation can be printed for distribution to the students.

(3) The same set of slides can be easily updated each year. (As with any computer data, a habit of backing up important data on a regular basis will ensure that valuable data is not lost.)

(4) A large number of presentations can be stored on either a hard disk or a high-capacity removable drive, allowing an instructor to have easy access to a year's worth of graphics and text. For example, if the class needs to do a quick review of material from the previous quarter in order to solve a current calculus problem, a slide from a previous lesson can be quickly retrieved and displayed.

Drawbacks of using presentation software in the classroom include the cost of hardware and software, time for instructors to learn how to use a presentation program, and the time involved in creating the presentations. Some I-TV teachers may feel that unless they can use this technology in their regular classrooms too, it is not worth the trouble for one or two I-TV classes. Also, it is often difficult for I-TV teachers to utilize presentation software when their only computer access is in the I-TV room. This has led some I-TV networks to provide portable computers to their teachers, which allows for creation of documents and presentations at their convenience, including at home.

CD-ROM

Compact disks (CD) are modern alternatives to 8-track and audiocassette technologies. The use of CD technology has been widely expanded by its combination with computer technology in the form of CD-ROMs (Compact Disk-Read Only Memory). Computers equipped with a CD-ROM drive can read data—in the form of text, graphics, audio, video, or software programs—from a CD-ROM disk. One CD-ROM disk is capable of storing approximately 600 megabytes of data, or 65,000 pages of text. CD-ROMs are used for a wide variety of applications. Examples include:

- interactive multimedia programs (e.g., ADAM, which allows the user to explore human anatomy)
- multimedia encyclopedias that combine, text, graphics, video, and sounds in a searchable database
- distribution of programs for various computer types (one CD-ROM can hold hundreds or thousands of shareware and public domain programs)
- distribution of clip-art and photography collections for use in desktop publishing
- distribution of government databases and documents

CD-ROM technology is a valuable tool for the storage and distribution of large amounts of data. While most CD-ROMs do not have the ability to display high-resolution video, CD-ROM titles are widely available and are relatively inexpensive ($30 to $100).

Interactive Multimedia

Interactive multimedia refers to computer programs that allow users to explore topics in a non-linear way—that is, the program is designed so that the user can easily navigate to the information that he or she wants to access. In addition, multiple media elements are used. Interactive multimedia applications can be integrated into the classroom in much the same manner as any other media element (VCR tape, text, transparencies). As with traditional media, it is the content which should be of primary concern. I-TV teachers can use multimedia for a variety of purposes, including:

(1) A reference database, e.g., a CD-ROM encyclopedia, thesaurus, or dictionary
(2) Extension of concepts covered in the curriculum, e.g., an in-depth opportunity to explore a specific scientific concept
(3) Simulated lab experiments, e.g., in lieu of on-site labs, an I-TV chemistry teacher may utilize computer-simulated labs that allow students to perform all of the steps and make all of the decisions in reaching a desired end-point
(4) Virtual field trips, e.g., a multimedia trip through the Louvre or Smithsonian Institution

Interactive multimedia can be especially advantageous for student review and independent learning because of the ability for the user to customize the learning experience. Many multimedia titles have been designed specifically for this purpose and include questions for testing and for identifying areas the student needs to review.

As mentioned previously, interactive multimedia applications are often sold on CD-ROMs. Teachers can also create their own interactive multimedia applications. However, with teacher-created programming, the time and energy involved may be greater than their educational value. In fact, research in the use of multimedia in education has indicated that the greatest benefit comes from student design and creation of multimedia programs about a particular subject rather than presentation of a teacher-created application (Papert, 1992; Nix and Spiro, 1990). In the I-TV classroom, for example, teachers can assign their students to produce a computer-based multimedia presentation, provided the computer resources are available. The class may be divided into groups responsible for different tasks in the multimedia production process: media collection (photos, video clips, sounds), scripting (narration and text), fact-checking, programming, editing, etc. (Vaughan, 1994).

World Wide Web (WWW)

The Internet-based information tool known as the World Wide Web (WWW) is another form of multimedia that can be used to publish student-designed ''pages'' of information via computer. For the I-TV teacher, this offers an excellent way to retrieve assignments from remote students while simultaneously extending student knowledge of Internet access and use. Reports, papers, and assignments published on the World Wide Web can be accessed by a remote instructor, remote student, or anyone on the Internet. Moreover, accompanying sounds, photographs, videoclips, and files can be linked to the student-created page of information, allowing quick and easy creation of multimedia reports and papers. Access to student-published information can, of course, be restricted. A number of excellent books about designing WWW documents are available, for example, *HTML Manual of Style, HTML Source Book, Teach Yourself Web Publishing in a Week,* and of course, *HTML for Dummies.*

Photo CD, Digital Camera

Photo CD is a format developed by the Kodak Company for digital storage of photographs. Although not really a computer multimedia product in the strictest sense, Photo CDs can be a valuable resource for the I-TV teacher. Most photolabs can take slides and photographs, developed or undeveloped, digitize them, and place the images on a CD-ROM in Photo CD format. The images can then be viewed using a computer CD-ROM drive or a consumer device such as a Photo-CD player.

Alternatively, teachers can use a digital camera to bypass the use of film altogether. Images captured with a digital camera can be viewed directly over the I-TV network, incorporated into computer-based multimedia presentations, or downloaded to a computer for printing, archiving, and/or later viewing. Purchase of at least one digital camera for I-TV teacher use is a worthy investment.

MAKING I-TV COURSES ACCESSIBLE

The Americans with Disabilities Act (ADA) clearly indicates that schools have a responsibility to provide accommodations that allow individuals with visual, hearing, speech, and cognitive disabilities to participate as fully as possible in all classes.

The University of Maine at Augusta (1993) has developed a *Guidebook for Accessible I-TV Programs* for use by that state's I-TV networks. (See Appendix 2 for ordering information.) This guidebook is an excellent resource for any network attempting to make I-TV programs more accessible to students with hearing, visual or cognitive disabilities.

Visual Disabilities

The University of Maine recommends the following alternative formats for visual information:

(1) *Braille:* Braille refers to a system of raised dots which allows people with visual impairments to read text. There are several different Braille formats, including ones for musical scoring. A number of production houses will translate text and documents into Braille and print them on a Braille printer. (See University of Maine, 1993, for a listing of such services.) Alternatively, a school or network may decide to purchase a Braille printer.

(2) *Large print:* Large print allows persons with some visual ability to read text more easily.

(3) *Computer format:* This allows visually impaired persons to use a speech synthesizer to listen to text documents. There are a number of very sophisticated add-on programs for personal computers that allow voice translation of documents and also provide voice assistance for word processing by blind persons. If it is acceptable to the student, the purchase and use of such a computer system is the most versatile and cost-effective alternative.

(4) *Audio cassette tape:* Text is recorded on a tape for later listening.

(5) *Audio description:* Text, graphics, plays, movies, and other visual media are described or recorded onto an audio tape.

Audio

Two techniques are commonly used to adapt audio information for students with aural disabilities.

(1) *Interpreter services:* This involves having a professional sign language interpreter translate in real time. This has the advantage of allowing the student to interact with the teacher and fellow students via the interpreter.

(2) *Captioning services:* This involves having a captioner type the audio information into a device which encodes the text into the video stream. The text appears on the bottom of the screen at the sites that need captioning. (Note: As of July 1, 1993, all television sets sold must be able to display captioning. However, in digital networks, captioning options may have to be engineered into the system to ensure that captioning information is passed correctly through the CODECs.)

TECHNOLOGICAL "STYLE"

A teacher's success in utilizing computer multimedia in the I-TV classroom is dependent on the willingness of the teacher to take risks. Self-confident teachers who are comfortable experimenting in front of students are most likely to utilize the technology than are those who are reluctant to appear less than fully knowledgeable. It is crucial to provide the means and time for I-TV teachers to learn and "polish" their technology skills. It is easy for administrators to assume that once a teacher has learned to manipulate the buttons in an I-TV classroom, there is not a need for continuing professional development. Just as in any classroom, the quality of instruction will be enhanced by continually providing opportunities for teacher experimentation with new technologies.

Audiovisual communication lies at the heart of two-way interactive television technology. It should not be assumed that I-TV is merely a mechanism by which the teacher-delivered lecture can be transmitted to passive students. I-TV technology offers the opportunity to improve on the instruction found in the traditional classroom, rather than merely replicating it. I-TV need not be an extension of the 15,000 passive, TV-watching hours already accumulated by the average sixteen-year-old child.

Unlike watching television, I-TV can and should be a demanding and engaging process in which students are participants in their own learning. The ability to send a video image from a microscope, pinpoint a cat's aorta during a dissection under the document camera, display the outline of a lesson, or consult a CD-ROM encyclopedia are only a few of the options available to the I-TV teacher. The technological tools covered in this chapter, in the hands of a capable teacher, can ensure that the full potential for stimulating interactive teaching and learning in the I-TV classroom is realized.

CHAPTER 7

Teaching and Learning in the Virtual Classroom

WHEN personal computers first became widespread a decade ago, there was an obvious, but superficial, similarity to the television set—both provide video and audio information to people watching the device's screen. Many people wrongly equated the quality of interaction with a computer with that of a television—the television viewer is engaged in a passive experience, whereas the computer user is engaged in a much more active and self-directed experience. Today with the increasing adoption of two-way interactive television, it is again easy to assume that the I-TV is just another extension of television watching and that the same behaviors apply. This chapter explores the fundamental differences between television and two-way I-TV in the areas of teaching and learning style.

DISTANCE EDUCATION AND THE TELEVISION

Video-based distance education—in the form of one-way broadcasts such as instructional television, videotaped instruction, and instruction by satellite—initially appealed to educators, who could see its great potential for combining the ability of television to convey ideas and emotions with quality instructional content. Educators knew that students were familiar with the medium and, in fact, enjoyed it immensely. Some students spent countless hours watching television at home. Children, even of preschool age, were renowned for being able to recite verbatim most every current television commercial. Why not put this powerful influence on young minds to good use?

Many educators believed that if they could take this popular medium and simply alter its content, students would become "educated" by doing just what they wanted to do anyway—watch television. Unfortunately, there were several flaws in this thinking.

Early developments in instructional television involved a lecture from a teacher framed in the traditional "head and shoulders" view common to the nightly news. To students, teachers on instructional television programs became known as "talking heads." Much of early educational television, videotape, and satellite programming consisted simply of a talking head imparting information. For students, it lacked the immediate gratification of a half-hour TV sitcom or the intriguing storyline of an hour-long drama or soap-opera. And it definitely lacked the activity and visual bombardment of commercials.

For students, instructional television wasn't anything like watching TV. Students were used to the multisensory engagement of commercial television and younger children were familiar with educational television in the form of fun, participatory programs such as *Sesame Street*. In addition, instructional television in the school required students to be responsible for tests and homework, responsibilities not required by regular TV watching. In other words, students saw right through it! It didn't look like TV to them, it didn't cause the gratification that TV watching did. So, students took advantage of the one commonality that instructional television had with commercial TV—they could tune out.

ACKNOWLEDGING THE "TV" IN "I-TV"

Two-way interactive television is similar to instructional television in that both are based on television technology; early forms of I-TV were called "talk-back TV" since you could "talk back" to the television. With I-TV, however, most of the limitations that are present with educational television, videotaped, or satellite programming are overcome by the ability of I-TV teachers and students to interact spontaneously, as well as use a multitude of additional instructional technologies. I-TV represented a transition in video-based distance learning from a passive to an interactive medium. Instruction was no longer to be watched, it was to be directed and engaging.

An I-TV class is a fundamentally different experience than other video-based distance learning media. In two-way interactive television, the television is simply the vehicle through which geographically dispersed individuals and classes can see, listen, talk, and engage each other. Viewing a television is not the "ends" for I-TV, but the "means" for utilizing a much more powerful communication tool. In other words, the I-TV teaching and learning experience is not focused on or limited by the television.

Teachers and students in I-TV classes have access to almost every form of communication that was present in the traditional classroom — everything except touch! As such, it is important that I-TV students and teachers understand the differences between "TV-watching" and "I-TV participation." One cannot participate in an I-TV class with the same set of behaviors used when simply watching television.

Sidebar 7.1. Interaction in a Distance Learning Classroom

In the traditional classroom, ideas are exchanged, knowledge is imparted, and feedback can be immediate through instructor-student interaction and peer interaction. In distance education, the student and instructor rarely meet face-to-face. Interaction between a teacher and student can impact student satisfaction and learning in the televised classroom. Teachers who encourage involvement, offer feedback, and use strategies to increase social presence are viewed more favorably by the students (Rifkind, 1993). Therefore, interaction has emerged as a vital element in distance education (Klinger & Connet, 1992). Although many believe the myth that interaction between faculty and students is limited within distance education, interaction has significantly increased through the variety of new telecommunications technologies (Annenberg/CPB Project and the PBS Adult Learning Service, 1992). Today's learners have a different perspective of communication because learners are more accustomed to communicating with and structuring communication around the media (Krebs & Pease, 1993). For example, interacting with another person using a telephone or computer on a daily basis is considered normal for most learners today.

New telecommunications technologies allow for increased interaction among peers, learners, and instructor (Moore, 1989). Interaction can also occur on-site between students or facilitators before, during, and after the class (Dillon, Confessore, Gibson, 1993). The various types of communication mediums include telephone conferencing, the most widely used form of technology-assisted communication. Telephone conferencing can include audiographic conferences, picture phones, computer conferences, and electronic keypads. Other types of interaction include fax machines, voice mail, and e-mail. However, through the use of two-way video and audio, interaction can be very similar to face-to-face interaction except the communicators are geographically dispersed (Annenberg/CPB Project and the PBS Adult Learning Service, 1992).

To facilitate interaction within a distance education classroom, teachers may consider structuring lessons for cooperative learning. Through cooperative learning, the students are assigned a specific task and are placed into a group sink-or-swim situation (Damyanovich, 1987). Other ways that teachers can increase interaction is to ask for comments from sites rather than individuals (Scollon, 1981). Teachers can utilize humor, ask questions, praise student contributions, keep a relaxed expressive nonverbal manner, and involve students. Most students enjoy communicating via distance education and find answering questions easier when they are encouraged to do so (Rifkind, 1993). According to Rifkind, "students perceive there to be higher levels of rapport with instructors when they were asked questions and encouraged to speak, as well as the instructor smiled at individuals in class" (p. 36). Utilizing other technologies such as e-mail in conjunction with the existing network whether it is satellite, microwave, or videotape based, may bring classes together and provide easier access to other students and the teacher (Kendall & Oaks, 1992).

Interaction is an "essential element of the teacher-learning process, whether in a classroom or at a distance" (Kruh & Murphy, 1990, p. 1). In examining the teachers' perceptions of classroom interaction, Gehlauf, Shatz, and Frye (1991) found that teachers stressed the importance of interaction with students at distant locations. In fact, Ritchie and Newby (1989) concluded that several investigations have indicated that classrooms that have higher levels of interaction may have higher levels of achievement.

This is excerpted from Olivieri (1993) with permission.

Sidebar 7.2. Me? Replaced by a TV Set! Never! by Carol J. Swinney, Hugoton High School, Hugoton, Kansas

Five years ago when my school district proudly announced that we were going to become a part of an interactive television network, my heart nearly stopped beating. After nearly twenty years in the traditional classroom, I felt a strange sensation deep in the pit of my stomach. Oh, yes, I had seen those television teachers. In fact I had a personal favorite, a gorgeous dark haired Spanish teacher broadcast from San Antonio, Texas. Her dark, curly hair bounced lightly on her shoulders, and when she wanted her TV students to repeat the phrase she had just modeled, the camera zoomed in to provide a close-up of her sparkling, chocolate brown eyes framed in luxurious dark lashes. Privately, I called her Wink-Um, and I enjoyed her television antics, but me, on TV? Why I don't even have the necessary equipment! Was I to be replaced by a TV set?

Yet after the initial shock wore off, I realized that the sensation growing in the depths of my body was not fear, but excitement. Here was a chance to make the walls of my classroom invisible, to provide my students with experience in tomorrow's technology today, and to test the teaching skills I had developed so carefully for two decades.

As a foreign language teacher, I believe that interactive television provides an amazing opportunity to promote my love of communication beyond my school and to expose my students to experiences that will be valuable in the telecommunications workplace of the 21st century. In addition, I have been noticing the past couple of years that students require more energy and more visualization to stay "tuned in" to class. I was startled to discover that my students do not recognize life before TV. Television with its action, color, and fast-paced energy is a not so silent member of their families, more available than live human contact much of the time. And so I began my interactive television teaching experience on the premise that I could capture the students' imaginations and stimulate their desire to learn a language as easily as they recite TV commercials or hum the words to theme songs.

Yet I stubbornly held on to the belief that techniques I had successfully used in the traditional classroom would translate to interactive television instruction. And I was right, sort of. I quickly learned that the elements of successful instruction were variety, visualization and vigor. In fact, teaching interactive television had enlivened my traditional classroom as I have come to view my students, not as a captive audience, but as active participants in the process of communication and learning.

Looking back on my five years as a teacher using interactive television, I have learned five valuable lessons.

(1) *Adaptability*: Virtually anything that can be done in the traditional classroom can be adapted to I-TV. We have learned songs, played "restaurant" with the waiter in one town and customers in three other locations, produced fashion shows, and paraded for Mardi Gras. We have cooked simultaneously in four locations. Using the technology of I-TV we can now integrate multi-media effects into our efforts.

(2) *Origination*: The key to daily success is simply "being ready." All students at all sites must have materials in time for use in class. Testing and grading must be coordinated with all sites and technologies. Of course, variations in school calendars and schedules pose their own unique challenges.

(3) *Flexibility*: Coping with change is essential for both success and sanity. Interruptions, a carefully designed activity which doesn't quite translate, a technical glitch—all demand that a Plan B, even a Plan C be available for immediate use.

(4) *Humor*: To meet the ever present challenge of technical difficulties and human error, the instructor must be quick with a smile, ready to shrug her shoulders and laugh at her own humanity. Remember: Murphy's Law is the fine print in the I-TV contract.

(5) Enthusiasm: As noted by Ralph Waldo Emerson, "Nothing great was ever achieved without enthusiasm." The successful I-TV teacher must eagerly explore new possibilities for her students and her curriculum. Technology is only intimidating until we understand how it can enhance the educational process.

A final word of warning: It would be easy to become so enamored with the technology that one forgets the purpose of Interactive Television is to expand the learning opportunities of our students. Fiber optic technology is a valuable tool in the educational process, but it is not the teacher. In fact, in the successful I-TV classroom, the technology is transparent.

So, after five years as an interactive television instructor, the sensation of excitement still motivates me to explore new ways to use interactive television to educate my students. Me? Replaced by a TV? Never! But you can bet that I welcome the power of this technology to expand the world of learning for me and my students.

Note: Carol Swinney was the 1995 F.R.E.D. Telecommunications Teacher of the Year.

I-TV AND TEACHING STYLE

Many people, especially superintendents and principals, initially believe that I-TV teaching does not require modifications in teaching style and that a teacher can continue to teach just as he or she has in the traditional classroom. To some extent this is true. A teacher who predominantly lectures, who provides little opportunity for student interaction, and who teaches by consecutive page in the textbook can teach in exactly that way over I-TV, with little accommodation other than having to fax worksheets or collect tests by mail. But what about the teacher who conducts more interactive instruction? How can an "authentic," cooperative, or participatory curriculum survive the physical dispersion of students in an I-TV classroom? Or how can cooperative learning techniques be utilized among remote students? What changes are required to adapt a curriculum based on research and inquiry to the I-TV medium?

These and other questions are among the issues in which I-TV educators are most interested. I-TV is often purported to be a transparent technology allowing for the replication of the traditional classroom across distance. However, I-TV educators have recently realized that they may have been shortsighted in adopting the goal of duplicating the traditional classroom and are now using the technology as an opportunity to modify their teaching techniques. Unlike other forms of distance learning, I-TV teachers are not limited to a single instructional method. For example, in the context of a single class session, I-TV can accommodate traditional lecturing, individualized research, and small-group problem solving. This flexibility is what makes I-TV an exciting distance learning medium; it is the only distance learning technology in which such a wide variety of teaching techniques and instructional methods can be utilized.

I-TV teachers quickly become accustomed to the instructional capabilities of the overhead camera and other media tools. For example, an I-TV anatomy teacher has the flexibility of being able to immediately switch from a view of an outline of a lab procedure, to a multimedia slide show showing the process, to a videotape showing a demonstration of a particularly tricky step in the procedure, to finally conducting the lab experiment as each site sees the work of other sites simultaneously. Many I-TV teachers use the necessity for adapting their curriculum to I-TV as an opportunity to modify their teaching techniques in ways that they can carry back to their traditional classroom. In fact, some instructors use I-TV as the excuse for abandoning traditional instructional methodologies in favor of creating classrooms in which student products become the criteria by which students are assessed. In this way, the I-TV teacher can become the efficient facilitator of learning rather than the plodding purveyor of knowledge. It is this role—the efficient facilitator of learning—to which I-TV teachers are aspiring when they use the technological tools available in their classrooms.

Sidebar 7.3. Learning Theories of Particular Relevance to I-TV Instruction

Component Display Theory

Merrill (1983) classifies learning in two dimensions—content and performance. Content includes the facts, concepts, procedures, and principles learned by the student, while performance refers to the integration of content into practical use. Merrill's distinction between content and performance in his component display theory is very applicable to the I-TV classroom and to the integration of instructional media. I-TV students have the opportunity to learn content and exhibit their application of the knowledge through the use of the media tools in the I-TV classroom.

Constructivist Theory

Constructivist theory can also form a solid basis for I-TV instruction (Duffy and Jonassen, 1991; Bednar et al., 1991). Kemp and Smellie (1994) state the assumptions on which constructivism is based:

- Knowledge is constructed from experience.
- Learning is an active process, with experience leading to meaning.
- Learning should occur in realistic settings.
- Growth in understanding concepts comes from experiencing many perspectives relative to a situation, then adjusting beliefs in response to new perspectives.
- Testing should be integrated with the task, not treated as a separate activity.

Each of these assumptions holds special meaning and applicability in the I-TV classroom. Because of the geographical dispersion of students, an I-TV instructor has to help students build knowledge from experience in different ways. By effectively utilizing the technology in the I-TV classroom, however, it can be done. For example, a laserdisk segment of artwork from the Louvre or other art museum can be the "next best thing to being there" for I-TV students.

From a constructivist viewpoint, it is worthwhile to examine the three themes around which the American Psychological Association and the Mid-Continent Regional Educational Laboratory's twelve principals of instructional design and educational reform are based (Wagner and Mc-Combs, 1994):

- Learners operate holistically as a function of intellectual, emotional, social, and physical characteristics.
- The learner's behavior is based on his or her perceptions and evaluations of situations and events from a self-orientation that interprets meaning and value relevant to personal goals and interests.
- The learner's development across all domains of functioning is never static and unchanging, but is a dynamic growth process that serves inherent needs for mastery, control, and belonging.

These themes represent a very solid foundation on which I-TV instruction can be based.

Motivation Theory

Four elements of learner motivation are directly applicable to the I-TV learning environment (Keller, 1983):

(1) *Interest:* The ability to engage and sustain learner curiosity and attention directly impacts the degree to which commitment to learning will occur.

(2) *Relevance:* Being able to relate learned information and concepts to individual needs or goals is important. Instructional content should be related to the world of work, higher education expectations, or to practical skills.

(3) *Confidence:* Learners must perceive some likelihood that they will be successful.

(4) *Satisfaction:* Reinforcement of the learning process is vital. By combining extrinsic rewards and intrinsic motivation, students will be more likely to pursue or continue to pursue learning goals. [Note: the I-TV teacher has the benefit (at least for the first few years of network operation) of capitalizing on the newness of the technology and the attention placed on students by the media, community, and others.]

Interestingly, Wagner and McCombs (1994) found that distance educators are more likely to consciously incorporate the concepts on motivation theory in their classrooms than instructors in traditional classrooms. They conclude:

All learners benefit from instruction in which they are motivated, feel that they exercise control over their learning experience, are respected and are accountable for their own learning outcomes. However, because there is the perception that these variables tend to distinguish distance education learning experiences from traditional learning experiences, there appears to be a greater willingness on the part of distance educators to consider employing instruction designs, models, and techniques to accommodate these variables than on the part of traditional educators.

Sidebar 7.4. Basic Questions a Beginning I-TV Teacher Needs to Ask, by Sheryl Melton, Beaver High School, Beaver, Oklahoma

1. *Do I really want to teach over I-TV?* If you enter the I-TV program thinking it will not work, guess what? It probably will not work. If, however, you are determined to make the system work, it probably will perform beyond all expectations. Teachers are amazingly inventive people and so are students. I've discovered that most problems can be solved with just a little creative thought and determination.
2. *Do I feel confident about my teaching style and command of my subject area?* I truly feel that a beginning I-TV teacher needs to have two or more years of teaching the particular subject under his/her belt. The I-TV teaching experience is challenging enough without trying at the same time to master a new subject.
3. *How do I feel about the loss of privacy within my class?* You are no longer teaching in one isolated classroom. You will be teaching in several schools with numerous monitors that have taping capabilities. You may not even be aware of some of the people who are watching you teach.
4. *Can I handle the restriction of my classroom movement?* If you are a walker and a pacer, you may find staying within the camera view very restricting.
5. *Am I prepared to handle the extra load of students?* Not only will you be adding more students to your teaching load, you will be adding extra grading and bookkeeping.
6. *Is there time in my schedule to visit other sites?* While it usually isn't required, it is always helpful for students at the other sites to see you in person occasionally.
7. *How will tests and homework be transferred back and forth?* The fax machine may be a partial solution, but it takes time to fax the material and it can be expensive. Mailing is another option, but the turn-around time keeps students from benefiting from the immediacy of grading results. Couriers are the best solution if you can find people in your community who commute to other sites.
8. *Am I flexible enough not to be frustrated with interruptions from not only my school, but also from other schools in the system?* Be prepared for fire drills, pep rallies, assemblies, yearbook pictures, daily announcements, class meetings, etc. Multiply whatever interruptions occur in your school by however many schools are in your network.
9. *Will I be able to adapt my teaching methods to the different communities?* Remember that every school has its own personality, just as every student has his/her own personality, and you will be asked to mesh those personalities into one I-TV class.

Note: Sheryl Melton was the 1993 F.R.E.D. Telecommunications Teacher of the Year.

The Cooperative Classroom

Cooperative learning simply refers to one of the many methods of student organization that encourage social interaction and cooperation among students, and discourage the individualistic, competitive arrangements found in the typical classroom. Although much more comprehensive in its total scope, an example of a cooperative learning technique can be seen in student questioning.

In a traditional classroom, a teacher may ask the whole class a question as a way of determining whether a concept is understood. Only some students will raise their hands, indicating that they think they know the answer. Still fewer students—usually one—will be selected to respond. This method pits student against student. Those not called on may wish they had been and those who didn't raise their hands are able to "get by" without having to know or find the answer. An alternative would be to divide students into teams of learners with each team comprised of a heterogeneous mix of students, e.g., high, low, and average achievers. As a question is posed to the class, students know that they will be given a brief period of time to confer with their teammates to discuss the question and to insure that all team members are equally up to speed on the answer and the process used in determining it. The teacher then calls on a student from any team with the full expectation that an informed (correct) response will be given, but more importantly, that all students in a team will be equally capable of responding. The intended outcome of this process, of course, is to actively engage all students and to not allow students to "not know" how to get the correct answer.

Cooperative learning techniques can be easily used in the I-TV classroom with some small accommodation to remotely situated students. The two major tenets of cooperative learning—positive interdependence and individual accountability (Brandt, 1990)—can be used with students at several remote sites. Some suggestions for incorporation of cooperative learning techniques in the I-TV classroom include:

(1) *Creation of cooperative learning teams within each site:* Where more than two to four students are present at each site, multiple teams may be formed. Where two to four students are enrolled at a site, one team may be formed. Where only one student is present at a site it is possible to combine that student with students at other sites.

(2) *Incorporation of "jigsaw" techniques:* One student in each team

becomes an expert on one topic. Each team member is responsible for teaching the topic to their teammates.

(3) *Involvement of students in "group investigation" techniques:* Students independently take responsibility for one or more components of the research and then are responsible for presenting their findings to the rest of the class.

(4) *Cross-site teaming:* In this technique, team members across all sites are given the opportunity to meet and hold discussions over the network for a portion of a class period. Other students may alternatively be given time to conduct related research in the local library or on the Internet. This method is particularly useful in preparation for class projects. Cross-site teaming allows each team to prepare, work out strategies and divide duties.

Instructional Media: Supplementary or Integral to Instruction?

Instructional media tools – such as VCRs, laserdisk players, audiotape players, and CD-ROMs – can be viewed as either supplementary to or supportive of education. It is more accurate, however, to view them as an integral part of the instructional process. This viewpoint implies a responsibility on behalf of the teacher to utilize and develop only those media resources which directly contribute to learning. It also implies that media tools and support are available to teachers.

This brings up a major issue for teachers: the time and effort required to assemble or develop the media resources for use in the I-TV classroom. Overcome with a wealth of opportunities, the novice I-TV teacher may feel compelled to develop a multimedia slide show for every class presentation or find relevant videotapes and laserdisks on every topic, resulting in extensive preparation time. Instead, the first-time, I-TV teacher should begin slowly, utilizing only those resources which are most pertinent, and taking the time to develop only those resources that will provide a unique improvement over existing resources.

Instructional Media as a Learning and Assessment Tool

There is little hard research proving the ability of multimedia to enhance learning (Townsend and Townsend, 1992). However, there is a great deal of experience that attests to the usefulness of multimedia as an instructional, learning, and assessment tool. As an instructional tool, multimedia can be utilized by the instructor to convey information. As a learning tool, multimedia may be used by the student to explore a particular concept. As an assessment tool, multimedia can serve as the means through which the instructor can gauge the student's ability to communicate understanding of the subject matter.

TEACHING THROUGH MULTIMEDIA

The use of multimedia in the I-TV classroom—that is, the convergence of text, graphics, sound, animation, or video through computer presentation—lends itself well to instructional use. Integration of multimedia presentations with lectures and other forms of instructional media provides the I-TV instructor with an expanded opportunity to efficiently and effectively convey the nuts and bolts of course content.

In considering the use of multimedia in the I-TV classroom it may be helpful to think of multimedia resource development as falling into one of three levels (Kemp and Smellie, 1994):

(1) *Mechanical level:* routine processes such as the conversion of existing information into a suitable format, for example, printing text in the appropriate font size and aspect ratio for easy viewing on the TV monitor

(2) *Creative level:* planning and integration of graphics with text and/or sound, for example, producing a short, lesson-based multimedia slide show

(3) *Design level:* conceptualizing, integrating, and aligning information with instructional objectives, for example, developing a CAI (computer-assisted instruction) module which branches to related topics of student interest

The Need for Content-Confident Teachers

Clay and Grover (1995) indicate that distance education can force teachers into shifting their self concept away from being a "content specialist" toward being a "methods novice." The first-time I-TV teacher can momentarily find the I-TV classroom as an intimidating, or at least, preoccupying, environment in which more thought will initially be required to switch camera views than to impart wisdom (or facilitate learning). It is therefore preferable to select I-TV teachers who are already content-confident and who can concentrate on gaining experience with the delivery method.

While there is a need for content-confident teachers, content cannot be the sole focus in the I-TV classroom. Again, Clay and Grover (1995) indicate that it may be more important to "uncover" learner interest and understanding of subject matter than it is to "cover" the content. The opportunities inherent in the I-TV classroom for broadening instruction beyond textbook and worksheets should not be wasted.

I-TV AND LEARNING STYLE

As a distance learning technology, two-way I-TV lends itself well to incorporating the principles of accepted learning theory. I-TV can be used to promote learner participation, enable student feedback, and actively engage the learner. In fact, there are some qualities of the two-way interactive television medium that can positively change classroom behaviors. For example, most I-TV teachers agree that the I-TV classes require a greater level of teacher preparation and organization, because of the perceived need to remain on task; lack of audio or video interaction seems awkward in the I-TV classroom. Additionally, many I-TV teachers feel compelled to spend all of their time engaged with their students and do not provide class time for reading assignments or other homework because those activities don't directly utilize the technology. This can lead to a more simulating classroom environment for the students.

How Learning Occurs

There are three formal ways that most learning takes place: presentation of information, self-paced study, and instructor-learner or small-group interaction (Kemp and Smellie, 1994). Because of its interactive capabilities, all three are easily adapted to two-way interactive technology.

Learner Characteristics and I-TV

Learner characteristics can be grouped into three domains—cognitive, affective, and physiological (O'Keefe, 1982). Every learner has a different combination of these characteristics.

In the cognitive domain, according to Townsend and Townsend (1992), there are seven "stages" in the learning process: apprehending, acquisition, retention, recall, generalization, performance, and feedback. These stages are based on the six levels of intellectual activity outlined by Bloom (1956): knowledge, comprehension, application, analysis, synthesis, and evaluation. In such a hierarchy of cognitive learning, students should be challenged to go beyond the rudimentary knowledge and comprehension level. Students should be able to apply what they have learned, analyzing and synthesizing their knowledge into a meaningful whole, and be able to evaluate their own knowledge for gaps and inconsistencies.

Affective characteristics such as motivation and interest level also contribute to the level of learning among individuals. Apart from the course subject, I-TV students may be enticed by the technological learning environment or they may be leery of it. While such attitudes toward technology may be altered by experience, they should be taken into account.

In addition, the physiological characteristics of each learner is affected by environmental factors such as lighting, noise levels, temperature, and space. Attention must be given to these factors in the I-TV room. Poor audio quality, feedback, light reflecting on monitors, or a continuing speaker hum can significantly decrease learning.

Successful I-TV instructors are aware of the differences in learner style among students at all sites and plan their instruction accordingly. Three particularly insightful learning theories were outlined in Sidebar 7.3.

Sidebar 7.5. The Beaver County Interactive TV Cooperative
by Denise Coldwater, Beaver County, Oklahoma

Settling into my first teaching job in 1975, I soon realized I was expected to teach those students who had a history of "falling through the cracks" while also teaching the mainstream individual. My standard teacher-ed classes had not prepared me for this challenge. I struggled, the students struggled and a few lights came on. The next year I moved into a classroom where more freedom was allowed, more students' needs were actually met, and I felt like education was actually taking place. Emphasis was still placed on a standard testing system, well manicured lesson plans and a structured, traditional style of teaching. I knew I was not meeting the needs of many of my students but I did not know specifically what was missing in my teaching style.

Leaving teaching in 1978, I knew that there had to be more teacher training but what it was or where it was, I didn't know. I knew that I learned better by doing and I knew people who learned well by simply being lectured to! While retired from teaching, I spent my years with my three sons and husband on our farm and ranch. Once again I was faced with some very interesting factors when it came to different learning styles. What was once considered "being bullheaded" was starting to look as if it was not just a personality trait but also a learning style within itself. What was the educational future for those students who seemed to do better in a classroom setting not dominated by straight-back desks, chalkboards, and lecture podiums?

Years later, when Cletus Carter, Executive Director of the Oklahoma REAL (Rural Entrepreneurship thru Action Learning) project called me to ask whether I would be interested in facilitating a REAL classroom in Beaver County, Oklahoma, these questions still stirred in my mind. I said yes and so ended fourteen years of diapers, doctor's visits, household chores and an occasional afternoon bridge game.

A few minutes of I-TV familiarity were given to me before classes started in August of my first year back in teaching. Which buttons controlled what TV monitor, where the sound controls were, how to run the fax machine, how to turn the whole system on and off, what switch controls the three cameras and a brief warning not to allow the students to discuss their school's sports programs over the airways. That was it, I was supposed to be ready to go!

Fear, excitement, anticipation and dread preceded my first day of my return to the classroom. My teaching career that I had ended fourteen years earlier and my goals and dreams in the education field were very far removed from those I had in the previous decade. New feelings stirred inside my head as I realized that I had an opportunity to expose students to a life-altering curriculum via the very latest in high technology.

The first day of school came and went and I survived. Between all four schools on my network and two separate hours of classes I had acquired thirty-six lively and receptive entrepreneurial students. We spent the first day establishing ground rules, signing Interactive Television Contracts and trying to match faces and names. I found it very chaotic watching three television monitors and a classroom all at the same time. Time took care of that problem just as it took care of learning all the buttons and switches associated with the system.

I quickly discovered as every first time I-TV teacher does, that I felt out of control because of my inability to reach out and physically come in contact with each of my students. The students have the same insecurities because they wonder if they will be able to establish a learning relationship with an instructor that they cannot personally get to know and they wonder how much can they get by with via the television monitor. Prospective I-TV instructors are reluctant to assume the role of instructional facilitator because they fear that they will lose control of the teaching process. With equal fears on both sides, students and teacher are put on equal ground. My students and I found ourselves working together and establishing a stimulating, learning relationship of the 1990's type. Hi-tech does not have to be impersonal and distance learning is a wonderful mechanism to remove the boundaries between communities. I chose to ignore the warnings about letting students discuss school sports over I-TV and we have found it very supportive as all four schools basically wanted the best from all the teams and even visit other schools' games now.

Our classrooms were equipped with telephones and fax machines. I highly recommend these conveniences in all I-TV classrooms. All paperwork moves through the fax and through the postal system. All private conversations between myself and the students or administrators happen via telephone. All REAL I-TV students quickly learned fax and phone skills, another life skill that better prepared them for the real world.

Faxes are great but slow. I soon learned to copy lessons that require some form of paperwork and mail or delivered them myself. An oddity of my I-TV class is the opportunity that I have to travel to all my schools every week and teach from different sites during the week. Traveling from school to school helped the paperwork dilemma. Traveling also provided my students and myself with a unique opportunity to get to know each other and develop a relationship. To walk into a classroom and be openly welcomed by the students is every secondary teacher's dream.

Preparing copy work well in advance was just one of the different teaching techniques that I learned to utilize with the interactive television. REAL is taught by experiential methods and that made it a perfect course on the network, it also presented some trying challenges. The experiential learning cycle makes it possible for students to learn at their optimum level because they are learning in the way that best suits their needs. In order to exercise all sides of the cycle, each lesson plan should allow time for experience, reflection, expansion and application. REAL curriculum is already prepared for the instructors, so I found that other than preparing well ahead of time, most lessons were ready to use. The experiential learning cycle required student interaction and I made a seating chart that I copied for each week and marked each day as I was able to get interaction from all the students. I also used the chart to make notes for future reference concerning each student.

Note: Denise Coldwater directs the R.E.A.L. (Rural Entrepreneurship thru Action Learning) Program in rural Oklahoma.

Molding I-TV Instruction to Learner Style Preference

Students do not learn all concepts equally well in a given medium. For example, a visually oriented student will be able to understand the functioning of a set of heart valves through an animation, whereas a student more oriented to text and audio may benefit more from a text description of the process that is also read aloud by the teacher. O'Neil (1990) stressed the value of providing instruction tailored to the individual learning styles of students. Perrin (1990) similarly found that adjusting teaching strategies to student learning styles can produce significant gains in student achievement.

In the I-TV classroom, instructors have both the opportunity to take learner style preference into account and the ability to instruct through a variety of media, incorporating visual, auditory, and kinesthetic learning. For example, a lesson about different architectural styles can be illustrated using several media: the history of architecture can be easily reviewed via videotape or laserdisk; ancient and modern building materials can be shown under the overhead camera; a blueprint can be faxed to each remote classroom for use in a group project activity; and students' understanding can be assessed through the preparation of a multimedia presentation on architecture in a specific geographical region and time period.

Instructors that wish to have more knowledge about the learning styles of their students can use one of the several learning preference inventories to profile student learning styles. These tests determine whether a student is primarily a visual, auditory, kinesthetic, or combination learner. Additional learning preferences, such as whether a student learns best in individual or group situations or whether a student prefers oral or written expression, can likewise be measured through a learning inventory.

PART FOUR

IS IT WORTH IT? ASSESSING INVESTMENT AND RETURNS

CHAPTER 8

Issues in Human and Social Capital

WITH most educational technologies, the economic concept of "return on investment" is often considered irrelevant to the question of technology adoption or too difficult to accurately ascertain. Educational technologies are frequently adopted based on educator experiences and community, school board, or administrator interest. Rarely is educational technology subjected to the same tests of fiscal scrutiny as might occur in business or industry; education operates in an arena where the economic rationale of the marketplace is largely absent.

This chapter discusses the adoption of I-TV technology in the context of the spread of innovation/technology and social and human capital. This chapter takes a more theoretical and holistic approach to the development of two-way interactive television networks; those wanting a more nuts and bolts discussion of financial issues surrounding I-TV should turn to the next chapter.

THE ADOPTION-DIFFUSION MODEL

How then is educational technology passed on from school to school? How is its proliferation assured? It is important to understand this process in order to fully appreciate the complexities of measuring impacts and returns on investment.

Rogers (1983) defines diffusion as "the process by which an innovation is communicated through certain channels over time among the members of a social system." He further defines social change (of which diffusion is one example) as "the process by which alteration occurs in the structure and function of a social system." The study of the diffusion of innovation stems largely from a forty-year research tradition in the study of adoption of technology. Most diffusion studies are based on a model of linear communication in which a single agent informs a potential adopter about an innovation. Rogers and Kincaid (1981) broadened this model to a "convergence model" of diffusion in which information and knowledge was exchanged and created among participants (potential adopters, early adopters, etc.) until a mutual understanding was reached. In other words, one entity or person need not be the sole agent of change; a group can come together to form the critical mass needed to drive change.

Adoption of I-TV technology encompasses both technology diffusion and social change. I-TV involves a change in the social system (i.e., the school) in that schools must change class times, student make-up procedures, teaching paradigms, etc., to accommodate I-TV. In addition, the function of the school (i.e., social system) may also be changed; high schools may now be the central point in the community for the provision of undergraduate, graduate, and continuing education courses as well as advanced and dual-credit courses for K − 12 students.

The Innovation-Decision Process

Those who have already adopted two-way I-TV technologies will recognize the following five steps in the innovation-decision process (Rogers, 1983):

(1) *Knowledge:* learning about the innovation
(2) *Persuasion:* forming an attitude toward the innovation
(3) *Decision:* adopting or rejecting the innovation
(4) *Implementation:* bringing the innovation into use
(5) *Confirmation:* reaffirming the previous decision to adopt the innovation

The innovation-decision process for I-TV usually proceeds as follows. First, an administrator, board member, teacher, or someone connected with the school learns of the existence of instructional two-way interactive television. The persuasion stage usually occurs as a result of visiting one or more operating I-TV networks. At that point, certain intuitive reactions are generated, e.g., it looks like it works, education appears to be occurring, students seem engaged, etc. As positive (or negative) feelings and opinions are reinforced, the decision-making process begins. This usually happens at two levels. First, the superintendent (or other administrator) must decide for him/herself that this technology is worth pursuing. Second, a process develops by which the school board and others are brought up to speed and the final decision to adopt or not adopt is made. The process of implementation may actually be the shortest of the steps involved, but is highly intensive and consumptive of administrator time. The last step in the innovation-decision process is not always a conscious step. Indeed in many instances, confirmation isn't carried out through a formal evaluation. Nevertheless, informal confirmation does occur if the decision makers have a feeling of comfort that they have made the right decision.

When an organization, rather than an individual, is responsible for an innovation decision, Rogers (1983) alters the description of the innovation process to include:

(1) Initiation
  - *agenda setting:* defining the need for the innovation
  - *matching:* linking a problem with an innovation solution
(2) Implementation
  - *redefining/restructuring:* modifying the innovation to meet the specific need and altering organizational structures to accommodate the innovation
  - *clarifying:* defining the relationship between the innovation and organization more clearly
  - *routinizing:* melding of the innovation into the organization such that the innovation ceases to be a new or separate activity

It is not always clear which process—individual or organizational decision making—is at work in I-TV adoption. The size and nature of the bureaucracy of the educational institutions involved affect whether decisions are made by an individual or by an organizational process. For example, the smaller the school, the greater the probability that decisions will be made by a superintendent who will subsequently try to convince the school board that he/she is making the "right" decision.

Rates of Adoption

The rate of technology and innovation adoption follows an "S-curve" when the number (or percent) of adopters is plotted over time (see Figure 8.1). The point at which the innovation seems to catch on and a rapid increase in adopters occurs is sometimes called the "take-off" point. This point occurs at the ten- to twenty-five percent adoption level (Rogers, 1983). This "take off" effect is generated by several factors: at this time interpersonal networks have spread the news about the new technology or innovation (i.e., "word of mouth"), and the technology or innovation is widely visible to potential adopters. For I-TV, the

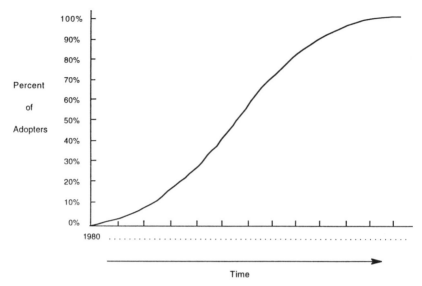

Figure 8.1. The "S-curve" of technology and innovation adopt rate (adapted from Rogers, 1983).

"take-off" point has yet to be reached in most states. In Minnesota, however, the diffusion of two-way interactive television technology is well under way.

Between 1980 and 1991, forty percent of Minnesota's 430 school districts became I-TV adopters. In Figure 8.2, the time of adoption of I-TV is plotted during this eleven-year time period. The S-curve for

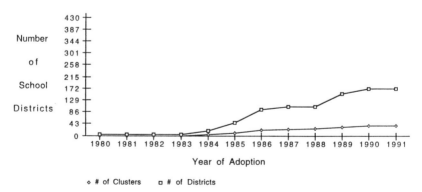

Figure 8.2. The rate of adoption of I-TV technology in Minnesota [data from Distance Learning in Minnesota (1991)].

Minnesota is elongated, but the shape is still evident. The plot in Figure 8.2 is distorted by two major waves of state funding for I-TV development, one in the mid-1980s and another in the early 1990s. These funding cycles are known in the diffusion literature as "adopter incentives" which tend to artificially shape the rate of adoption.

In addition to adopter incentives, several other factors influence the rate of adoption. Rogers (1983) reports that five characteristics of an innovation or technology determine its rate of adoption: (1) relative advantage, (2) compatibility, (3) complexity, (4) trialability, and (5) observability.

Relative Advantage

The relative advantage of I-TV lies in the extent to which it is perceived to be better than previous methods. Proponents of I-TV, the authors included, differentiate I-TV from its distance learning predecessors (e.g., audiographic tele-learning and instruction by satellite) by its unique capacity for simultaneous, two-way audio and video interaction between teacher and students. Potential adopters of I-TV evaluate the relative advantage of the technology in economic terms, but also consider less tangible factors such as image (e.g., being educationally "up to date"), convenience (e.g., avoiding the need to transport students or teachers), and satisfaction (e.g., feeling a sense of accomplishment with having introduced the innovation). More important to the rate of adoption than the actual advantage gained through I-TV, however, is the perceived value. Rogers (1983) states, "the greater the perceived relative advantage of an innovation, the more rapid its rate of adoption is going to be."

Compatibility

Rogers (1983) reports that "compatibility is the degree to which an innovation is perceived as being consistent with the existing values, past experiences, and needs of potential adopters." I-TV is clearly compatible with several of the values prevalent in education today. For example, the perception that technology is good; that there is a widespread need among small rural schools for equality of access to advanced courses; and that entry into post-secondary coursework should be accelerated.

Complexity

I-TV is a relatively complex innovation; its technical details may be beyond the scope of understanding of many school administrators. Even the most technologically sophisticated educators will not have sufficient knowledge to embark on the planning, development, equipment selection, and installation of an I-TV network without significant technical assistance. This is perhaps the biggest reason for the relative slowness of I-TV technology diffusion. Fifteen years have passed since the development of the Freshwater I-TV Network in Eagle Bend, Minnesota. By educational diffusion standards, this falls somewhere between the fifty-year time span it took for complete adoption of kindergarten (from 1900−1950, Mort, 1953) and the five-year time span (from 1958−1963) it took modern mathematics to reach widespread use (Carlson, 1965). Technological and organizational assistance, from state departments or other intermediate agencies, can clearly accelerate the rate of I-TV adoption in some states.

Trialability

Rogers (1983) refers to trialability as the degree to which an innovation or technology may be tested or experimented with prior to adoption. For example, in a classic study of innovation diffusion, Ryan and Gross (1943) found that Iowa farmers adopted hybrid seed corn only after each farmer first tried it on a small portion of their acreage. Ryan and Gross concluded that if hybrid seed corn adoption had been dependent on an ''all or none'' decision, i.e., no chance to try a small amount, the rate of adoption would likely have been much slower. The inability of schools to partially build an I-TV network is a factor in the slow rate of I-TV diffusion.

Observability

The extent to which an innovation such as I-TV is visible to others is also directly related to the rate of adoption. Observability can be measured in two ways: (1) the extent to which the technology itself is visible to others, and (2) the extent to which the results of the technology are visible. In the seed corn example above, farmers could readily see the growth, maturity, and vigor of their hybrid corn. Moreover, they could readily see the differences in yield from their test plots.

The visibility of an I-TV network will not be great unless there is knowledge as to its existence and a conscious effort to allow visitors to view the system. Even less visible to outsiders will be the results of I-TV: improved student achievement, increased access to colleges of choice, and greater success rates at the post-secondary level. These results are much less tangible and visible than those of many other innovations and technologies.

(Note: Rural and urban schools may have somewhat different rationales for I-TV adoption. For example, small schools might use I-TV to electronically combine students in an advanced course such as Physics, while larger urban schools might use I-TV provide multiple sections of an existing course such as Russian IV. Other motivations may also come into play. One astute urban principal remarked that urban schools may feel forced to adopt I-TV technology simply out of a fear of being "one-upped" by their rural counterparts.)

MEASURING RETURN ON INVESTMENT

As mentioned earlier in this chapter, educational technology has generally not been subjected to the same cost-benefit analysis that businesses make regarding acquiring new technology: few educators sought to measure the return on investment for the large numbers of computers purchased in the last decade for student use in schools; few states considered it necessary to justify multi-million dollar expenditures for placing a satellite dish on every school's roof. The common thread in all of these "non-decisions" was that it simply "made sense." The technology afforded opportunities to students that they did not otherwise have. The expenditures were justified largely as a necessary and expected cost of school reform.

The authors feel an obligation to temper their enthusiasm for I-TV technology and its capabilities with a justifiable economic rationale for I-TV adoption. Chapter 9 details a method by which any current or potential adopter can quickly calculate the economic costs and benefits of two-way I-TV, based on the intended or actual uses of the network. The intent of this cost-benefit analysis is to enable the adopter to quantify the benefits resulting from the technology, thereby providing a more rational approach for decision making.

Chapter 9 details the measurement of return on investment at a strictly financial level. The rest of this chapter, however, deals with two additional theoretically based methods of gauging the value of I-TV: social and human capital.

SOCIAL CAPITAL

Social capital is a prominent theoretical perspective in sociological literature. It has been variously defined as:

- the kinds of interpersonal connections that can enhance one's professional advancement (Bourdieu, 1977)
- a variety of entities with two common characteristics: one, some aspects of social structures, and two, efforts facilitating action within that structure (Coleman, 1988)
- those expectations for action within a collective effort that affect both economic goals and goal-seeking behavior of its members even when these expectations are not oriented toward an economic sphere (Portes and Senserbrenner, 1993)

Emma Theuri (1995) extrapolates four major characteristics of social capital from these and other definitions. She asserts that social capital is:

(1) Based on the social connectedness of any institution either internally (e.g., in the family) or externally (e.g., in the community)

(2) Backed by a collective effort of all the players involved

(3) Based on intrinsic motivation toward some expected and well defined gains

(4) Embedded within broad social factors including cultural, ethnic, class, and academic orientations

A somewhat less academic definition of social capital might include: the values and characteristics possessed by an individual or group which are widely accepted within that group as desirable or from which emanate power and/or respect. Social capital in one setting or group is different from that in other groups and situations. For example, the social capital in a corporate board room is much different from that in a street gang or a small rural school.

Schools have historically concentrated on gains in teacher certification, school financial support, and curriculum standardization as methods for increasing student achievement (Hobbs, 1989). Factors outside the school that affect student achievement have also been studied at length: socioeconomic status of the family, parental education level, parent involvement in the school, race, gender, etc. While both sets of achievement-related variables are measurable and informative, Theuri (1995) points out that educational policy has failed to recognize the factors embedded in sources of family and neighborhood social capital. More importantly, she contends that ''policy makers need to recognize how the cultures of the three institutions interact (school, family and neighborhood) and the role each plays in affecting student performance.'' Bridging areas of school, family, and neighborhood social capital improves the chances for increased student achievement (Theuri, 1995).

Whether or not we adhere to the theoretical implications of social capital, it clear that a combination of social values and capital drawn from each institution in which a student interacts (school, parents, and community) is more conducive to student achievement than if each of the entities maintains its own, independently held notions of social values and capital. For example, studies have shown that in a comparison between student achievement levels in public vs. parochial schools, while holding other variables constant, parochial students outperform their public school counterparts (Chandra, 1993). The explanation for this difference is based in social capital (Coleman, 1988). In parochial schools, a family's social capital — that is, their perspectives, their values, and their expectations — are doubly reinforced by the school and the community, thus, students reach higher levels of achievement than where conflicting or non-reinforcing values are present.

I-TV has the potential to play a large role in bringing together the social capital from several spheres, thereby reinforcing the factors that positively affect student achievement. In other words, I-TV technology is not limited to the provision of high school or dual-credit classes, it is also a vehicle for building community. The conscious integration of school, family, and community values, i.e., social capital, in a two-way I-TV program can be accomplished through a number of after-hours and alternative uses (see Chapter 10 for alternative uses of I-TV networks). I-TV networks can be used to facilitate cross-community meetings; provide regional social services to students, families, and others; facilitate professional organization meetings; and provide college or community education classes, etc. The use of I-TV networks by families and communities strengthens the connection between school, family, and community, thereby using social capital to reinforce student achievement.

A HUMAN CAPITAL PERSPECTIVE

The concept of human capital is founded on the principle that education is an investment in the future of society. Human capital is defined economically as the idea that human beings possess skills and abilities, over and above their physical labor, that contribute to economic growth (Hobbs, 1986). Attention was focused on human capital following World War II, as economists found that the classic economic models used to account for economic growth through increases in land, labor, and physical capital were not adequate to explain the sustained economic growth that was occurring (Williamson, 1979). This caused some researchers to begin studying not just the quantity of labor produced, but also its quality. Inherent in this notion is that there is an economic payoff—to the individual, to the community, and ultimately to society—associated with higher educational attainment. Of course, for education to produce a return, there must also be jobs which use the education. This is a particular problem for rural communities that often lack the employment opportunities that utilize and reward higher levels of education (Bluestone and Harrison, 1982; Lichter and Costanzo, 1987; McGranahan and Ghelfi, 1990). In the absence of local opportunities, highly educated individuals may be forced to move out of their home communities in order to realize a return on their educational investments. In this instance, both the individual and the human capital become mobile and displaced from the locale that made the investment.

In rural America, urban-based economic growth has been subsidized through rural investment in education as educated people leave rural areas to seek jobs in urban areas. In other words, rural America's investment in human capital has rarely been realized at the level at which the investment took place, i.e., the local community. Those leaving the community take the community's (as well as their own) human capital investment with them. In short, education represents only half of the human capital story—the job that uses and rewards the education is the other half.

If there is substantial societal benefit from the production of human capital in the educational system, and rural communities continue to subsidize urban economic development (because highly skilled employment opportunities are disproportionately located in metropolitan America), then for rural America investment in I-TV offers two possibilities:

(1) The capital investment in two-way I-TV technologies in rural areas will merely provide additional economic benefit to urban areas.

(2) Rural America can build sufficient capacity, i.e., human capital to attract economic resources that will productively engage highly skilled rural workers, thereby contributing directly to the economic gain of the communities having made the educational and financial investment in I-TV.

Only the second possibility offers a guaranteed return on investment for rural, K − 12, I-TV networks. McGranahan and Ghelfi (1990), Lichter and Costanzo (1987), and Hobbs (1995) argue that caution should be used in assuming that rural economic development is likely to result from a simple expansion of rural educational resources. Rather, increasing the potential for production of human capital must be linked to ongoing community and economic development efforts.

In rural areas with I-TV capabilities, access to high-speed telecommunications can make an area attractive to business and industry. Through telecommunications, workers in a small farm community can have access to the same information and communication resources as they would in a metropolitan area. The economic potential of rural areas has already been increased by the capability of telecommunications to deliver the information resources needed by business. What may become the new limiting factor is the ready availability of human capital, and /or the capacity to generate human capital. For example, if a company can provide training for its employees in a rural town from a home office in another state via an I-TV link, the attractiveness of locating employees in rural areas is much greater. Similarly, the availability of high school graduates with advanced vocational training can also attract the interest of business and industry. In summary, one of the less tangible benefits of the educational opportunities afforded by I-TV is its potential for generating a sustainable source of human capital for rural America.

Conducting an I-TV
Cost-Benefit Analysis

DISCUSSIONS of whether to adopt two-way interactive TV inevitably focus on the question: "Is it worth the money?" Schools may be able to justify I-TV costs on the basis of offering courses that they could not otherwise afford, however, schools will also need to have an economic rationale for implementing I-TV technology if a plan for I-TV development is to proceed.

In an attempt to provide an economic decision-making tool for prospective and current adopters of I-TV, one of the authors, Vicki Hobbs, has collaborated with Dr. Curtis Braschler of the University of Missouri-Columbia Department of Agricultural Economics in designing a cost-benefit spreadsheet for I-TV. (Consult the following section for details on how to obtain a copy.) This computer spreadsheet allows the user to determine the costs and benefits of implementing and operating an I-TV network for a single school, a district, or a consortium of schools. Instead of providing set costs and benefits, this model allows the user to enter either estimated or precise figures for any given local situation; I-TV costs differ greatly from one implementation, state, and transmission technology to another.

This analysis spreadsheet can be used at several stages. For example, schools may use it early in the planning process to determine the economic rationale for implementing or not implementing two-way interactive television, while more exact numbers may be used for a second analysis during the implementation phase. The adopter can conduct a third analysis after the first year of operation in order to determine the ongoing economic viability of the technology.

OVERVIEW OF THE COST-BENEFIT
ANALYSIS SPREADSHEET

The spreadsheet is divided into four sections: costs (Section A), benefits (Section B), cost-benefit summary (Section C), and break-even analysis (Section D).

Nine categories of costs are designated. The analysis distinguishes between fixed costs, which can be spread over several years, and variable costs, which occur on an annual basis. The first three cost items—classroom renovation, classroom construction and classroom equipment—are fixed costs which can be spread over several years. The next four cost items—line lease, teacher training cost, teacher stipends, and equipment maintenance—are variable costs.

While costs are usually easy to compute, the calculation of benefits is a more subjective estimate of economic benefits accruing to the school and community. Benefits are divided into ten categories. The model is designed so that the user needs to estimate only the number of students enrolled and the value to each student of each course to be offered through I-TV. The "value per student" should be locally determined and should reflect either the economic value to each student completing the course, or the cost of offering the course through conventional means.

Section C of the spreadsheet incorporates data from sections A and B to compute total costs, total benefits, and the ratio of benefits to costs. The number of students in the various categories is also automatically computed.

The final section of the worksheet (Section D) allows the user to determine the level of student enrollment at which a "break-even point" is reached, that is, the point at which costs equal benefits.

The value of a computer-based analysis is that the user can input variables for a particular scenario, allow the spreadsheet to perform the computations, and then print a hard copy of the analysis for comparison with printouts from different scenarios. This allows the user to observe how the costs and benefits are affected by changes in key variables.

While the spreadsheet is reproduced in the figures of this chapter, the complexity of the mathematical formulas in the spreadsheet prevents easy hand calculation. The intention of this chapter is to provide an annotated review of the spreadsheet; the reader can easily obtain a copy and use it to make the actual calculations. In the figures, the cells where data is entered appear in Column G and are designated by shading. The cells in which automatic calculations are made are designated by alternating white and black lines and usually appear in Column H.

A copy of the spreadsheet is available on disk from the authors for a $5 shipping and handling fee; send request and fee to Scott Christianson,

411 Central Methodist Square, Fayette, MO 65248. Alternatively, the file can be downloaded from the Internet via the world-wide-web from < http://cmc2.cmc.edu/mite.html >. The spreadsheet is available in both MS-DOS (Lotus 1-2-3 and Excel for Windows) and Macintosh formats (Microsoft Works and Excel).

COSTS

Figure 9.1 lists the costs involved in renovating a classroom for use as an I-TV classroom. The usual costs include room remodeling, carpeting, air conditioning, sound soak material for walls, lighting addition/modification, and riser and/or teacher console construction. Costs are dependent on the extent of the modifications required, but can range from as little as $1000 to more than $10,000 per room. There is a cell

	A	B	C	D	E	F	G	H
63		A COST-BENEFIT ANALYSIS OF TWO-WAY INTERACTIVE TELEVISION						
64				FOR THE				
65					SCHOOL DISTRICT			
66								
67								
68								
69								
70								
71								
72								
73								
74								
75								
76								
77								
78	A. COSTS:							
79	A1. CLASSROOM RENOVATION:							
80	a.	Remodeling						
81		Enter cost estimate in G81:						
82	b.	Carpeting						
83		Enter cost estimate in G83:						
84	c.	Air Conditioning						
85		Enter cost estimate in G85:						
86	d.	Sound Soak for Walls						
87		Enter cost estimate in G87:						
88	e.	Lighting						
89		Enter cost estimate in G89:						
90	f.	Riser and/or Teacher Console						
91		Enter cost estimate in G91:						
92	g.	Other Renovation Costs						
93		Enter cost estimate in G93						
94								
95		SUBTOTAL CLASSROOM RENOVATION COSTS						
96	h.	Amount of Renovation Costs Borrowed:						
97		(Enter in G97)						

Figure 9.1. Section A1, classroom renovation.

	A	B	C	D	E	F	G	H
99	A2.	CLASSROOM CONSTRUCTION:						
100	a.	General Construction						
101		Enter cost estimate in G101:					▓▓▓▓▓	
102	b.	Carpeting						
103		Enter cost estimate in G103:					▓▓▓▓▓	
104	c.	Air Conditioning						
105		Enter cost estimate in G105:					▓▓▓▓▓	
106	d.	Sound Soak for Walls						
107		Enter cost estimate in G107:					▓▓▓▓▓	
108	e.	Lighting						
109		Enter cost estimate in G109:					▓▓▓▓▓	
110	f.	Riser and/or Teacher Console						
111		Enter cost estimate in G111:					▓▓▓▓▓	
112	g.	Other Construction Costs						
113		Enter cost estimate in G113:					▓▓▓▓▓	
114								
115		SUBTOTAL CLASSROOM CONSTRUCTION COSTS						▓▓▓▓▓
116	h.	Amount of construction costs borrowed:						
117			(Enter in G117)				▓▓▓▓▓	

Figure 9.2. Section A2, classroom construction.

(G 93) for "Other Renovation Costs" in which any costs not covered in the first six categories can be entered. The subtotal of classroom renovation costs will automatically appear in cell H 95. If borrowed funds are used in the renovation of the classroom, that amount should be included in cell G 97. If a classroom must be constructed, the amounts in this section should be left blank and the costs of construction should be entered in the portion of the spreadsheet shown in Figure 9.2.

The Classroom Construction portion of the spreadsheet, Figure 9.2, need only be completed if it is not possible to renovate an existing classroom. Classroom construction costs include subcategories for general construction costs, carpeting, air conditioning, sound soak for walls, lighting, riser and/or teacher console construction, and other construction costs. Precise or estimated amounts should be included in cells G 101 to G 113; borrowed funds used for classroom construction should be entered in cell G 117. The subtotal of the classroom construction costs will be automatically calculated in cell H 115.

Figure 9.3 deals with the costs of equipping an I-TV classroom (either renovated or constructed). Included are costs for monitors, microphones, speakers, cameras, the control system, the sound system, the video cassette recorder(s), the facsimile machine, and the echo canceller (if necessary). The typical cost range for all the required classroom equipment (monitors, cameras, sound system, and control system), except the CODEC in a digital system or the fiber termination box in an analog system, is $25,000 to $35,000 per classroom. Installation and wiring costs should be included in cell G 134, while any

	A	B	C	D	E	F	G	H
119	A3. CLASSROOM EQUIPMENT							
120	a.	Monitors						
121		Enter cost estimate in G121:					▨	
122	b.	Microphones/speakers/sound system						
123		Enter cost estimate in G123:					▨	
124	c.	Cameras						
125		Enter cost estimate in G125:					▨	
126	d.	Audio/video control system, (e.g.,AMX controller)						
127		Enter cost estimate in G127:					▨	
128	e.	VCR						
129		Enter cost estimate in G129:					▨	
130	f.	Fax						
131		Enter cost estimate in G131:					▨	
132	g.	Echo Cancellor						
133		Enter cost estimate in G133:					▨	
134	h.	Installation and wiring						
135		Enter cost estimate in G135:					▨	
136	i.	Other equipment(e.g., computer, laserdisk, etc)						
137		Enter cost estimate in G137:					▨	
138								
139		SUBTOTAL CLASSROOM EQUIPMENT COSTS						▥
140	j.	Amount of Equipment Costs Borrowed						
141			(Enter in G141)					▨

Figure 9.3. Section A3, classroom equipment.

additional equipment, such as a computer or laserdisk player, can be included in cell G 137. As above, any borrowed funds used for classroom equipment purchase should be included in cell G 141. Classroom equipment costs will be automatically subtotaled in cell H 139. [Note: If classroom equipment is leased rather than purchased, the equipment lease rates should be added to the annual line lease and entered in the following section (long-term annual line lease)].

If transmission lines are not owned by the I-TV cluster, line leases will have to be paid. The costs section in Figure 9.4 includes the cost of the line lease figured on an annual basis. Costs will typically include the

	A	B	C	D	E	F	G	H
143	A4. LONG-TERM ANNUAL LINE LEASE							
144	a.	Amount of annual line lease: (Enter in G144)					▨	
145	b.	Estimated length of line lease (in years)						
146			(Enter in G146):				▨	
147								
148	A5. COST TO TRAIN ONE TEACHER							
149		NOTE: If necessary, divide the total estimated						
150			training costs by the number of teachers					
151			requiring training in your school.					
152	a.	No. of I-TV teachers who will teach						
153		from your site (Enter in G153):					▨	
154	b.	Your cost to train one teacher						
155			(Enter estimate in G155):				▨	
156								

Figure 9.4. Section A4, long-term annual line lease, and Section A5, cost to train one teacher.

transmission equipment (CODEC or fiber termination box) along with the monthly line lease for the telecommunications network. This amount varies widely from one provider and state to another. Typically line lease costs fall between $1000 to $2000 per month per site. Enter the annual line lease costs in G 144. The length of the line lease, in years, should be included in cell G 146.

Section A.5 in Figure 9.4 calculates the teacher training costs. This will be minimal for established networks, and more substantial for networks just starting up. There are several distance learning institutes around the country where teacher training can be acquired. Alternatively, training can be provided at the local sites by a person(s) involved in an I-TV network elsewhere in the state or country, for example, a network director and teacher from a network operating on the same type of I-TV technology. Projected costs should include salaries for the I-TV teachers during their training time. The training cost per teacher will likely range between $500 and $1000. Enter the number of I-TV teachers who will teach from the site for which the analysis is being conducted in cell G153. Insert the estimated or actual cost for training one teacher in cell G 155.

Sidebar 9.1. Funding I-TV

Schools can attempt to reduce or defer I-TV costs in several ways.

Telecommunications Company Support

Several telephone and cable companies around the country have played a vital role in the financing of two-way initiatives within their communities. Telecommunication companies may be convinced to support a local school-based I-TV network in a number of different ways, from hiring a full-time industrial developer with specific expertise in financing development projects to actually providing the funds for local schools to begin an I-TV network.

Community Contributions

Involvement of the community has been stressed as essential throughout this book. With respect to funding, there are two possibilities for incorporating the community:

(1) An I-TV funding campaign can be initiated in the community to solicit contributions toward classroom equipment purchase. Major employers, businesses, organizations, agencies, etc., may be guaranteed a certain number of hours of network use per week in return for their contributions.

(2) A second possibility for recouping network costs is the creation of an hourly usage rate which would apply to all non-school use of the network

by the community. (Note: The issue of resale of telecommunications services may be a source of contention among the larger telephone companies; be sure that this point is adequately addressed in any long-term lease negotiated.)

External Grant Funds

Federal, state, and/or private funds may be available. Two current federal sources are (1) Rural Utility Services (Previously Rural Electrification Administration) Distance Learning and Medical Link Grants; and (2) National Telecommunications and Information Administration (NTIA) grant funds. Private foundations may also be a source of funding, but attracting such funding is often a time-consuming venture. For most schools, fund-raising and grant writing efforts will be most effective on the local or state level.

The portion of the spreadsheet shown in Figure 9.5 is used to calculate the cost of paying teachers that will be teaching over the network. The salaries of the I-TV teachers are entered in cells B−G 172, i.e., the salary for the first teacher is entered in cell B 172, the salary for the second teacher is entered in cell C 172, etc. Remember that only those teachers for whom the local site assumes a salary commitment should be included here. Other teachers on the network would be included in their own schools' spreadsheet, unless the spreadsheet is being used to analyze an entire network's costs and benefits.

Section A.6.a. in Figure 9.5 pertains only to those high school and dual-credit courses that are already being taught at the local site, i.e., I-TV courses that would have been taught locally anyway. In rows 178−194 are listed seventeen possible I-TV courses. List the percent of salary (or time) allocated for each teacher for each course taught in the appropriate column and row. For instance, if Teacher 1 teaches Algebra II as one of six classes which he or she teaches, 16.7 (percent) would be entered in cell B 183. This process should be repeated for each teacher and each course taught from your local site. If necessary, the course name may be replaced with that of a new class name.

Section A.6.b. in Figure 9.6 lists new dual-credit courses offered as part of the I-TV curriculum, that is, only those dual-credit courses which were previously not taught locally within the school system. List the percentage of time taught by each teacher for new dual-credit courses, taking care to keep the percentage entries in the appropriate column for each teacher (refer to row 172 in Figure 9.5). Section A.6.c. of this figure is for listing the percentage of teacher time devoted to teaching new high school courses which will be offered as part of the I-TV

	A	B	C	D	E	F	G	H
157	A6. TEACHER SALARY COSTS							
158								
159								
160								
161								
162								
163								
164								
165								
166								
167								
168								
169								
170								
171		TEACHER1	TEACHER2	TEACHER3	TEACHER4	TEACHER5	TEACHER6	
172	TEACH SAL.							
173								
174	a. EXISTING LOW-ENROLLMENT, HIGH SCHOOL (OR DUAL CREDIT) COURSES							
175	WHICH ARE TO BE OFFERED OVER I-TV							
176								
177		PERCENT OF TIME SPENT BY EACH TEACHER ON EACH COURSE						
178	SPAN.I	0	0	0	0	0	0	
179	SPAN.II	0	0	0	0	0	0	
180	SPAN.III	0	0	0	0	0	0	
181	COL ENG	0	0	0	0	0	0	
182	CREAT. WR	0	0	0	0	0	0	
183	ALG.II	0	0	0	0	0	0	
184	PHYSICS	0	0	0	0	0	0	
185	PRE-CALC	0	0	0	0	0	0	
186	PROB/STAT	0	0	0	0	0	0	
187	CHEM.I	0	0	0	0	0	0	
188	CHEM.II	0	0	0	0	0	0	
189	ANAT/PHYS	0	0	0	0	0	0	
190	CHILD DEV.	0	0	0	0	0	0	
191	AG.ECON.	0	0	0	0	0	0	
192	SOC/PSYCH	0	0	0	0	0	0	
193	AM.GOVT.	0	0	0	0	0	0	
194	COMPUTER	0	0	0	0	0	0	

Figure 9.5. Section A5, teacher salary costs.

	A	B	C	D	E	F	G	H
197	b. NEW DUAL CREDIT COURSES OFFERED AS PART OF THE I-TV CURRICULUM							
198								
199		PERCENT OF TIME SPENT BY EACH TEACHER ON EACH COURSE						
200	ALGEBRA	0	0	0	0	0	0	
201	CONT MATH	0	0	0	0	0	0	
202	COL ENG	0	0	0	0	0	0	
203	SPANISH	0	0	0	0	0	0	
204	GERMAN	0	0	0	0	0	0	
205	ACCOUNT.	0	0	0	0	0	0	
206	BIOLOGY	0	0	0	0	0	0	
207	SPEECH	0	0	0	0	0	0	
208	OTHER	0	0	0	0	0	0	
209								
210	c. NEW HIGH SCHOOL COURSES OFFERED AS PART OF THE I-TV CURRICULUM							
211								
212		PERCENT OF TIME SPENT BY EACH TEACHER ON EACH COURSE						
213	CALCULUS	0	0	0	0	0	0	
214	JAPANESE	0	0	0	0	0	0	
215	FRENCH	0	0	0	0	0	0	
216	BUS.LAW	0	0	0	0	0	0	
217	ADV ACCT	0	0	0	0	0	0	
218	BR.JOURN.	0	0	0	0	0	0	
219	SPEECH II	0	0	0	0	0	0	
220	OTHER	0	0	0	0	0	0	
221	OTHER	0	0	0	0	0	0	
222	OTHER	0	0	0	0	0	0	

Figure 9.6. Section A5, teacher salary costs, continued.

curriculum, that is, those courses which were not taught locally before the implementation of the I-TV network. Note: In either section any course name may be replaced with a new course name.

The automatic calculation of total teaching costs for each course listed in the previous sections (Figures 9.5 and 9.6) appears in the cells shown in Figure 9.7; no data entry is required in this section.

Figure 9.8 shows the portion of the spreadsheet used for entering any additional costs related to salary, such as any additional stipend for teaching an I-TV course (entered in cell G 281) and any portion of a network director salary and expenses which will be paid by the local district (entered in cell G 286). The subtotal of additional salary expenditures appears in cell H 288.

Section A.8, shown in Figure 9.9, deals with equipment maintenance costs. Two options are given for handling such expenses. Either the district (or consortium) will enter into an annual maintenance contract (the district's portion of which should be entered in cell G 297) or there will be an annual contribution to an I-TV maintenance budget (the district's portion of which should be entered in cell G 299). The subtotaled equipment maintenance costs appear in cell H 301.

Depreciation schedules and interest rates are covered in Section A.9 (Figure 9.10). If any borrowed funds are used in the construction of the

	A	B	C	D	E	F	G	H
228	EXISTING HS/DUAL CREDIT COURSES							TOT COST
229	SPAN.I	0	0	0	0	0	0	0
230	SPAN.II	0	0	0	0	0	0	0
231	SPAN.III	0	0	0	0	0	0	0
232	COL ENG	0	0	0	0	0	0	0
233	CREAT. WR	0	0	0	0	0	0	0
234	ALG.II	0	0	0	0	0	0	0
235	PHYSICS	0	0	0	0	0	0	0
236	PRE-CALC	0	0	0	0	0	0	0
237	PROB/STAT	0	0	0	0	0	0	0
238	CHEM.I	0	0	0	0	0	0	0
239	CHEM.II	0	0	0	0	0	0	0
240	ANAT/PHYS	0	0	0	0	0	0	0
241	CHILD DEV.	0	0	0	0	0	0	0
242	AG.ECON.	0	0	0	0	0	0	0
243	SOC/PSYCH	0	0	0	0	0	0	0
244	AM.GOVT.	0	0	0	0	0	0	0
245	COMPUTER	0	0	0	0	0	0	0
246								
247	SUBTOTAL							
248								
249								
250	NEW DUAL CREDIT COURSES							TOT COST
251	ALGEBRA	0	0	0	0	0	0	0
252	CONT MATH	0	0	0	0	0	0	0
253	COL ENG	0	0	0	0	0	0	0
254	SPANISH	0	0	0	0	0	0	0
255	GERMAN	0	0	0	0	0	0	0
256	ACCOUNT.	0	0	0	0	0	0	0
257	BIOLOGY	0	0	0	0	0	0	0
258	SPEECH	0	0	0	0	0	0	0
259	OTHER	0	0	0	0	0	0	0
260								
261	SUBTOTALS							
262								
263								
264	NEW HIGH SCHOOL COURSES							TOT COST
265	CALCULUS	0	0	0	0	0	0	0
266	JAPANESE	0	0	0	0	0	0	0
267	FRENCH	0	0	0	0	0	0	0
268	BUS.LAW	0	0	0	0	0	0	0
269	ADV ACCT	0	0	0	0	0	0	0
270	BR.JOURN.	0	0	0	0	0	0	0
271	SPEECH II	0	0	0	0	0	0	0
272	OTHER	0	0	0	0	0	0	0
273	OTHER	0	0	0	0	0	0	0
274	OTHER	0	0	0	0	0	0	0
275								
276	SUBTOTALS							
277								

Figure 9.7. Subtotals of teacher salary costs.

	A	B	C	D	E	F	G	H
279	A7. ADDITIONAL SALARY COSTS							
280	a. Additional stipend for I-TV teaching (per teacher)							
281			Enter stipend in G281:				▓▓▓▓	
282								
283	b. The portion of any I-TV Network personnel salary							
284	(or personnel expenses) which you will pay, e.g.,							
285	Network Director salary and/or travel expenses							
286			Enter estimate in G286:				▓▓▓▓	
287								
288		SUBTOTAL ADDITIONAL SALARY COSTS						▓▓▓▓
289								

Figure 9.8. Section A7, additional salary costs.

	A	B	C	D	E	F	G	H
290	A8. EQUIPMENT MAINTENANCE COSTS							
291	NOTE: You will likely handle maintenance in one of two ways.							
292			You will either enter into a maintenance contract					
293			or you will contribute to a maintenance fund to be					
294			tapped into as necessary. You will therefore likely					
295			enter an amount into only ONE of the categories below.					
296								
297	a. Annual Maintenance Contract (Enter in G297)						▓▓▓▓	
298	b. Estimated Annual I-TV Maintenance Budget							
299			Enter in G299:				▓▓▓▓	
300								
301		SUBTOTAL EQUIPMENT MAINTENANCE COSTS						▓▓▓▓
302								

Figure 9.9. Section A8, equipment maintenance costs.

	A	B	C	D	E	F	G	H
303	A9. DEPRECIATION SCHEDULE/INTEREST RATES							
304	a. Insert Interest Rate on borrowed money in G304:						▓▓▓▓	
305			(enter as a decimal, e.g., ".06"					
306	b. Estimated no. of years over which classroom							
307	renovation or construction will be depreciated							
308			Enter in G308:				▓▓▓▓	
309		SUBTOTAL RENOVATION—$ + PRINCIPAL + INTEREST						▓▓▓▓
310		SUBTOTAL CONSTRUCTION—$ + PRINCIPAL + INTEREST						▓▓▓▓
311								
312	c. Estimated no. of years over which classroom							
313	equipment will be depreciated—Enter in G313:						▓▓▓▓	
314		SUBTOTAL EQUIPMENT—$ + PRINCIPAL + INTEREST						▓▓▓▓
315								
316	d. Estimated no. of years a trained teacher							
317	will remain with the network: (Enter in G317)						▓▓▓▓	
318								

Figure 9.10. Section A9, depreciation schedule/interest rates.

	A	B	C	D	E	F	G	H
319	A10. ANNUALIZED COST SUMMARY:							
320								
321	TOTAL ANNUAL COST OF CLASSROOM RENOVATION							|||||||||||
322								
323	TOTAL ANNUAL COST OF CLASSROOM CONSTRUCTION							|||||||||||
324								
325	TOTAL ANNUAL COST OF CLASSROOM EQUIPMENT							|||||||||||
326								
327	TOTAL ANNUAL COST OF TRAINING ALL TEACHERS							|||||||||||
328								
329	TOTAL ANNUAL COST FOR TEACHER STIPENDS							|||||||||||
330								
331	TOTAL ANNUAL CAPITAL COST							|||||||||||
332								
333	TOTAL ALL ANNUAL COSTS RELATED TO I-TV							|||||||||||
334								

Figure 9.11. Section A10, annualized cost summary.

I-TV classroom or for equipment purchase, the interest rate should be entered in decimal form in cell G 304. For example, 12.5% would be entered as 0.125. The number of years over which classroom renovation or construction will be depreciated should be entered in cell G 308. Renovation subtotals are automatically included in cell H 309 and the subtotals for construction appear in cell H 310.

The estimated number of years over which the classroom equipment will be depreciated should be entered in cell G 313. The estimated number of years a trained teacher is likely to remain with the network is entered in cell G 317; this allows for calculating the ongoing training costs for new I-TV teachers.

The cells in column H in Figure 9.11 calculate the total annual costs by category: classroom renovation, classroom construction, classroom equipment, teacher training, teacher stipends, and capital cost. (No data is entered in this section.) A summary of all annual costs related to I-TV appears in cell H 333.

BENEFITS

The next section of the spreadsheet deals with the benefits of I-TV. Several parts of this section require the user to estimate the number of students involved in I-TV courses and the value of each course per student. The concept of ''value per student'' is a way of estimating the value of each I-TV use. The value per student included in each subsection should be consistent with the projected economic value to the student of having taken the course. Alternatively, the cost per student for offering the course through conventional means can be used as a proxy for "estimated value per student."

The sections of the spreadsheet shown in Figures 9.12a through 9.14 are used to calculate the benefits for a number of different types of I-TV courses (existing high school, existing dual-credit, new high school, and new dual-credit). Subsections "a" through "q" of Figures 9.12a and 9.12b list seventeen of the most common I-TV courses, however, any course name can be substituted. At the end of each subsection a "Total Value for this Class" is automatically calculated in Column H. At the end of the section a subtotal of benefits for the entire category of courses is automatically calculated. For example in Figure 9.12b the "Subtotal Benefits from High School Courses Added" is calculated and appears in cell H 436.

As with all other sections, in Figures 9.12a, 9.12b, 9.13, 9.14, and 9.15, it is important to enter only those numbers that pertain to the entity for which the cost-benefit analysis is being done, for example, the local school. That is, only the estimated number of students enrolled in the local school should be included, not the total number across the network unless the analysis is being conducted for the entire network.

Figure 9.16 shows section B.5 of the spreadsheet. This section uses data on the estimated number of students per year, and the average savings in transportation costs for each student, to calculate the value of decreased transportation costs. This is especially useful where transportation had previously been required to area vocational schools, where students were transported to an area or community college for dual-credit courses, or where students or teachers were transported to another high school for high school courses.

Benefits section B.6 (shown in Figure 9.17) attempts to quantify the "good will" and "community savings" generated by community use of the network, for example, by agencies, businesses, organizations, or government. Any income which is generated from community use of the network is entered in cell G 566. While it may be very difficult to give an economic value to community "good will" or aggregate community savings attributed to I-TV, the opportunity exists for quantifying these values in whatever way is most appropriate. Alternatively, cells G 566 – 570 can be left blank.

Figure 9.18 shows the portion of the spreadsheet used for estimating the benefits of community access to adult, college, or community education courses. The estimated number of persons per year is entered

	A	B	C	D	E	F	G	H
338	B. BENEFITS:							
339								
340								
341								
342								
343								
344								
345								
346								
347								
348	B1. EXISTING LOW-ENROLLMENT, HIGH SCHOOL (OR DUAL CREDIT) COURSES							
349	WHICH ARE PLANNED TO BE OFFERED OVER I-TV							
350								
351	a.	SPAN.I						
352		Estimated no. of students: (Enter in G352)						
353		Estimated Value per Student: (Enter in G353)						
354		Total Value for this class:						IIIIIIIIIIIII
355								
356	b.	SPAN.II						
357		Estimated no. of students: (Enter in G357)						
358		Estimated Value per Student: (Enter in G358)						
359		Total Value for this class:						IIIIIIIIIIIII
360								
361	c.	SPAN.III						
362		Estimated no. of students: (Enter in G362)						
363		Estimated Value per Student: (Enter in G363)						
364		Total Value for this class:						IIIIIIIIIIIII
365								
366	d.	COL ENG						
367		Estimated no. of students: (Enter in G367)						
368		Estimated Value per Student: (Enter in G368)						
369		Total Value for this class:						IIIIIIIIIIIII
370								
371	e.	CREAT. WR						
372		Estimated no. of students: (Enter in G372)						
373		Estimated Value per Student: (Enter in G373)						
374		Total Value for this class:						IIIIIIIIIIIII
375								
376	f.	ALG.II						
377		Estimated no. of students: (Enter in G377)						
378		Estimated Value per Student: (Enter in G378)						
379		Total Value for this class:						IIIIIIIIIIIII
380								
381	g.	PHYSICS						
382		Estimated no. of students: (Enter in G382)						
383		Estimated Value per Student: (Enter in G383)						
384		Total Value for this class:						IIIIIIIIIIIII
385								
386	h.	PRE-CALC						
387		Estimated no. of students: (Enter in G387)						
388		Estimated Value per Student: (Enter in G388)						
389		Total Value for this class:						IIIIIIIIIIIII
390								
391	i.	PROB/STAT						
392		Estimated no. of students: (Enter in G392)						
393		Estimated Value per Student: (Enter in G393)						
394		Total Value for this class:						IIIIIIIIIIIII

Figure 9.12a. Section B1, benefits for existing courses.

	A	B	C	D	E	F	G	H
396	j.	CHEM.I						
397		Estimated no. of students: (Enter in G397)					▓▓▓	
398		Estimated Value per Student: (Enter in G398)					▓▓▓	
399		Total Value for this class:						‖‖‖‖‖‖‖‖‖
400								
401	k.	CHEM.II						
402		Estimated no. of students: (Enter in G402)					▓▓▓	
403		Estimated Value per Student: (Enter in G403)					▓▓▓	
404		Total Value for this class:						‖‖‖‖‖‖‖‖‖
405								
406	l.	ANAT/PHYS						
407		Estimated no. of students: (Enter in G407)					▓▓▓	
408		Estimated Value per Student: (Enter in G408)					▓▓▓	
409		Total Value for this class:						‖‖‖‖‖‖‖‖‖
410								
411	m.	CHILD DEV.						
412		Estimated no. of students: (Enter in G412)					▓▓▓	
413		Estimated Value per Student: (Enter in G413)					▓▓▓	
414		Total Value for this class:						‖‖‖‖‖‖‖‖‖
415								
416	n.	AG.ECON.						
417		Estimated no. of students: (Enter in G417)					▓▓▓	
418		Estimated Value per Student: (Enter in G418)					▓▓▓	
419		Total Value for this class:						‖‖‖‖‖‖‖‖‖
420								
421	o.	SOC/PSYCH						
422		Estimated no. of students: (Enter in G422)					▓▓▓	
423		Estimated Value per Student: (Enter in G423)					▓▓▓	
424		Total Value for this class:						‖‖‖‖‖‖‖‖‖
425								
426	p.	AM.GOVT.						
427		Estimated no. of students: (Enter in G427)					▓▓▓	
428		Estimated Value per Student: (Enter in G428)					▓▓▓	
429		Total Value for this class:						‖‖‖‖‖‖‖‖‖
430								
431	q.	COMPUTER						
432		Estimated no. of students: (Enter in G432)					▓▓▓	
433		Estimated Value per Student: (Enter in G433)					▓▓▓	
434		Total Value for this class:						‖‖‖‖‖‖‖‖‖
435								
436	SUBTOTAL BENEFITS FROM HIGH SCHOOL COURSES ADDED:							‖‖‖‖‖‖‖‖‖
437								

Figure 9.12b. Section B1, benefits for existing courses, continued.

225

	A	B	C	D	E	F	G	H
438	BENEFITS:							
439	B2. NEW DUAL CREDIT COURSES OFFERED AS PART OF THE I-TV CURRICULUM							
440								
441	a.	ALGEBRA						
442		Estimated no. of students: (Enter in G442)						
443		Estimated Value per Student: (Enter in G443)						
444		Total Value for this class:						▓▓▓▓▓▓▓
445								
446	b.	CONT MATH						
447		Estimated no. of students: (Enter in G447)						
448		Estimated Value per Student: (Enter in G448)						
449		Total Value for this class:						▓▓▓▓▓▓▓
450								
451	c.	COL ENG						
452		Estimated no. of students: (Enter in G452)						
453		Estimated Value per Student: (Enter in G453)						
454		Total Value for this class:						▓▓▓▓▓▓▓
455								
456	d.	SPANISH						
457		Estimated no. of students: (Enter in G457)						
458		Estimated Value per Student: (Enter in G458)						
459		Total Value for this class:						▓▓▓▓▓▓▓
460								
461	e.	GERMAN						
462		Estimated no. of students: (Enter in G462)						
463		Estimated Value per Student: (Enter in G463)						
464		Total Value for this class:						▓▓▓▓▓▓▓
465								
466	f.	ACCOUNT.						
467		Estimated no. of students: (Enter in G467)						
468		Estimated Value per Student: (Enter in G468)						
469		Total Value for this class:						▓▓▓▓▓▓▓
470								
471	g.	BIOLOGY						
472		Estimated no. of students: (Enter in G472)						
473		Estimated Value per Student: (Enter in G473)						
474		Total Value for this class:						▓▓▓▓▓▓▓
475								
476	h.	SPEECH						
477		Estimated no. of students: (Enter in G477)						
478		Estimated Value per Student: (Enter in G478)						
479		Total Value for this class:						▓▓▓▓▓▓▓
480								
481	i.	OTHER						
482		Estimated no. of students: (Enter in G482)						
483		Estimated Value per Student: (Enter in G483)						
484		Total Value for this class:						▓▓▓▓▓▓▓
485								
486	SUBTOTAL BENEFITS FROM DUAL CREDIT COURSES ADDED:							▓▓▓▓▓▓▓
487								

Figure 9.13. Section B2, benefits for new courses.

226

	A	B	C	D	E	F	G	H
488	BENEFITS:							
489	B3. NEW HIGH SCHOOL COURSES WHICH ARE LIKELY ADDITIONS							
490	TO THE I-TV CURRICULUM							
491	a.	CALCULUS						
492		Estimated no. of students: (Enter in G492)						
493		Estimated Value per Student: (Enter in G493)						
494		Total Value for this class:						|||||||||||
495								
496	b.	JAPANESE						
497		Estimated no. of students: (Enter in G497)						
498		Estimated Value per Student: (Enter in G498)						
499		Total Value for this class:						|||||||||||
500								
501	c.	FRENCH						
502		Estimated no. of students: (Enter in G502)						
503		Estimated Value per Student: (Enter in G503)						
504		Total Value for this class:						|||||||||||
505								
506	d.	BUS.LAW						
507		Estimated no. of students: (Enter in G507)						
508		Estimated Value per Student: (Enter in G508)						
509		Total Value for this class:						|||||||||||
510								
511	e.	ADV ACCT						
512		Estimated no. of students: (Enter in G512)						
513		Estimated Value per Student: (Enter in G513)						
514		Total Value for this class:						|||||||||||
515								
516	f.	BR.JOURN.						
517		Estimated no. of students: (Enter in G517)						
518		Estimated Value per Student: (Enter in G518)						
519		Total Value for this class:						|||||||||||
520								
521	g.	SPEECH II						
522		Estimated no. of students: (Enter in G522)						
523		Estimated Value per Student: (Enter in G523)						
524		Total Value for this class:						|||||||||||
525								
526	h.	OTHER						
527		Estimated no. of students: (Enter in G527)						
528		Estimated Value per Student: (Enter in G528)						
529		Total Value for this class:						|||||||||||
530								
531	i.	OTHER						
532		Estimated no. of students: (Enter in G532)						
533		Estimated Value per Student: (Enter in G533)						
534		Total Value for this class:						|||||||||||
535								
536	j.	OTHER						
537		Estimated no. of students: (Enter in G537)						
538		Estimated Value per Student: (Enter in G538)						
539		Total Value for this class:						|||||||||||
540								
541	SUBTOTAL BENEFITS NEW HIGH SCHOOL COURSES ADDED							|||||||||||
542								

Figure 9.14. Section B3, benefits for new courses, continued.

	A	B	C	D	E	F	G	H
543	BENEFITS:							
544	B4. ABILITY TO GRADUATE STUDENTS FULLY MEETING COLLEGE							
545	ENTRY REQUIREMENTS BECAUSE OF I-TV							
546		Est. no. of students/year: (Enter in G546)					▓▓▓	
547		Estimated Value per Student: (Enter in G547)					▓▓▓	
548		SUBTOTAL VALUE OF MEETING COLLEGE REQUIREMENTS						‖‖‖‖‖‖‖
549								

Figure 9.15. Section B4, benefits of meeting college entry requirements.

	A	B	C	D	E	F	G	H
550	BENEFITS:							
551	B5. DECREASED TRANSPORTATION COSTS AS A RESULT OF I-TV COURSE OFFERINGS,							
552	E.G., DECREASED VOC-TECH SCHOOL TRANSPORTATION, ETC.							
553		Est. no. of students/year: (Enter in G553)					▓▓▓	
554		Estimated Value per Student: (Enter in G554)					▓▓▓	
555		SUBTOTAL VALUE OF DECREASED TRANSPORTATION COSTS						‖‖‖‖‖‖‖
556								

Figure 9.16. Section B5, decreased transportation costs.

	A	B	C	D	E	F	G	H
557	BENEFITS:							
558	B6. INCOME/GOOD WILL/COMMUNITY SAVINGS GENERATED FROM COMMUNITY USE OF							
559	THE NETWORK, E.G., BY AGENCIES, BUSINESSES, ORGANIZATIONS,							
560	GOVERNMENTAL UNITS, ETC.:							
561								
562								
563								
564								
565								
566	a.	Enter estimated annual income in G566:					▓▓▓	
567	b.	Enter annual estimated economic value of					▓▓▓	
568		community good will in G568:					▓▓▓	
569	c.	Enter estimated annual community savings					▓▓▓	
570		in G570:					▓▓▓	
571		SUBTOTAL VALUE OF INCOME/GOOD WILL/SAVINGS						‖‖‖‖‖‖‖
572								

Figure 9.17. Section B6, income, good will, and community savings generated from community use of the network.

	A	B	C	D	E	F	G	H
573	BENEFITS:							
574	B7. COMMUNITY ACCESS TO ADULT/COLLEGE/COMMUNITY EDUCATION COURSES, E.G.,							
575	SAVINGS IN TRANSPORTATION COSTS, VALUE OF TIME SAVED, ETC.							
576		Est. no. of persons/year:(Enter in G576)					▓▓▓	
577		Estimated Value per Person: (Enter in G577)					▓▓▓	
578		SUBTOTAL VALUE OF ADULT/COL/COM ED COURSES:						‖‖‖‖‖‖‖
579								

Figure 9.18. Section B7, access to adult, college, and community education courses.

228

	A	B	C	D	E	F	G	H
580	BENEFITS:							
581	B8. JOINT TEACHER PROFESSIONAL DEVELOPMENT/INSERVICE PROGRAMMING, E.G.,							
582	SAVINGS IN TRANSPORTATION COSTS, WORKSHOP FEES, VALUE OF							
583	ADDITIONAL TRAINING, ETC.							
584		Est. no. of teachers/year:(Enter in G584)						
585		Estimated Value per Teacher: (Enter in G585)						
586								
587		SUBTOTAL VALUE OF PROF DEVELOPMENT						|||||||||||||
588								

Figure 9.19. Section B8, benefits of professional development opportunities.

in G 576 and the estimated value to each person is entered in G 577. The numbers for "value to each person" can include estimated savings in aggregate transportation costs, value of time saved by persons enrolled locally rather than at distant sites, and increased employee skills, wages, and productivity.

The benefits associated with joint teacher professional development programming is included in the part of the spreadsheet shown in Figure 9.19. Savings in transportation costs, workshop fees, value of additional training, etc., can be used as the basis for estimating the value per teacher involved. The estimated annual number of teachers involved in such activities should be entered in cell G 584.

The benefits of access to specific college or university services through I-TV, such as special education services, diagnostic testing, speech therapist services, etc., are calculated in benefits Section B.9 (shown in Figure 9.20). The estimated annual value of such services should be included in cell G 592.

The last benefits section (Section B.10, Figure 9.21) involves the benefits to students of graduating from high school with some accumulation of college credit. Estimated values may be obtained by including savings in college tuition as a result of earning college credit while in high school and savings in college expenses because of early graduation. In cell G 600, the estimated number of students per year realizing this type of benefit should be entered. Into cell G 601 the estimated value per

	A	B	C	D	E	F	G	H
589	BENEFITS:							
590	B9. ACCESS TO SPECIFIC COLLEGE/UNIVERSITY SERVICES, E.G., SPECIAL							
591	EDUCATION SERVICES, DIAGNOSTIC TESTING, ETC.							
592		Est.annual value of services: (Enter in G592)						
593								
594		SUBTOTAL VALUE OF COLLEGE SERVICES						|||||||||||||
595								

Figure 9.20. Section B9, benefits of access to specific services.

	A	B	C	D	E	F	G	H
596	BENEFITS:							
597	B10. BENEFIT OF GRADUATING FROM HIGH SCHOOL WITH COLLEGE CREDIT							
598	E.G., SAVINGS IN COLLEGE TUITION, SAVINGS IN COLLEGE							
599	EXPENSES BECAUSE OF EARLY GRADUATION, ETC.							
600			Est. no. of students/year: (Enter in G600)				▓▓▓▓▓	
601			Estimated Value per Student: (Enter in G601)				▓▓▓▓▓	
602			SUBTOTAL VALUE OF GRADUATING W/COLLEGE CREDIT:					▐▌▐▌▐▌▐▌
603								

Figure 9.21. Section B10, savings in college.

student is entered. As with other sections, the benefit subtotal will automatically appear in column H (cell H 602).

COST-BENEFIT SUMMARY

The third section of the spreadsheet is the cost-benefit summary (see Figure 9.22). All the numbers in this section are calculated automatically from the values entered in the previous two sections; the calculated values appear in column H. The summary data includes (1) Total Benefits

	A	B	C	D	E	F	G	H
605			C. COST-BENEFIT SUMMARY					
606								
607	TOTAL BENEFITS							▐▌▐▌▐▌▐▌
608								
609	TOTAL COSTS							▐▌▐▌▐▌▐▌
610								
611	TOTAL BENEFITS LESS TOTAL COSTS							▐▌▐▌▐▌▐▌
612								
613								
614								
615	TOTAL PROJECTED I-TV ENROLLMENT—EXISTING CURR. OFFERINGS							▐▌▐▌▐▌▐▌
616								
617	TOTAL PROJECTED I-TV ENROLLMENT—NEW DUAL CREDIT COURSES							▐▌▐▌▐▌▐▌
618								
619	TOTAL PROJECTED I-TV ENROLLMENT—NEW HIGH SCH COURSES							▐▌▐▌▐▌▐▌
620								
621	TOTAL STUDENTS MEETING COLLEGE REQUIREMENTS DUE TO I-TV							▐▌▐▌▐▌▐▌
622								
623	TOTAL STUDENTS IN REDUCED TRANSPORTATION COSTS							▐▌▐▌▐▌▐▌
624								
625	TOTAL STUDENTS IMPACTED BY PROGRAM (DUPLICATED COUNT)							▐▌▐▌▐▌▐▌
626								
627								
628	AVERAGE $ BENEFIT PER STUDENT							▐▌▐▌▐▌▐▌
629	AVERAGE $ COST PER STUDENT							▐▌▐▌▐▌▐▌
630	AVERAGE $ BENEFIT OVER $ COST							▐▌▐▌▐▌▐▌
631								
632	AVERAGE BENEFIT-COST RATIO PER STUDENT							▐▌▐▌▐▌▐▌
633								

Figure 9.22. Section C, cost-benefit summary.

(cell H 607), (2) Total Costs (cell H 609); and (3) Total Benefits Less Total Costs (cell H 611). Cells H 615−623 include the total projected enrollments for existing curriculum offerings, new dual-credit courses, and new high school courses, as well as the total number of students meeting college entry requirements and realizing reduced transportation costs due to I-TV. Cell H 625 includes the total number of students (duplicated) impacted by the I-TV program. (Note: The number in cell H 625 is a duplicated count. For example, if a student is enrolled in two I-TV courses, the student would be counted twice.)

The average benefit per student, average cost per student, and resulting average benefit over cost are calculated and presented in cells H 628−630. The final calculated entry in this section (cell H 632) is the average benefit to cost ratio per student. The point at which costs equal benefits, i.e., the break-even point, is denoted by a benefit-cost ratio of 1.00. A ratio greater than 1.00 will indicate greater benefits than costs; a ratio of less than 1.00 will indicate that costs outweigh benefits. This way, the extent to which benefits exceed costs or costs exceed benefits can be easily determined.

Note: It is important to quantify benefits to the same extent that costs are quantified. It is easier to insert the direct costs associated with room renovation or teacher salaries than to approximate the dollar value associated with transportation or time savings; for some there will be a temptation to underestimate the benefits relative to the costs. Leaving a benefits section blank for a reason other than non-applicability to the local situation may result in a cost-benefit analysis which does not present an accurate picture of the economic impact of the technology.

BREAK-EVEN ANALYSIS

The final section in the spreadsheet (Section D, Figure 9.23) is the "Break-Even Analysis." This section determines the level of student enrollment required to reach the break-even point−the point at which costs equal benefits, holding all other variables constant. Summary totals are carried down from Sections A (Costs) and B (Benefits), resulting in the calculation of the number of students that need to be enrolled in I-TV courses locally (cell F 660) in order to economically justify the development or continued existence of an I-TV program. (Note: This section does not include uses of the network other than for K−12 education, i.e., community usages are not included.)

	A	B	C	D	E	F	G	H
641		D. BREAKEVEN ANALYSIS						
642								
643								
644								
645								
646	AVERAGE VALUE PER STUDENT—EXISTING HS/DUAL CREDIT COURSES							‖‖‖‖‖‖‖‖
647	NO. OF STUDENTS ESTIMATED ABOVE							‖‖‖‖‖‖‖‖
648	AVERAGE VALUE PER STUDENT—NEW DUAL CREDIT COURSES							‖‖‖‖‖‖‖‖
649	NO. OF STUDENTS ESTIMATED ABOVE							‖‖‖‖‖‖‖‖
650	AVERAGE VALUE PER STUDENT—NEW HIGH SCHOOL COURSES							‖‖‖‖‖‖‖‖
651	NO. OF STUDENTS ESTIMATED ABOVE							‖‖‖‖‖‖‖‖
652	AVERAGE VALUE PER STUDENT—ALL COURSES							‖‖‖‖‖‖‖‖
653								
654	TOTAL BENEFITS (AS CALCULATED ABOVE)							‖‖‖‖‖‖‖‖
655		BASED ON	‖‖‖‖‖‖‖‖	STUDENTS				
656								
657	TOTAL COSTS (AS CALCULATED ABOVE)							‖‖‖‖‖‖‖‖
658								
659	**							
660	* YOUR BREAKEVEN ENROLLMENT POINT WOULD BE				‖‖‖‖‖‖‖‖	STUDENTS *	
661	**							

Figure 9.23. Section D, break-even analysis.

Sidebar 9.2. An Alternative Method of Determining Cost-Effectiveness

Using data from three typical analog fiber I-TV networks in Minnesota, North Dakota, and Kansas, a per pupil cost was calculated by taking the total cost of the system over a 10-year period and dividing by the current number of students enrolled in high school courses across all network schools multiplied by 10 (to approximate the minimum number of students

Table SB9.2.1. Comparison of Costs per I-TV Student.

	Minnesota (8 Sites)	North Dakota (4 Sites)	Kansas (4 Sites)
Total # of high school students enrolled in I-TV classes	451	129	191
Estimated # of total high school students enrolled over 10-year period	4,510	1,290	1,910
Total cost of network over 10 years	$1,835,000	$751,264	$866,388
Cost per school per year*	$22,938	$18,782	$21,660
Total per pupil cost of the I-TV network over 10 years	$407	$582	$454

*The cost/school year/school assumes that all costs are prorated across 10 years. In reality, each cluster paid some money up front, leaving monthly expenditures which varied from $9,200 to $12,711 to $18,500 per year per school.

served over that time period). These calculations yielded a projected 10-year average per pupil cost of $481. These costs are based on students enrolled in high school courses in each cluster (with the exception of the Kansas cluster which did include high school students enrolled in three summer college courses). The calculated cost does not include those students enrolled in dual-credit courses, nor does it include a value for the benefit of network use for staff meetings, in-service workshops, special education assessments, remedial classes, adult continuing education or college courses, or a multitude of community and other uses.

The costs per I-TV student (Table SB9.2.1) compare very favorably with the cost of providing advanced courses traditionally. For example, if it were possible to hire an experienced master teacher to teach only advanced classes for six periods per day at a salary of $25,000 (including benefits), the per pupil cost, assuming an average of 8 students per class, would be $521.

CONCLUSION

Instead of imposing an economic value for all of the various I-TV uses, this spreadsheet allows the user as much flexibility as possible in determining the local value of each I-TV application. All schools or networks will not use the technology for identical purposes nor will they assign an identical value to each use; it is left to the user of the cost-benefit analysis to control the quality of the input data.

PART FIVE

REALIZING THE POTENTIAL OF I-TV

Global Technology, Local Application: Economic and Community Development via I-TV

THE benefits of two-way interactive television technology are not limited to the provision of advanced classes for high school students. I-TV has the potential to increase the links between schools and communities on a regional basis. In fact, most I-TV networks immediately develop a significant amount of "after-hours" use by community groups and training organizations. Networks will tend to be more motivated to fully utilize the system if their costs are based on twenty-four hour availability of the network. After-hours applications for an I-TV system include:

- adult, GED, or community education classes
- combined-school staff development training
- inter-community meetings or public forums
- medical, legal, and other professional continuing education or re-certification courses
- consumer safety courses
- agricultural extension and community development activities
- intergovernmental or interagency meetings
- business training seminars
- community drug and alcohol abuse prevention and other health-related activities
- emergency response training
- job skills training or retraining

TELECOMMUNITIES

The economic development potential of I-TV is enhanced by the creation of telecommunities across a region. The idea of a "Rural Telecommunity" comes from the expansion of "community" to encompass a region (rather than one town or city) and viewing a "telecommunity center" as a place in each community where a variety of telecommunications capabilities can be tapped (Internet access, I-TV, facsimile, data transfer, etc.). Several educational networks have expanded to include a second I-TV facility and computer network in each community for this purpose, housed either within the school or in the city hall, library, or other public building. These connections have been utilized in a variety of ways, from business videoconferencing and telemarketing to use by residents for word processing, faxing, browsing the Internet, and sending e-mail to children away at college. (The notion of an urban telecommunity center has been supported by several major telephone companies around the country. These centers provide ''one-stop shopping'' where urban dwellers and businesspersons can tap into a variety of telecommunications resources.)

A slightly different version of the ''telecommunity center'' was established in 1992 by the Blue Earth Valley Telephone Company in Blue Earth, Minnesota. They constructed an interactive videoconferencing center for use by schools, businesses, hospitals, and other institutions in the surrounding area. This telecommunity center, along with sixteen other public videoconferencing rooms in Minnesota are connected to the MEANS (Minnesota Equal Access Network Services) network. The MEANS network serves as a means of interconnecting telecommunity, school, hospital, and private I-TV networks. And through POLARIS Telecom, interconnection with the University of Minnesota and other long-distance carriers is made available.

A telecommunity network can expand the reach and power of communities, rural and urban. A myriad of applications can be envisioned for such networks: accessing government agencies in other communities; providing adult education; seeking assistance from regional service organizations; linking similar institutions, e.g., banks, across multiple communities; organizing groups (4H, commodity producers, etc.) across a region; etc.

The sections in this chapter chronicle some of the potential community and alternative applications of telecommunity and K−12 interactive television networks.

CONTINUING EDUCATION

Many professions require access to continuing education. Fire fighters, medical personnel, farmers, law enforcement personnel, and others need the opportunity to participate in continuing education courses to keep up-to-date in their fields. I-TV can provide continuing education programs to multiple communities at the same time, thereby eliminating the overhead and costs associated with conducting workshops at multiple locations or the time and travel expenses associated with requiring all participants to attend a workshop at a central site. In addition, courses conducted via I-TV can be offered at times which might not be feasible if lengthy transportation was involved; participants can attend workshops in their home towns at night via I-TV, increasing the convenience for participants and thereby increasing rates of participation. For example, the Vermont Interactive Television (VIT) system offers continuing education courses for realtors, engineers, members of the national guard, and business professionals (Bunting, 1994). VIT sites are plentiful enough that no resident is more than 25 miles from an I-TV site. (However, not all of VIT's sites can be involved in the same session.)

While other distance learning technologies can be used for providing continuing education (cable, satellite downlink, videotapes), I-TV can provide the direct interaction between instructors and participants that is critical to a high level of participant satisfaction and understanding in continuing education programs.

Examples of I-TV-based continuing education include:

- training for nurses and nursing home personnel
- dental assistants' workshops
- EMT training/training updates
- pesticide use training
- firearms safety training

ADULT/COMMUNITY EDUCATION

Adult education courses are a natural for after-hours use of a school-based network. Adult education programs range from formal degree programs to personal enrichment courses. For example, Brainerd Community College in Minnesota offers a "Degree in Three" program via I-TV for working adults who want to pursue an associate degree. In addition, they offer I-TV programs such as "Perennial Gardening," "All About Auto Insurance," and "Bow Hunting for Deer" to the surrounding communities. Such a diversity of offerings can draw a large portion of the community into I-TV courses.

One of the best ways to generate interest in I-TV courses is to offer a short course introducing the community to the possibilities afforded by I-TV and telecommunications. Brainerd Community College, for instance, offers "Business Applications of Interactive TV," and a "Seminar on Going Back to School" as introductory courses for the community.

Community interest in college courses and personal enrichment classes can be gauged by distributing a survey to area residents. Surveys can be distributed by publication in the local paper, by sending them home with students, or by enclosure with public utility bills, if permissible. This type of survey should provide information on goals (Do residents want to take courses leading to a degree or just for personal interest?), specific subjects and courses of interest (e.g., foreign language, psychology, business, etc.), and the amount that the individual is willing to pay for courses. Offerings can then be tailored to meet the needs of the community. In addition, support from local government and businesses can be built for the program. For example, if there is a large demand for a course in entrepreneurship, but the potential participants cannot afford the tuition, local extension or county government might be convinced to provide a grant to offset the cost of the course. Local banks may join together in order to offer low or no interest loans to cover tuition costs for adults seeking a degree via I-TV. Service organizations may underwrite the costs associated with specific professional enhancement courses for their members or for the community at large.

Networks with a connection to a college or university can easily provide undergraduate and graduate courses for adults in rural communities. Distance learning is often the only means for non-traditional students to balance an inflexible work schedule with furthering their education. For teachers, after-hours programs can be a means for earning college credit toward a master's degree or additional certification.

Other possibilities for adult education programs include job training and retraining. Private Industry Councils working with Job Training and Partnership Act (JTPA) programs can use I-TV to provide regional job readiness and job counseling programs. Where specific job training is required, displaced workers can be linked with a training facility in another community, eliminating the need for travel. An I-TV link can also be established between a large, regional industry and outlying I-TV sites for the provision of customized training opportunities on an ongoing basis.

JUDICIAL AND CORRECTIONAL SYSTEMS

I-TV networks can also be extended to correctional institutions. Provision of remedial, secondary, GED, and vocational classes for inmates can be conducted cost-effectively because the costs associated with transportation, surveillance, and security for traditional courses are eliminated. In addition, other services, such as psychological and job counseling services, can be offered to correctional institutions through I-TV.

While the provision of courses to inmates via I-TV is increasing, the judicial system has been experimenting with using videoconferencing for remote arraignments for over a decade. Remote arraignments are extremely cost-effective in large cities in which the jail and courthouse are separated by many miles, thereby requiring costly high security transportation of inmates for only a few minutes of appearance time before a judge. Other court proceedings can also be conducted via I-TV. For example, the *Chronicle of Higher Education* (June 23, 1995) reports that a Georgia case was recently argued before that state's Supreme Court via I-TV. "The lawyers, Lisa Gunn and Mark Johnson, presented their arguments in front of television cameras and monitors at Kennesaw State College, while the justices heard and watched the arguments from a similarly equipped room at the Georgia Supreme Court. The lawyers, who were arguing a property rights case, live close to Kennesaw campus—one of 215 sites in the state with this type of technology. The justices and lawyers interacted just as they would have during typical oral arguments."

EXTENSION AND GOVERNMENTAL AGENCY SUPPORT

I-TV can be an effective means of linking with university extension services in areas such as community development, youth programs, and business, industry, and agricultural support forums. Extension community development specialists, business and industry specialists, home economists, agricultural specialists (e.g., agronomy, horticulture, live-stock, etc.) may be able to utilize the technology extensively.

I-TV can also be a tool for the integration of human resource agency services across communities. A pilot project in Howard County, Missouri, is experimenting with the potential for inter-community linkage of juvenile justice, health and mental health, family services, and other county-level agencies through two-way interactive television.

I-TV linkages can also be used in government. For example, in Alabama the Intercampus Interactive Telecommunications System (IITS) has installed a site in the capitol, allowing state legislators to meet with their constituencies at any of the twenty I-TV sites in the IITS.

I-TV may be useful for a variety of organizations and agencies, including:

- Farm Bureau, Soil Conservation Service, Farmers' Home Administration, State Conservation Commission, Agricultural Stabilization and Conservation Service, and federal Crop Insurance Offices
- Health & Human Service Agencies, Social Security Administration, Juvenile Justice, Vocational Rehabilitation, Employment Security
- commodity groups, such as the Pork Producers Association and the Livestock Association
- rural fire protection districts, rural emergency medical boards and regional library boards

TELEMEDICINE

Chapter 1 examined some of the limitations of schools in small communities and ways of overcoming these limitations through I-TV. Health care is another area in which rural communities are often at a disadvantage. C. Everett Koop (1994), former U.S. Surgeon General, has pointed out the two main problems confronting rural health care — the lack of primary care physicians and the isolation of physicians working in rural areas:

> The shortage of primary care physicians confronts us at a time when we need them more than ever. The "managed competition" health care plan . . . is suitable only for the 60 percent of Americans who live in areas of high population density, because the theory of managed competition requires a large population base to foster the competition that is supposed to keep costs in check. Forty percent of Americans — spread across 90 percent of the United States — will still depend on the dwindling number of primary care doctors.

> Perhaps even more discouraging is the way primary care physicians — often practicing medicine in rural America, the inner city or small hospitals or clinics — feel isolated from the larger world of medicine. Primary care physicians, even though they are often paid the least, are

expected to know the most, since they are expected to diagnose and then treat or refer elsewhere, any and every health problem a patient brings into their offices. With medical knowledge expanding every day, no physician can keep up without help.

Now, we can remove the sense of isolation by using high-tech medical communication – high performance computers, high-resolution television and video and fiber-optic information highways. These technologies help us put the entire world of medical science at the fingertips of even the most isolated rural family doctor. A telecommunications health information network allows doctors not only to seek information on a puzzling case before them, but also to pursue lifelong learning.

I-TV can be used by rural hospitals and doctors for a variety of applications. Rural doctors can link with major regional health facilities for remote diagnostics, medical consultation, and staff seminars via I-TV. Telemedical sub-fields are developing rapidly, including teleradiology, telecardiology, telepathology, and others.

K – 12 networks can help their communities explore telemedicine by providing scheduled times for use of the network by area physicians, health care workers, patient support groups, and for community medical education forums. Once again, schools will need to educate the surrounding community regarding the capabilities and limitations of I-TV.

On a larger scale, telemedicine is also a means for exporting medical expertise to other nations. For example, the *Los Angeles Times* (1994) reports that physicians at Massachusetts General Hospital and the Mayo Clinic are using I-TV to advise patients in Jordan and Saudi Arabia. In another example, the *Los Angeles Times* reports "Dr. Jim Troxell unwinds the bandage from his patient's foot to reveal gangrene, which has eaten away much of the heel. A consulting orthopedist takes a close look, and after a few questions, endorses Troxell's treatment. It's the kind of consultation that takes place in medicine all the time. But in this case, Troxell and his patient are in Kwajalein, an atoll in the South Pacific. The orthopedist is 2,200 miles away at Honolulu's Tripler Army Medical Center."

Telemedicine has the potential to be one of the fastest growing uses of telecommunications technology. The ability to visually link hospitals or clinics with the homes of chronically ill patients could provide a substantial advance in patient care. For example, the Medical College of Georgia is testing a system that provides care to the homes of twenty five seriously ill patients. The Medical College of Georgia estimates that by carefully monitoring asthma and high blood pressure of patients at home, the number of hospitalizations, each with an average cost of $15,000 – $20,000, can be significantly reduced.

Telemedicine has the potential to markedly decrease response time and improve ease of access to specialized medical services. Several legal issues, however, prevent immediate use across the country. Since states license physicians individually, a new range of licensing, insurance, and liability problems will arise when a patient and physician are in different states, or for that matter, different countries. Maintaining patient confidentiality over the network is another important issue, requiring much greater control than in the educational arena. Payment issues also have not been fully resolved. For example, how should compensation for remote consultations be handled, and what obligations do insurance companies incur in such arrangements?

Perhaps the biggest challenge facing telemedicine today is the issue of liability. For example, when an incorrect diagnosis is made via a telemedicine network, the fault could lie with the remote physician making the diagnosis, the local physician concurring with and acting on the diagnosis, the technology itself, or a combination of all three. If the technology is found to not provide the remote physician with sufficient information, could the equipment and transmission line provider be held liable?

> Malpractice liability may prove to be one of the most vexing problems and could impede the general application of telemedicine. Obviously, any analysis of "what might be" will only gain validity from the outcomes of precedent setting cases. Clearly, a preventative approach to liability is the best defense. It must be stressed to the physician that if the visual and audio links do not provide adequate information to allow for appropriate diagnostic interpretation, none should be given. (Sanders, 1994)

These are issues which must be resolved within the medical community before wholesale adoption of telemedical technologies can occur.

BUSINESS AND ECONOMIC DEVELOPMENT

Many communities across the country – urban and rural – are taking advantage of telecommunications for economic development. Services which require communications, such as processing and management of data, telemarketing, and customer service are locating in rural areas. Sometimes in partnership with local telephone companies, telemarketing companies often find that a rural location can reduce the cost of doing business and provide a ready employee base.

Opportunities for telecommuting are becoming more widely available as home-based access to advanced telecommunications improves. The day rural workers no longer need to migrate to urban areas or commute on a daily basis is rapidly approaching.

Sidebar 10.1. I-TV Entertainment and the Electronic Cafe

No longer do entertainers and audiences have to be in the same place in order to interact with one another. For example, in 1993, musician Graham Nash played guitar in Los Angeles, California, accompanied by Todd Reynolds on fiddle in New York. Audiences in both locations were able to enjoy the real-time combination of audio and video from the sites. Recently a similar event was sponsored by the Electronic Cafe International between Austin, Texas, and Santa Monica, California, in which "Team Fat," an Austin-based surf band, played to audiences in both locations. The two-way audio and video connection allowed the band to receive requests and answer questions from members of the "virtual" audience.

The Electronic Cafe International is an affiliate-based organization founded on the idea that telecommunications can remove geographic and social barriers. The Electronic Cafe began in 1984 as a project commissioned by the Los Angeles Museum of Contemporary Art for that year's Olympic Festival. The project established a telecommunications link between five diverse ethnic Los Angeles communities and the museum, allowing visitors to "trade video and still images, collaborate in writing and drawing on a common virtual canvas, transmit musical pieces, retrieve information and communicate in dynamic ways" (Rico, 1990; Hart, 1994; Pagel, 1995). The Electronic Cafe now has over 40 affiliates throughout the world.

ADDITIONAL SCHOOL, PARENT AND STUDENT CONNECTIONS

Opportunities also exist for the provision of special services to remote areas through I-TV. Linkage of psychological assessment clinic services with outlying school districts can provide much needed diagnostic and assessment services for students with special needs, e.g., learning disabled, behaviorally disordered, etc. Connections with special services can also be used for organizing parenting forums, training for school district special services teachers, and/or direct consultation with school psychologists regarding individual student clients.

Also connections to statewide student and community service organizations can be made via I-TV For example, I-TV can be used by 4H for leader training, inter-community demonstrations and project reviews, and as a means for rural chapters to interact with their urban counterparts.

The potential linkages and uses for school-based I-TV networks and telecommunities are virtually limitless. As James Chadwick, early I-TV pioneer and now superintendent of Haven Public Schools in Kansas said, ''Our only limitation is the collective imagination of all those involved.''

CHAPTER 11

You Can't Get There from Here: Impediments to I-TV Adoption

I-TV technology was first introduced by AT&T Bell Labs as a demonstration at the 1964 World's Fair in Flushing Meadow, New York. The major difficulty in setting up the demonstration was a lack of high-speed telephone lines to connect one site to another (Trowt-Bayard, 1994). Today's challenge is the same: the lack of a high-speed telecommunications infrastructure to support bandwidth intensive applications such as I-TV. While there are other reasons why I-TV has not been widely adopted, e.g., lack of school and community awareness of the technology's capabilities, a primary reason is the lack of an available telecommunications infrastructure.

CURRENT INFRASTRUCTURE

Developing a comprehensive picture of the current telecommunications infrastructure is a nearly impossible task. Telephone companies (both local exchange carriers and interexchange carriers), cable TV, utility companies, and others (e.g., state highway departments) are the primary holders and developers of the public land-based telecommunications infrastructure in the United States. However there are a number of other means of transmitting information: satellite, radiowaves, microwaves, etc. In addition, an increasing amount of infrastructure is held by private entities, among them competitive access providers (CAPs), business and industry, and educational institutions, none of whom are required to report their telecommunications capabilities to regulatory agencies. Further compounding any infrastructure inventory is that public long-distance companies are not required to disclose full information about their infrastructure, to protect them from such information being used by competitors. New technologies are also emerging that can greatly increase the bandwidth of existing telecommunications lines, making assessment of current capabilities misleading. Overall, the U.S. has a diverse and sporadically deployed system of interconnected, and non-interconnected, telecommunications capabilities.

The University of Southern California's Global Telecommunications Infrastructure Research Project is currently working with industry groups to conduct an assessment of the current and developing telecommunications infrastructure, both in the United States and globally. While this study doesn't attempt to directly inventory overall infrastructure, it will provide a means for comparing telecommunications abilities between companies and nations. For industry, the study will hopefully produce a uniform set of tools and common methodology for measurement of investments in telecommunications.

Around the globe, the expansion of high speed fiber optic systems is proceeding at a rapid pace (Helms, 1993):

- Singapore is planning fiber optic lines to every home by the year 2005.
- In East Germany, efforts are under way to link 1.2 million homes with optical fiber by 1996.
- Japan is planning to spend $450 billion in the next twenty years to expand their current fiber optic network to homes and apartments.

Sidebar 11.1. Telecommunications Regulation: The Beginning of the End, by Peter W. Huber

The telecommunications industry is in a period of enormous transition. The world that was dominated by a highly regulated phone monopoly and consisted of numerous distinct communications sectors no longer exists. The world of a fully competitive and highly integrated communications and information system is still a vision. To discover the best path to this new world, we need to understand where we are coming from and how far we have traveled.

For the most of this century, telephony was viewed as a natural monopoly. The high cost of fixed plant, the steadily declining average cost of service, and the need for all customers to interconnect with one another made it seem sensible, perhaps unavoidable, to have a single monopoly provider. The Bell System was born on that premise and with it an elaborate body of regulation designed to reconcile private monopoly with the public good.

The old regulatory paradigm contained three basic elements: First, the protected franchise: Would-be competitors were barred from competing or even interconnecting with the enfranchised carrier; natural monopoly thus became a self-fulfilling prophecy. Second, the quarantine: The monopolist was restricted to its regulated sphere and barred from exporting its expertise (and the corrosive influence of its monopoly) into adjacent competitive markets. Third, cradle-to-grave regulation: Prices, term, and conditions of the monopolist's services had to be approved by regulators before they could be imposed on customers.

This system served the county adequately for more than 50 years, permitting the Bell System to deploy the most technologically sophisticated telephone system in the world.

Today, the two overarching technological trends are fragmentation and convergence. There are more switches, more lines, more networks, many more levels of interconnection; the old integrated, centralized media are being fragmented into many smaller and more independent parts. At the same time, interconnections are proliferating and becoming much more seamless. The media themselves are converging. Television is leaving the air in favor of wires; the telephone is leaving the wires in favor of the air. And any given service can be provided by a variety of means. TV networks, cable companies, long-distance phone companies, and others are all becoming information and communications companies.

Regulators must adapt to this evolving market to ensure that it becomes as open and competitive as possible. The problem is that the incumbents on opposite sides of the traditional regulatory fence have quite different views about which kind of competition should come first. Thus, television broad-casters want to contain phone and cable companies, just as radio broad-casters want to contain phone and cable companies, just as radio broadcasters once hoped to contain television and just as newspapers once hoped to contain radio.

Nevertheless, the dynamics of the new technologies have forced regulatory change. The protected phone franchise has eroded as new entrants have been permitted first to serve niche markets and later to engage in more extended competition. The quarantine has been partially lifted as the boundaries between regulated and competitive markets have eroded. Pervasive regulation of prices and conditions is gradually giving way to competition.

A new paradigm of unfettered competition—without entry barriers, quarantines or unnecessary regulatory restrictions—is now beginning to emerge. But the transition is by no means complete. In fact, regulation today is at its apogee, because a smooth transition between paradigms requires that new rules be erected before the old ones can be dismantled.

Under the old model, for example, there was no need for interconnection or equal access standards; the only interconnection was between customers and their monopoly carrier. We may likewise anticipate a day when inter-connection regulation will once again become unnecessary; competitive forces will balance out, and interface standards will then be set as they are in other industries—through market forces, voluntary agreements, and evolu-tionary consensus. Today, however, while dominant carriers still mingle with fledgling competitors, interfaces must be regulated along with everything else. And day by day the interfaces multiply, as equipment providers, long-distance carriers, information providers, wireless providers, and others all clamor for new forms of access—steadily blurring the lines between customers and providers.

Regulators are increasing the pace of their shift from managing monopoly to managing competition. Indeed, this is one of the most important—if least appreciated—regulatory initiatives of our day. Our ability to compete in the new global markets will turn, in significant part, on how—and how quickly—critical disputes are resolved.

Reprinted with permission from *Issues in Science and Technology*, Huber, "Telecommunications Regulations: The Beginning of the End," Fall 1993, pp. 50–58. Copyright 1993, by the University of Texas at Dallas, Richardson, TX.

The United States has one of the most advanced telecommunications systems in the world. However, deployment of advanced services in the U.S. has thus far been driven sporadically by market demand, rather than by a comprehensive plan of government or telecommunications companies.

The promise of fiber optic based technologies will not be realized in large sections of the U.S. for many years to come. However, much can be done with existing technologies. An important step in integrating the country's telecommunications infrastructure is to ensure that access to copper, microwave or other high bandwidth technologies is available in areas where fiber is not or will not be deployed. In addition, such technologies should be seamlessly interconnectable with more advanced fiber optic technologies. To use a popular analogy, the information superhighway cannot consist of only four-lane divided highways. There must be on-ramps from the state highways, county roads, and country lanes in order to fully integrate the citizenry.

THE NEED FOR INFRASTRUCTURE EXPANSION

There is clearly a need to expand the telecommunications infrastructure in rural America—rural communities may have the most to gain from distance-dissolving telecommunications technologies. The inequity of access to advanced telecommunications services between rural and urban areas is becoming increasingly clear. Earlier in this century, the rural electrification effort was driven by the inequities that existed between rural and urban areas in the availability of electricity.

As late as 1935, farmers had been denied electricity not only in the Hill Country [of Texas] but throughout the United States. In that year, more than 6 million of America's 6.8 million farms did NOT have electricity. Decades after electric power had become part of urban life, the wood range, the washtub, the sad iron and the kerosene lamp were still the way of life for almost 90 percent of the 30 million Americans who lived in the countryside. All across the United States, wrote a public-power advocate, ''Every city 'white way' ends abruptly at the city limits. Beyond lies darkness.'' The lack of electric power, wrote the historian William E. Leuchterberg, had divided the United States into two nations: ''the city dwellers and the country folk''; farmers, he wrote, ''toiled in a nineteenth-century world; farm wives, who obviously eyed pictures in the Saturday Evening Post of city women with washing machines, refrigerators, and vacuum cleaners, performed their backbreaking chores like peasant women in a preindustrial age.'' (Caro, 1982)

While the need for rural electrification may have been a bit more dramatic, there is much in common between the rural electrification efforts of the 1930s and the development of telecommunications technology in the 1990s. Today, however, we don't have the telecommunications equivalent of the Tennessee Valley Authority to take the initiative in bringing a national policy for the deployment of advanced telecommunications to fruition.

In 1933, when legislation created the Tennessee Valley Authority, a giant step was taken through the rural electrification program. The TVA legislation was important in three respects (Ellis, 1966):

(1) It gave preference in the sale of low-cost wholesale power for distribution to states, cities, counties, and cooperative organizations.

(2) It authorized TVA to construct transmission lines to carry the wholesale power to points of need.

(3) It specified that the power should be sold at the lowest possible cost.

Lacking a national public works agenda similar to the TVA for deployment and expansion of the telecommunications ''superhighway,'' it is unclear whether the work of scores of private companies will result in an integrated, fully deployed network in either a regulated or an increasingly deregulated environment. Much has changed since 1933, including the notion that rural development is too important and urgent to be left to free market enterprise. Indeed, Clyde Ellis (1966) and others saw the national government as the only entity which could foster rapid, efficient, and low-cost power. Confidence in the capabilities of federal government have waned over time, as has the ability of government to rise to the occasion. Today, we seem to be willing to bet the future of rural telecommunications on the deregulation of the telecommunications industry, hoping that what government can't or won't do, private enterprise will accomplish.

There are several basic problems with deregulation as legislated. For example, many assume that deregulation will reduce rates for telecommunications services. There may indeed be some short-term, or perhaps even long-term, reduction in basic telephone rates in metropolitan areas, where multiple providers will find it worth their time to vie for customers. It is less certain whether rate increases can be avoided in rural areas where competitors may not exist.

Sidebar 11.2. Evolving Interactive Television for Distance Education in North Dakota, by Ron Stammen

In 1989, The North Dakota Educational Telecommunications Council, a funding agency created by the state legislature in 1989, commissioned Federal Engineering of Fairfax, Virginia, to study the state's telecommunication needs. This study helped set the stage to fund planning grants for technology projects, statewide distance education telecommunications infrastructures, and subsequent training workshops. This first study was bolstered by Hobbs (1990) who provided a comprehensive educational analysis about statewide distance education services. By November 1990 a series of regional needs assessments were completed for the Council's consideration during competitive grant applications. A study by Stammen (1990) helped launch the SENDIT statewide K–12 computer network which became an extension of the state's Higher Education Computer Network. Both computer networks serve as a communication link between I-TV instructors and students and provided needed library services.

Through these processes, school district personnel throughout the state had identified needed high school distance education courses, particularly foreign languages, and a wide variety of educational needs for staff development. The data were used to build a distance education infrastructure which was funded top-down by the council and bottom-up from local matching funds supported by several state and federal supporting grants.

Two-Way Interactive Television Networks

A number of telephone-line-based, two-way interactive networks were established during the 1990–1992 time period. Funds were acquired for cooperating school districts by combining the North Dakota Educational Telecommunications Council grants, state block-grant restructuring funds, and regional vocational state entitlements. In 1994, 36 percent of rural high schools had access to instruction delivered via two-way interactive television. The principal objective of these networks is to provide students curricular choices that would not otherwise be available due to limited faculty, gaps in expertise, or insufficient student enrollment to conduct a course at one school or campus.

The development of these community high school systems indicates that North Dakota schools were quick to see the possibilities of interactive television as a means of expanding the offerings of rural schools. Network Resources and Hezel, Inc. (1994) found that the Educational Telecommunications Council had recognized the potential of such I-TV systems to strengthen small schools. The earlier adopters were also encouraged by

- the necessity to promote cooperation and possible consortium-building among smaller districts
- the need to help link smaller schools to stronger partners
- the opportunity to consider video network planning as part of a state-funded "rural school restructuring initiative" promoted by the Department of Public Instruction

The high school video technology varies from two-way microwave to voice-activated T-1 compressed video to switched DS-3 digital; however, most high schools utilize two-way analog fiber interactive television networks. Adoption of this technology was fostered by the rapid deployment of fiber optic cabling by the state's telephone companies, the strong advocacy of such systems by the state's Vocational Education Technology Consultant, Ted Renner, and the willingness of many rural telephone cooperatives to negotiate moderately priced video service contracts.

The University System's (two-way) Interactive Video Network (IVN) is a T-1 digital telephone routing system which connects the state's eleven colleges and universities, the five Native American Community Colleges, the State Capitol, and several high school networks.

The primary purpose for university-secondary school connections is to provide staff development opportunities for teachers and school administrators. However, several arrangements are made each year for high school students to enroll in college courses. Consequently, the networks are also scheduled late afternoon, evening, and most weekends. As an example, the Great Northwestern Network (an analog network), which is connected to the University System's IVN T-1 digital system, also has an analog, fiber optic classroom installed adjacent to a university T-1 classroom at Bismarck State College. This analog I-TV classroom was purposely not connected to the university system so the local post-secondary institution could concentrate on meeting regional school and community needs without being encumbered with the University System's statewide scheduling environment.

The Great Northwest Network is the largest system in the state with a cluster of nineteen high schools and connections to two statewide networks. It was reorganized in 1994 by area networks which surround the state's

capital city, one of which was the first to operate in the state during the
1989–1990 term. The Educational Telecommunication Council initially
provided funds to help pay for development and construction of three
separate two-way interactive television networks. Then, during subsequent
funding cycles, the Council fully funded the costs for the interconnections
between these original three clustered networks. The network is managed
by one coordinator responsible to the consortium governing board whose
members are school administrators. The Council provided funds for this
network to also operate a VSAT (two-way audio/visual satellite) system
which will be connected in 1996 to several rural, remote high schools located
one to two hundred miles away from the Great Northwest Network.

These high schools met most benchmarks outlined by the Hobbs' (1990)
study. They are offering three to six courses in every academic or vocational
area; however, foreign language became the most common offering among
all distance education curricula. The networks helped further the process of
interschool cooperation and have surpassed expectations in meeting the
academic objectives. A variety of non-instructional but highly valued uses
include interschool meetings and co-curricular activities, from crop judging
to college admission counseling. These networks are utilized for adult education more each year as the population is becoming more aware of the
opportunities available on these networks and the providers are becoming
more able to adapt to the technology. Network administrators are pleased
with their networks and see them as providing new opportunities for their
students, staff, and communities at a reasonable price.

Broadcast Telecommunication Services

North Dakota has three satellite uplink systems which have been funded,
for the most part, by various federal funding agencies made possible by
congressional legislative acts. University-based transportation and
aeronautical programs have a regional support base in the nation. The third
uplink, installed with congressional funds through the Agriculture Department, is Prairie Satellite Network. This network was completed in 1994 and
provided satellite dishes to 70 of the 190 secondary school districts. Two
satellite studios can broadcast programs to be developed by educators
and/or entrepreneurs.

In addition, this public telecommunication group offers school television
services over their statewide microwave system to offer "Habemos
espanol!" (Spanish I & II) to about one percent of the rural pupils. Spanish
III was piloted nationwide during 1993–94 by funds from the nationwide
SERC STAR School funding. Spanish Broadcast services are available to
any school district or individual (adult) because they are aired over the
public broadcasting network during the daytime.

North Dakota Educational Telecommunications Infrastructure

North Dakota's 1995 developing educational telecommunications infrastructure is comprehensive. It is composed of interactive television net-

works, broadcast telecommunications services, and supporting computer-mediated networks. The Council found during the past 5 years that accessing libraries through SENDIT or Online Dakota Information Network (ODIN) is an integral function for serious Interactive Television students. The North Dakota telecommunication infrastructure for education and statewide meetings is robust in a state with a total population of 638,000. The following governmental and educational telecommunications systems, except for the multistate satellite systems, are interconnected through either physical connections or coordinating committees:

(1) Higher Education Computer Network

(2) Online Dakota Information Network (university library access)

(3) Information Service Division for state government telecommunications

(4) North Dakota Information Network (frame relay connections to all counties)

(5) North Dakota University Systems (two-way) Interactive Video Network

(6) SENDIT, a K-12 statewide computer-mediated communication network

(7) Ten wide area, secondary two-way interactive television networks

(8) Prairie School Satellite Network and Prairie School Television (microwave towers)

(9) Multistate satellite studio production facilities at University of North Dakota's Aerospace Center and North Dakota Rural Health Continuing Education Network, Northwest VSAT Network, and the Transportation Education Center at the North Dakota State University

(10) Local area cable services (Mandan-Bismarck area and others)

These ten categories explain the extent to which telecommunications are evolving in the state. Various agencies in North Dakota have cooperated to a large extent in developing these educational networks; however, efforts continue with intra-agency cooperation following another detailed statewide study prepared by Federal Engineering in 1995. Local telephone cooperatives completed a major purchase of US WEST properties in the state during 1995. They immediately initiated the development of a statewide vendors network to provide more bandwidth for rural areas, especially targeting K−12 schools. These types of endeavors provide evidence that connectivity with technological enhancements for interactive television will continue to evolve as they have since 1990.

REGULATORY ISSUES

The Communications Act of 1934, with some amendments, has been the basis for telecommunications regulation in the United States for the last half century. The act allowed for regulated monopolies to provide telephone service at a ''just and reasonable price.'' An important component of the act was the requirement for universal service, which meant that phone companies were obligated to provide service to rural areas, in which the market was not always profitable, in exchange for restrictions on competition. Telephone companies were considered to be "natural" monopolies, and consumer protection from monopolistic practices, e.g., price fixing, price gouging, etc., was sought through the creation of public utility commissions in each state. The Federal Communications Commission (FCC) was charged with regulating long-distance carriers. The goal of regulatory oversight was to ensure that prices charged and profits received were not excessive.

Prior to 1976 there was virtually no competition within the telephone industry. The monopolistic principles under which the telephone industry was created held true, chief among them being the avoidance of wasteful duplication of infrastructure and the efficient service coverage of an entire nation. In 1976 the Federal Communications Commission began the move away from monopolistic telecommunications services by opening the long-distance market to competition. This model was further eroded in 1983 with the breakup and divestiture of AT&T.

When AT&T was broken up into AT&T Long Distance and the seven Regional Bell Operating Companies (RBOCs), Local Access and Transport Areas (LATAs) were created across the country to define the areas within which the RBOCs were allowed to carry long-distance calls, i.e., only within a LATA. Most states now allow interexchange carriers to compete with the RBOCs for the intraLATA long-distance market, but RBOCs are prevented from providing long-distance services across LATA boundaries.

A New Age in Telephone Regulation

At the federal level, numerous telecommunications bills have been bandied about in Congress. Since the passage of precedent-setting legislation to deregulate the telecommunications industry, major changes will occur before the end of the century. There are two major stakeholders in the current deregulation debate: the interexchange (long-distance) carriers who wish to retain major portions of the 1983 divestiture stipulations, thereby limiting competition; and the regional Bell operating companies who want to be allowed to compete freely in all markets. Both parties are trying to place themselves in the best possible position for open competition. Other industries (cable television, satellite communications, wireless, broadcast television, etc.), are also fight-ing to protect their interests. Not since the Communications Act of 1934 has the protection of the public good in telecommunications legislation been more critical; as the industry stakeholders vie for position, it is the real stakeholders—the American people, wherever they reside—who stand to win or lose.

Sidebar 11.3. Is This Trip Necessary? by Daryl Hobbs, Professor of Rural Sociology, University of Missouri-Columbia

A philosopher once observed that nothing so persistently evades our attention as that which we take for granted. Nothing in contemporary American rural life is more taken for granted than driving. Virtually every need—a loaf of bread, breakfast, a machinery part, a doctor's visit or a day in school—means hitting the road. Driving is such a way of life, it is just done. That's the way things are. We don't ask why—we just do it. What is the alternative?

Like most technologies the full impact of improved private transportation did not happen overnight. The past 75 years have produced continuing improvements in cars and roads and along the way rural communities, institutions and life styles were transformed. Not all at once but little by little. But the changes have been so significant that the difference between rural and urban America is smaller. Improved transportation contributed directly to the pervasive school consolidation that relegated one-room country schools and high school graduating classes of fewer than 50 to the memories of today's senior citizens. Most of the doctors and businesses that once lined Main Street have now been replaced by regional clinics of medical specialists and regional shopping malls. It can be observed that the greatest public investment in rural health care has been roads—making it easier for rural people to reach the more distant and specialized services. The key concept in all these changes has been centralization. Improved roads and cars made it practical and feasible to centralize most of the services rural people depend on in larger towns. Transporting people to more centralized services has become a central organizing principle of contemporary rural America.

The cost of these changes to most rural communities has been great. Most American towns were established in the 19th century when transportation was slower and less dependable. Each was established for only one purpose—to provide nearby residents with the goods and services they needed. But as transportation improved and regional centralization of rural services occurred many of those small towns lost much of their original basis for existence and, along with it, much of the loyalty and affection of those who live there. Their loyalties have become divided among the several towns rural residents have grown to depend on for necessary goods and services. School consolidation had a particularly devastating effect on communities having lost their school in the process. Schools are typically the social heart of rural communities. As many of those communities have lost services they have also lost population and much of their hope for the future.

However, new telecommunications technologies now offer some hope for those rural communities that have resigned themselves to inexorable decline. While transportation technologies impose on rural communities the cost of regional centralization, new information technologies offer the prospect of substituting the exchange of information for the time, energy, and cost to travel to regional services. It allows rural people to question whether all the trips continue to be necessary. Instead of children traveling great distances to consolidated schools, interactive television has made it possible to offer the benefits of school consolidation, e.g., specialized courses that small schools could not afford to offer, without incurring the cost of transportation to even more consolidated schools. It is now possible for small town residents to have the benefit of specialized health care without making a trip to a regional clinic. New information technologies also make it possible for rural businesses to market their products on a regional, or even national or international basis from a remote rural location. Distance no longer need be the decisive factor in where new economic investment occurs. Consequently, new doors of opportunity for rural economic development are opening. But at this time the possibilities for rural communities are being realized in only a small number of rural places. To take advantage of these opportunities will require creative leadership in rural communities—local leaders, whether businessmen, school administrators, or citizens—leaders who realize that telecommunications technologies can contribute to reversing some of the trends rural people have come to take for granted. But before that occurs it will be necessary for rural leaders to think in terms of a new and different set of rules for the future and to set aside the inevitability of past trends that have been taken for granted.

The Rural Problem

The question of whether deregulation should occur is moot; it is clear that the FCC and Congress intend it to happen. The more relevant question is what effect will such legislation have on rural America and what will happen to the concept of universal service.

The costs of providing telephone service to rural America are much higher than the costs of providing service to urban areas (OPASTCO, 1994). Small, rural local exchange carriers (LECs) must provide service to a smaller number of subscribers who may be scattered over a large geographic area. The average number of subscribers per mile and per square mile in rural America is 6.3 and 4.4 respectively. Figures for the regional Bell operating companies (RBOCs) average 130 subscribers per mile and more than 330 per square mile (OPASTCO, 1994). For this reason alone, there must continue to be a viable mechanism for subsidizing the costs of rural telephone service and thereby equalizing the prices of telecommunications services regardless of geographic location.

In addition to the geographical dispersion of populations, three other factors contribute to the higher cost of providing telephone service to rural areas (OPASTCO, 1994):

(1) A higher proportion of residential versus business subscribers. In a 1992 Statistical Report of Rural Telephone Borrowers (REA, 1992), it was shown that among rural telephone companies, business subscribers accounted for 17.6 percent of the total telephone subscribers as compared to 25 percent among regional Bell operating companies. In addition, business subscribers in the RBOC areas were more likely to have multiple telephone lines by a factor of five to one, over those in independent telephone company areas.

(2) Because rural LECs cannot take advantage of economies of scale, they experience higher unit costs for usage-sensitive equipment. Although smaller telephone companies have smaller central offices, the set-up and maintenance of those facilities are not necessarily less expensive. Software upgrade costs are essentially the same regardless of central office size (software represents about 80 percent of the cost of a telephone switch). In addition, because LEC's purchase less equipment, they typically have less negotiating power with manufacturers than do their larger company counterparts.

(3) Higher loop-related investments are needed, due to longer loops and the remoteness of the areas they serve. Loop costs cover the cable and wire facilities from the subscribers' homes or business to the telephone company central office. Because of the greater distance involved and the low density of subscribers on rural "loops" such costs are greatly escalated.

Sidebar 11.4. What's in a Name? . . .

FRED is an unlikely name for a charitable foundation, but one which is rapidly making itself known in the area of rural telecommunications. Founded by the Organization for the Protection and Advancement of Small Telephone Companies (OPASTCO) in 1989, the Fund for Rural Education and Development—otherwise known as FRED—is a 501(c)(3) foundation whose aim is to sponsor programs that relate to the technological, social, and economic conditions of rural America. FRED strives to raise awareness that rural areas are not only the heart of a great past, but also the key to a thriving American future. Their contention is that new technologies, particularly in the area of telecommunications, are providing the means for tapping into the assets and strengths of rural America. Currently, six major initiatives comprise the FRED agenda:

(1) The FRED Scholarship Endowment provides educational opportunities for those who pursue careers in telecommunications, rural education, or rural development. The endowment fund is held in a separate account and generates interest to be used only for scholarship awards.

(2) *Rural Community Development: A Guidebook for Telephone Companies* is a unique, ongoing resource featuring development information and case studies designed to help telephone companies become successful community development leaders.

(3) The Rural Development Achievement Award honors the telephone company which, through service, volunteerism, and commitment, has made a positive impact on the well-being of its community.

(4) The Student Propelled Action in Rural Communities (SPARC) Grant works to activate rural America's number one resource—young people—by awarding small grants to innovative student projects in rural schools.

(5) *Rural America On Line* is a newsletter which serves as a forum for community development ideas and solutions for rural areas.

(6) The Rural Teacher of the Year in Telecommunications Award is given to an educator who is using telecommunications technology to expand educational opportunities for rural students.

Since its inception in 1993, the FRED Rural Teacher of the Year honors have been bestowed on Sheryl Melton of Guymon, Oklahoma (1993); Donna Toney of Ellettsville, Indiana (1994); and the most recent winner, Carol Swinney of Hugoton, Kansas (1995). Each of the honorees are pioneers in the field of two-way interactive TV and have contributed immensely, not only to the success of their own I-TV networks, but to the visibility and reputation of I-TV teachers around the country.

For additional information, contact the Fund for Rural Education and Development, 21 DuPont Circle, N.W., Suite 700, Washington, D.C. 20036 (202-659-5990).

Bringing I-TV Access to Rural America

In the midst of the telecommunications policy debate surrounding the Telecommunications Act of 1996, OPASTCO (1994) made several recommendations for addressing rural interests. It remains to be seen whether recent federal legislation and the legislative ''echoes'' at the state level will effectively uphold OPASTCO's recommendations.

- Rural subscribers are entitled to the same quality and types of telecommunications services as urban subscribers, at reasonable rates.
- Geographic toll rate averaging must remain a part of national telecommunications policy.
- In establishing future telecommunications policy, legislators and regulators must recognize that serving rural America is different than serving urban areas.
- Telecommunications policy must be designed to encourage the use of telecommunications, not discourage it.
- The modification of price support mechanisms in such a way that rural subscribers can no longer afford service is not acceptable.
- Universal service support should continue to be paid to LECs. The small LECs serving rural America provide the existing modern rural telecommunications infrastructure. They are committed to extending the information superhighway to rural areas and are in the best position to ensure that rural Americans continue to receive quality service and do not become information "have nots."

Economic viability is the key factor in determining whether rural communities prosper or cease to exist. For rural schools, two-way interactive television is a tool for achieving educational equity for students. For rural communities, interactive telecommunications technologies can make economic and community development a reality. Deployment of an advanced telecommunications infrastructure will not come easily, nor will it come cheaply. For rural America, it will also not come soon enough.

I-TV Sites for Visitation

MOST states in the U.S. have at least one I-TV network in place or in the process of development. State departments of education can provide information on networks in individual states. Additional information can be obtained from a yearly state-by-state survey of educational telecommunications published by Hezel and Associates; see the biography for reference information.

Listed below are a few of the many I-TV networks that are willing to host visitations and answer questions from potential adopters of I-TV technology. Networks are listed alphabetically; the information below was obtained directly from network representatives.

ALABAMA

Network Name: Intercampus Interactive Telecommunications System
(IITS)
Contact: Dr. Philip Turner, Assistant Vice Chancellor
Address: University of Alabama—Box 870102
              Tuscaloosa, AL 35487-0102
Phone: 205/348-9295
e-mail: PTURNER@UA1VM.VA.EDU

Network Description: We use primarily T-1 leased lines with telco devices at each site so we can use all of the T-1 capacity. If two sites are using the same line, we run at 1/2 T, etc. We began in 1991. Sites range from downtown big city to very rural. The system's primary use is to share graduate education resources. Secondary use is to provide access to unique graduate programs. Also used for dissertation meetings.

Soon we anticipate having twenty-one sites connected, including a connection to an existing four-site community college network.

Alabama's videoconferencing network (IITS) is possibly unique in the nation as it is a confederation of independent agencies.

ALASKA

Network Name: Matanuska-Susitna Borough School District/
Matanuska Telephone Assoc. Interactive Distance
Learning System
Contact: Mr. Richard Kenshalo, Transmission Engineer
Address: Matanuska Telephone Association
Palmer, AK 99645
Phone: 907/745-9575
Fax: 907/746-9678
e-mail: tsrmk@acad1.alaska.edu

Network Description: Our network is based on Grass Valley Group digital CODECS and uses DS-3, over fiber optic facilities. A DS-3 switch, controlled by a Sun Sparc workstation, controls the network. The system uses a scanning sequence, alternately scanning remote sites (sequential viewing). Any site can be an origination site. The system features remote camera control, question and answer (talk-back), picture in picture, and text on video. Both class and instructor cameras are motorized, allowing remote pan/tilt/focus/zoom.

The network first went on-line in 1993. It is utilized for both student and staff development. Network expansion plans are planned for at least one site, approximately 50 miles north. The areas served are all in rural Alaska. Gateway expansion is also tentatively planned. All expansions are pending PUC (Public Utility Commission) approval.

The system is a pilot project between the school district and the local telco co-op. The service is provided at nearly no cost to the school district. The state's PUC objected to the provision of this pilot project, under the premise that the service and costs were unduly discriminatory to the other rate-payers not associated with the school district. Final determination of tariffs, etc., are yet to be filed, and will largely determine the ultimate success, or failure, of this system.

ARIZONA

Network Name: NAUnet
Contact: Dawn M. Lewis, NAUnet Manager

Address: Northern Arizona University
                P.O. Box 5676
                Flagstaff, AZ 86011-5676
Phone: 520/523-9402
Fax: 520/523-9988
e-mail: dml@a1.ucc.nau.edu

Network Description: Northern Arizona University began operation in the Spring Semester of 1990 when we offered our original six courses to our first location in Yuma at Arizona Western College. Our network is comprised of home-run analog two-way interactive microwave circuits between all locations and our Master Control facility here in Flagstaff. We have four electronic classrooms on the main campus in Flagstaff from which we can deliver courses to any number of our connected sites and other sites via satellite uplink. Our classrooms on the main campus are connected to master control in several different ways. One classroom is connected directly with video cables, one is connected with a run of 1/2 inch video cable, and two are connected via two single mode fibers. Our fifth classroom, which will be built this summer will be connected via 1/2 inch video cable. In the near future, all of our buildings will be connected via fiber links. This fiber will be pulled this summer into our extensive tunnel system.

All of our statewide sites, except Prescott, Estrella, and Coolidge are connected via analog microwave. Those three are connected via T-1 over phone lines. The primary use of our network is to deliver University programs to those students who wouldn't otherwise be able to come to the main campus. We are currently delivering undergraduate – Junior/Senior – courses and graduate programs for those students. Our network also serves several purposes for the community and the university. The university is able to save travel dollars by holding meetings on the network, and by using the network to deliver training programs to its employees across the campus and across the state. The community uses our network to share ideas with other communities and to transmit city council meetings. The network is also used by city, county, and state government organizations to provide training to their employees across the state. It has been a very beneficial network and promises to be even bigger in the future. To date we are delivering sixty courses to these thirteen sites. Our expansion plans include seven more sites via analog microwave, the institution of two DS-3 circuits to carry another twenty eight sites' traffic and three more hubs where routing can take place.

AUSTRALIA

Network Name: South Australian TAFE Tele-learning Consortium
Contact: Paul Rixon, Manager
Address: 20 Light Square
                Adelaide, South Australia, 5000
Phone: 618/207-8527
Fax: 618/207-8552
e-mail: aulrix@tafe.sa.edu.au

Network Description: This network began in 1990, and has grown out of a need to provide classes to students, in a manner which is acceptable and effective for them. Most of our sites are in rural areas, areas in which we have traditionally had difficulty getting enough students to be able to cost-effectively run classes. Using videoconferencing we can supply a fairly traditional class, but aggregate enough students over three to four sites. Our usage pattern remains that 95% of use is dedicated to classwork.

In Australia, TAFE (Training And Further Education) deals with students after they have left secondary school, and offers a range of vocational and continuing education classes. It is funded by the Government, and has a mandate to provide training to students within its area; each State has its own TAFE department.

Our classwork has achieved a variety of goals:

- One of our rural Institutes now graduates 500% more students to diploma or certificate level than before.
- Our busiest sites are involved with up to 1,300 hours use per year, with 95% of that for class work (this translates to more than 44 hours /week in the busiest weeks).
- Last year our network generated 1,600 conferences, with over 2,600 hours of programming.

Our sites link in groups of three to four sites usually, providing class sizes of fifteen to twenty-five (which are similar to the class sizes in our normal classrooms). Each room is fitted out with an integrated package so that it looks like a classroom first, rather than a studio.

Each site uses a PictureTel 4000 as its basis, and the group owns two bridges, which we use very heavily (and are cascaded together). The network link is via Telecom Australia's ISDN link: we use their Microlink service for each room (which offers two B Channels, or

128 k). About half of the rooms utilize terminal adapters which can rate adapt to either 64 or 56 k per channel, so these rooms are able to link to American sites using switched fifty-six services.

CALIFORNIA

Network Name: TEN (Television Education Network)
Contact: Betty Benson
Address: San Jose University
             One Washington Square
             San Jose, CA 95192-0169
Phone: 408/924-2636
Fax: 408/924-2881
e-mail: bcbenson@sjsuvm1.sjsu.edu

Network Description: The Television Education Network has been in operation since 1985 using microwave line-of-site technology offering upper-division and graduate courses to off-campus sites. In 1992, we began offering professional development courses to business and industry. In 1993, we added the compressed video technology and four of the I-TV classrooms. Conference rooms are able to broadcast compressed video at 112 and 384 kbps. In 1994 the ATM technology (fiber) was introduced and is being used to offer the Masters in Library and Information Services to California State University at Fullerton. We broadcast to both rural and urban areas, serving a broad community both in the Silicon Valley and the farm community south of the University. The compressed CODEC is also used for committee meetings within the CSU system. Also through a partnership with the San Jose Medical Group, we offer a Wellness "Brown Bag" session once a month to all of our receive sites.

GEORGIA

Network Name: Center for Disease Control (CDC) WAN
Contact: Karl W. Branch
Address: 1600 Clifton Road
             Atlanta, GA 30333
Phone: 404/639-3001
Fax: 404/639-1733

Network Description: Transmission technology at CDC is either PRI, Switched 56 kb, or private network. The protocol is either SG3 (proprietary) or H.320 (standard). We run anything from 112 kbps to 384 kbps. All our sites are considered primarily urban with the exception of Ft. Collins which is rural. The private network consists of T1 and DS-3 sites and is interconnected by either T1 or DS-3. I-TV is used mainly for conferences, meetings, seminars, and some teaching.

ILLINOIS

Network Name: WIU College of Ed. and Human Services
Telecom. Network
Contact: Michael Dickson, Director
101 Horrabin Hall
Western Illinois University
Macomb, IL 61455
Phone: 309/298-1804
Fax: 309/298-2806

Network Description: Our network uses 1/4 T (384 Kbit) transmission with V-Tel equipment. Our network went on-line the summer of 1993 with Reading 569 (school district). Our communities are primarily rural community colleges through Western Illinois University and we also provide classes to Springfield Public School District 186. WIU and SPSD have a unique working relationship that allows us to do classroom observation from our electronic classroom without disturbing elementary classrooms for teacher training.

IOWA

Network Name: Iowa Communications Network (ICN)
Contact: Dr. Pamela Johnson, Director of
Educational Telecommunications
Address: Iowa Public Television
6450 Corporate Drive
Johnston, IA 50131
Phone: 515/242-4180
Fax: 515/242-3155
e-mail: pjohnson@po-1.star.k12.ia.us

Network Description: The ICN is a fiber optic (DS-3) digital SONET technology. First on-line in August 1993, the network serves urban and rural communities, but in most cases there is only one point of presence in each county, so if there is a community college—which is the regional hub—there is not a classroom at the high school even though it may be the largest school district in the region. The primary use of the network is education at all levels, K−12, community college, upper division college, graduate, continuing education, mandatory certification . . . (100,000 hours of programming last semester). In addition there are thousands of hours of meetings held regionally and statewide. Installation of fiber and transmission facilities were funded 100% by the state of Iowa. Classroom equipment was funded locally and/or with assistance from a Star Schools Grant from the United States Department of Education.

KANSAS

Network Name: The Learning Consortium
Contact: Dr. Sandra Thies
Address: Box 2000
Hesston, KS 67062
Phone: 316/327-7135
Fax: 316/327-7130

Network Description: The Learning Consortium is in its fourth year of transmitting high school and college classes. We are a fiber optic, fully-interactive (analog) network which also transmits data on a Novell, ICLAS network of 320 nodes in seven buildings in the four districts. The four districts partnering in TLC are Hesston, Moundridge, Canton-Galva, and Goessel. Total students in these four small, rural districts is 2000. Each high school I-TV classroom has equipment to allow use of videotapes, overhead projector (ELMO), slides, microscope, hand-held video camera, and laserdisk for instruction. Our next phase calls for computers in each I-TV classroom so software can be used across the network (picture within a picture would be part of this addition).

MINNESOTA

Network Name: Little Crow Telemedia Network
Contact: Pete Royer, Director

Address: Two Century Ave.
                    Hutchinson, MN 55350
Phone: 612/234-0267
Fax: 612/587-8063
e-mail: 6040Lctm@InforMNs.k12.mn.us

Network Description: Analog fiber, 100 miles, started 1989. Rural schools, primary purpose to deliver low incident—upper level high school courses. Also deliver post-secondary to graduate level courses, plus community education, county extension and business training and meetings. We are looking at linking up with another K – 12 I-TV network to share programming.

MISSISSIPPI

Network Name: Community College Network
Contact: Forrest Cooper, Manager
Address: Post Office Box 1162, HCC
                    Raymond, MS 39154
Phone: 601/857-3594
Fax: 601/857-3526

Network Description: Network uses T-1 transmission lines and first went on-line in July 1994. Situated in urban community college campus sites, through which both urban and rural segments of society are reached. The network is primarily used to deliver both community college and senior college courses. In addition, the network offers continuing education, including graduate instruction, agricultural, medical, private sector, and adult basic education training.

MISSOURI

Network Name: Education Plus Network
Contact: Nancy Steel, Director
Address: Putnam County R-I
                    801 South 20th
                    Unionville, MO 63565-9508
Phone: 816/947-2481

Network Description: Started in 1993 as one of the first I-TV networks in Missouri. Analog fiber optic system that is used mainly for high school courses. Three participating schools with one more to be added later this year.

NEW MEXICO

Network Name: Lea County Distance Education Consortium
Contact: Wayne Smith, Coordinator/Technician
Address: 5317 Lovington Highway
             Hobbs, NM 88240
Phone: 505/392-2600
Fax: 505/392-3737

Network Description: Lea County Distance Education Consortium links five public high schools and the College of the Southwest. GTE is the provider of the T1 service and the hardware is VTEL equipment. The I-TV system was implemented primarily to assist the public high schools in providing a broader offering of courses. Furthermore, New Mexico Junior College, NMJC, offers a variety of college courses during the evening.

NORTH DAKOTA

Network Name: Yellowstone Trail I-TV Cooperative
Contact: Steven Rassier, Superintendent
Address: Box 1188
             Hettinger, ND 58639
Phone: 701/567-4501
Fax: 701/567-2796

Network Description: The Yellowstone Trail I-TV System became fully operational on August 23, 1993. It is an analog fiber system. At this time it is being used to deliver high school courses to students in three rural communities. The total high school population of these three schools is 385 students (grades 9−12). In the 1994−95 school year we have offered courses in German, Advanced Composition, Creative Writing, World Geography, Farm Management, Art, and Senior Math.

The system has also been used for administrator meetings, teacher in-services, consortium board meetings, and meeting of the Yellowstone Trail Curriculum Council. Our hope for the future includes linking to other high school I-TV sites and a link to the North Dakota Interactive Video Network (NDIVN) which brings us into the statewide higher education network.

SOUTH DAKOTA

Network Name: South Dakota Rural Development
Telecommunications Network
Contact: Jim Protexter, Director
Address: 500 East Capitol
Pierre, SD 57501
Phone: 605/773-3333
Fax: 605/773-6581
e-mail: jimp@rdtn.state.sd.us

Network Description: The South Dakota Rural Development Telecommunications (RDT) Network began in December 1992 with six two-way interactive sites connected via a T-1 network. The state-owned RDT Network had developed out of a task force report commissioned by Governor George S. Mickelson. The primary purpose for the Network is to provide access to resources and information for South Dakota citizens. South Dakota is a rural state with a total populace of just over 700,000. The Network utilizes two technologies: T-1 fiber and digital satellite MPEG1. There are currently eighteen two-way interactive sites on the fiber system and nearly fifty satellite receive sites with another thirty to be added in Summer 1995. That will continue to grow to nearly 200 in the next few years. The Network also has interstate connectivity capability. This allows users to be connected to any two-way interactive system in the world.

RDT Network studios are located at a variety of facilities including state universities, technical institutes, hospitals, private universities, the State Capitol, and high schools. Although education is a priority on the network, it is available for anyone to use. This includes governmental agencies, private business, non-profit organizations, and individuals. The RDT Network is funded through user fees and does not receive an appropriation from the state's general fund. The network charges its users based on a three-tier rate structure: government/education, non-profit, and business. Government and education comprise the greatest majority of users. Their uses primarily include training, educational courses, department meetings, legislative hearings, and judicial proceedings. Other users have utilized the network for a variety of activities including job interviews, sales presentations, client support and field office meetings.

TENNESSEE

Network Name: University of Memphis TI
Contact: Sam Brackstone, Director – Extended Programs
Address: University of Memphis, Admin. Bldg. 382
               Memphis, TN 38152
Phone: 901/678-2991
Fax: 901/678-4049
e-mail: SBRACKSTONE@cc.memphis.edu

Network Description: TI net first started in March of 1993. Network links both urban and rural areas primarily providing college credit courses to distant sites from University Campus. Some administrative meetings are held over the links as well as some observation of elementary classes by students in the College of Education. We plan to expand our connectivity options by adding ISDN capability.

TEXAS

Network Name: East Texas Learning Interactive Network
              Consortium (ET-LINC)
Contact: Mary Fuller, Director
Address: Northeast Texas Educational Partnership
              Commerce, TX 75429
Phone: 903/886-5511
Fax: 903/886-5896
e-mail: mwf@tenet.edu

Network Description: ET-LINC came on-line in spring of 1995 (DS-3 network serving rural communities). Utilized for the delivery of advanced placement and dual-credit high school courses, teacher training, continuing education, and other university credit courses. Received a $1 million grant from Texas Education Agency to build interactive classrooms at nine rural high schools that will connect to ET-LINC for teacher training.

VERMONT

Network Name: Vermont Interactive Television
Contact: Judith Hastings, Program Manager
Address: Vermont Technical College
               Randolf Center, VT 05061
Phone: 802/728-1337
Fax: 802/728-3026
e-mail: jhasting@night.vtc.vsc.edu

Network Description: A total of twelve sites in Vermont, started in 1988. Main network is T-1; connection to U.S. Army is via two-way satellite. Serving all Vermont with primary mission of making education/training available to all areas of the state and enhancing communication for all organizations/institutions in the state. Network is used by (1) higher education for credit and non-credit courses; (2) K − 12 for special projects and AP courses; (3) state agencies for training and meetings; and (4) non-profits for training. In addition, the network is used for workforce training offered by many public/private entities and for legislative public hearings. May link with developing regional K − 12 video networks in the future. Communities currently directly served range from Burlington (largest city in Vermont) to Canaan (pop. 900). All sites serve their region. Goal is to have a site within twenty miles of every citizen.

WISCONSIN

Network Name: Northern Wisconsin Educational Communications
               System
Contact: Timothy K. Von Hoff
Address: 618 Beaser Avenue
               Ashland, WI 54806

Phone: 715/682-2363 ext. 154
Fax: 715/682-7244

Network Description: NWECS is a DS-3 network. Classroom equipment includes a VHS recorder/player, audio cassette recorder, document video camera, two classroom video cameras, and the capability of patching in other technologies as desired, such as computers and CDI devices. Our network serves a very sparsely populated area of Northern Wisconsin. We deliver high school, Technical College, and University Courses over the NWECS network. Enrichment programs, meetings, technology demonstrations, and some training have been held on NWECS.

I-TV Resources

DISTANCE LEARNING RESOURCES*

"WHERE do I go to get more information on distance learning?" is a question that I continually struggle with and am never able to fully answer. Of course, the best resource for educating yourself about I-TV and distance learning is to visit an ongoing project.

With this in mind, there are several other resources that can be of value. While there is no one publication that covers I-TV, there are several that address the topic from time to time. In addition, there are several conferences at which users of I-TV can be found leading sessions on technology implementation and effective I-TV teaching strategies.

(A word of caution: If you are getting information from a vendor, consultant, or telecommunication provider, be sure that you also get some unbiased information. In talking to consultants, visit or talk to three to four projects they have worked with in the last year or two.)

Conferences

Annual Conference on Distance Teaching and Learning. Held every summer in Madison, Wisconsin. Contact: Distance Teaching and Learning Conference, The Wisconsin Center, Room 105, 702 Langdon Street, Madison, WI 53706.

Minnesota Interactive TV Networks Annual Conference. Held every summer in Minnesota. Contact: Chris Dunrud, Support Services Network, 211 Jefferson Street North, Wadena, MN 56482.

Annual "Finding Our Way" Conference. Held every summer in Ohio. Contact: Center for Advanced Study in Telecommunications, 3106

*By Pete Royer, Director, Little Crow Telemedia Network, Minnesota.

Derby Hall, 154 N. Oval Mall, The Ohio State University, Columbus, OH 43210; 614/292-8444; cast@eng.ohio-state.edu

Organizations and Associations

The American Telemedicine Association, 1700 One American Center, 600 Congress Center, Austin, TX 78701.

Association for the Advancement of Computing in Education. Contact: AACE, P.O. Box 2966, Charlottesville, VA 22902; $65/yr.

Association for Educational Communications and Technology, 1025 Vermont Avenue NW, Suite 820, Washington, DC 20005; 202/347-7834.

Center for Advanced Study in Telecommunications (CAST), 3016 Derby Hall/154 N. Oval Mall, Columbus, OH 43210-1339; 614/292-8444.

Consortium for School Networking, P.O. Box 8387, Berkeley, CA 94707-8387; $500/yr.

Institute for the Transfer of Technology to Education (a division of the National School Boards Association), c/o National School Boards Association, 1680 Duke Street, Alexandria, VA 22314; 703/838-6722.

International Society for Technology in Education, 1787 Agate Street, Eugene, OR 97403-1923; 503/346-4414; $55/yr.

International Teleconferencing Association, 1650 Tyson Blvd. Suite 200, McLean Virginia, 22102; $100/yr.

Minnesota Interactive Television Networks, Two Century Ave, Hutchinson, MN 55350; $50/yr. per network.

National Coordinating Committee on Technology in Education and Training, P.O. Box 4437, Alexandria, VA 22303; 703/351-5243.

United States Distance Learning Association, c/o Applied Business teleCommunications, Box 5129, San Ramon, CA 94583; 510/606-5160. Annual meeting with Telecon on West Coast; vendor oriented; $100/yr. Publishes the *USDLA Funding Sourcebook* and *Education at a Distance*.

Periodicals

American Journal of Distance Education. Contact: College of Education, Pennsylvania State University, 403 South Allen Street, Suite 206, University Park, PA 16801-5202.

CAST Calendar and Newsletter. Available from the Center for Advanced Study in Telecommunications, 3106 Derby Hall, 154 N. Oval Mall, The Ohio State University, Columbus, OH 43210.

Education at a Distance. Contact: Applied Business teleCommunications, Box 5106 San Ramon, CA 94583.

Educational Technology. Contact: Educational Technology Publications, 700 Palisade Avenue, Englewood Cliffs, NJ 07632.

Educational Technology Research and Development. Contact: Association for Educational Communications and Technology, 1025 Vermont Avenue NW, Suite 820, Washington, DC 20005; 202/347-7834.

Electronic Learning. Contact: Scholastic, Inc., 555 Broadway, New York, NY 10012; 800/544-2917.

Electronic School. Contact: National School Boards Association, 1680 Duke Street, Alexandria, VA 22314; 703/838-6722.

International Journal of Educational Telecommunications. Available with membership in Association for the Advancement of Computing in Education. Contact: AACE, PO Box 2966, Charlottesville, VA 22902.

Tech Trends. Contact: Association for Educational Communications and Technology, 1025 Vermont Avenue NW, Suite 820, Washington, DC 20005; 202/347-7834.

TeleConference. Contact: Applied Business teleCommunications, Box 5106, San Ramon, CA 94583.

The Telemedicine Newsletter. Contact: Sheri Hostetler, Executive Editor, 600 Harrison Street, San Francisco, CA 94107.

T.H.E. Journal (Technical Horizons in Education). Occasional articles on I-TV and telecommunications. Contact: T.H.E., 150 El Camino #112, Tuscin, CA 92680.

Publications

Educational Telecommunications: The State-by-State Analysis ($150). Contact: Hezel & Associates, 1201 E. Fayette Street, Syracuse, NY 13210.

Interactive TV for Distance Learning: From Plan to Practice, by US

West and National School Boards Assoication. Available for $15 plus $5 shipping from NSBA, 1 P.O. Box 161 Annapolis Junction, MD 20701; 800/706-6722.

A Primer on Distance Learning and Intellectual Property Issues. Available free from Dow, Lohnes & Albertson, 1255 23rd Street NW, Washington, DC 20037-1194.

Distance Learning Primer. Available from Missouri School Boards Association, 2100 I-70 Drive Southwest, Columbia, MO 65203.

Teaching Tips ($10). Available from Minnesota Interactive Television Networks, Two Century Ave, Hutchinson, MN 55350.

Teaching at a Distance Over Interactive Television ($16) and *Guidebook for Accessible I-TV Programs* ($25). Available from the Center for Distance Education, University of Maine/Augusta, University Heights, Augusta, ME 04330.

INTERNET AND ELECTRONIC RESOURCES FOR INTERACTIVE TELEVISION**

The I-TV Internet Mail List

I-TV is an Internet mail list for the discussion of two-way video communications for education and community development. The mail list is open for subscription to anyone, and has significant membership from around the world. Subjects discussed include equipment manufacturers, equipment set-up and use, teaching paradigms, descriptions of I-TV networks, requests for help, conference announcements, book announcements, etc. Video communication using compressed digital (video teleconferencing), analog fiber, microwave, and satellite are discussed. The I-TV mail list is hosted by DPH Enterprises as a service to the community that it services.

The I-TV mail list is also available in a digest format (i.e., I-TV-digest), which includes approximately the previous two week's correspondence.

**By David Hart, Chief Engineer, DPH Enterprises, which offers the Galaxy Microsystems line of fiber optic connectivity products to education networks and community development networks. These low-cost, high-quality analog video systems connect local school systems into video networks, and offer community government a video link between offices. DPH Enterprises may be reached by e-mail at dhart@ offramp.com, postmail at 400 Del Robles, Austin TX 78727, or by telephone at 512/388-7465.

To Subscribe to the I-TV Mail List

From the e-mail address that you wish to receive your I-TV e-mail, send the following in the body of an e-mail message (the "Subject:" is ignored) to I-TV@cmc2.cmc.edu

subscribe i-tv
end

or

subscribe i-tv-digest
end

The majordomo mail list server will automatically subscribe you to the I-TV mail list. A "Welcome" message is sent to your e-mail address describing all the services available from the I-TV mail list. You are then a member. All subsequent e-mail correspondence from other members of the I-TV mail list will be sent to your e-mail address.

You are encouraged in the welcome message to submit a short introduction to yourself. If you are associated with an existing I-TV network, please include a description of this network. If you have a question about some problem your system is experiencing, please include a request for assistance. We like a good challenge.

The I-TV World-Wide-Web Pages

The I-TV mail list maintains a World-Wide-Web presence at "http://www.offramp.com/i-tv". These www pages point members, and others interested in the same subject materials, to the Internet resources available to web browsers. Included are URLs to member's home pages, I-TV network home pages, and resources appropriate to video communication. This is a new and growing aspect of the I-TV mail list. The back issues of the I-TV-digest are available through these web pages.

Other Mail Lists of Interest

Mail List: VIDNET-L@UGA.CC.UGA.EDU
Subscription Address: LISTSERV@UGA.CC.UGA.EDU
Owner: John R. Stephens, Jr. < JStephen@UGA.CC.UGA.EDU >

Description: VIDNET-L (Video Network Discussion List) was formed for the discussion of mutual problems and concerns which face all who are involved in the operation of a campus-wide video network. This includes any configuration which may be found in a campus environment — creation, operation, maintenance, programming, teleconferencing, rate structure, and videotext are some of the topics expected to be discussed.

Mail List: DEOS-L@PSUVM.PSU.EDU
Subscription Address: LISTSERV@PSUVM.PSU.EDU
Description: The American Center for the Study of Distance Education at Pennsylvania State University sponsors this list, which is an international discussion forum for distance education. The list's purpose is to promote communication among distance educators, and to disseminate information and requests about distance education around the world.

ERIC (Educational Resources Information Center)

ERIC is a federally funded national information system that provides access to an extensive body of education-related resources. The ERIC system can be accessed through gopher and world-wide-web.

Gopher

Point your gopher client toward ericir.syr.edu.

World-Wide-Web

Point your www client toward ericir.syr.edu.

Access   The ability to enter or connect to a telecommunications network.

Access Charge   The charge paid by local telephone subscribers and interexchange carriers (IXCs) to local exchange carriers (LECs) for connecting to the LECs' network. Telephone subscribers pay a monthly subscriber line charge, while IXCs pay usage-based access charges.

Amplifier   A device that increases the strength of an analog signal. *See* Attenuation.

Analog   A signal that is composed of a range of intensities instead of discrete units or integers.

Aspect Ratio   The relationship between height and width of a visual format. For example, letter-sized paper has an aspect ratio of 11 to 8.5 when viewed with the long side up. Common aspect ratios are two to three for 35 mm slides and three to four for video.

Asynchronous Transfer Mode (ATM)   A protocol for transferring digital information in cells, allowing for the simultaneous transmission of a number of different types of data (voice, video, computer, facsimile, etc.) along the same fiber optic line. Also known as cell relay.

Attenuation   The degradation of an analog signal (either video or audio). Can be caused by transmitting the signal over a great distance without proper amplification or by splitting the signal without amplification.

Audio Bridge   A device used in teleconferencing for mixing multiple audio signals and distributing the combined signal back to participants in the teleconference.

Authentic Instruction   Teaching that involves students in real-world problem solving and learning.

Bandwidth   The amount of information that can be transmitted through a communications channel. In digital communications, bandwidth is usually measured in bits per second (bps). Bandwidth of analog signals is measured in Hertz or cycles per second.

Bar Code Reader A device that uses an infrared light or a laser to read information from a bar code, often used with videodisks to index portions of the disk.

Bird Slang for a satellite in geosynchronous earth orbit (22,300 miles above the equator).

bps (bits per second) A rate used to measure the amount of digital information that can be transmitted through a particular medium.

Broadband Network A communications network, such as microwave, coaxial cable, satellite, or fiber cable, that transmits data without compression, or at gigabit per second speeds.

CCD (Charge Couple Device) A photosensitive microchip that is used in many modern video cameras; a CCD microchip replaces the traditional tube in the video camera and has better resolution for its cost and is less susceptible to damage or "burn in" that affects tube-type cameras.

Cell Relay *See* ATM above.

Central Office A hub on the telephone network where the lines for local circuits are switched and connected (either to circuits in the local area or to long distance circuits).

Coax, Coaxial Cable A cable in which a copper signal wire is placed in the middle of an insulating material and solid outer shield.

CODEC (COder-DECoder) A device that converts analog video and audio signals into digital form and compresses the data (Coding), as well as decompressing and converting a digital signal into an analog output (Decoding).

CODEC Conversion Converting a signal from one CODEC standard to another. Without dominant standards for interconversion, many CODEC converters are actually two CODECS that have been placed back-to-back and transfer data between the two units as NTSC video and line-level audio.

Competitive Access Provider (CAP) A company that has been authorized to compete with long distance and/or local carriers for providing telecommunications services.

Composite Video A video signal in which the RGB (see below) signals have been combined into one standard signal (*see also* NTSC).

Compressed Video A video signal that has been converted to a digital form which is then compressed for transmission over low bandwidth lines; such video is usually viewed at less than full-motion speeds.

Computer Assisted Instruction (CAI)   Use of a computer software program as a teaching and learning tool in a specific content area.

DACS (Digital Access Cross-Connect System)   A switching device used by phone companies to switch and connect T1 lines.

Depth of Field   The distance between the closest and most distant points that are in focus.

Digital   A signal that is composed of discrete units (either a 0, "off," or a 1, "on") instead of a range of variables. *See* Analog above.

Distance Learning   The provision of formal education to geographically dispersed individuals or groups through a communications medium, ranging from correspondence courses to live, fully interactive classrooms.

DS-3 (T-3) Digital Service Three   A standard fiber optic circuit that has a bandwidth of approximately 45 mbps.

Echo Canceller   A device that samples the audio coming into a site and then eliminates that signal from the outgoing audio, thereby eliminating audio "echo." See Chapter 2.

Elmo   The brandname of a manufacturer of video cameras. Commonly used to refer to a document or graphics camera that allows instructors to display objects that are on their desktop.

Equal Access   The ability to make a long-distance call using an identified long-distance carrier by dialing 1 plus 10 digits; sometimes called "1 +" dialing.

FAX (Facsimile Machine)   A device that scans documents and converts the information about the distribution of ink on the page to a signal that can be transmitted to remote sites via analog phone lines. The document is then printed at the remote site. Protocols for facsimile transmission are designed by group number, such as Groups 1, 2, 3, and 4.

FCC (Federal Communications Commission)   United States federal agency charged with regulating communications transmissions including telephone, cable, radio, television, and satellite.

Feedback   A build-up of signal in an audio system in which a signal is repeatedly amplified until it reaches an enormous volume.

Fiber Optic Cable   A flexible piece of glass or plastic fiber that can be used to carry pulses of light.

FM (Frequency Modulation) A means of transmitting information via analog radio waves in which the frequency of a carrier signal is varied in accordance with the signal being transmitted.

Focal Length A description of the design and capabilities of a camera lens.

gbps (giga bits per second) Rate of digital transmission equaling one billion bits per second.

Independent Telephone Company A local exchange carrier that never was a part of the former American Telephone and Telegraph system.

Instructional Media Audiovisual materials, or devices to utilize the materials, which contribute to instruction. Common forms of instructional media include video cassette players/recorders, laserdisk players, computer CD-ROMs, overhead cameras, audiotape players, etc.

Interexchange Carrier (IXC) A carrier providing long distance telephone service between LATAs (local access and transport areas).

International Telecommunications Union (ITU) A division of the United Nations that is responsible for overseeing the coordination of communications regulations between nations. *See* FCC above.

Internet The "Network of Networks" that ties together regional and local networks around the world using the TCP/IP suite of data transfer protocols.

Interoperability The ability to seamlessly translate data from one medium or protocol to another.

ISDN (Integrated Services Digital Network) A digital telephone standard that uses copper wire to deliver data, voice, and video at transfer rates up to 128 kbps.

ITFS (Instructional Television Fixed Service) A means of transmitting video and audio (one-way) via microwave radiation. Usually limited to regional areas of thirty-five miles. ITFS can be modified to provide two-way service.

I-TV A shorthand reference to two-way interactive television, a technology enabling simultaneous, two-way audio and video connections across multiple sites.

LATA (Local Access and Transport Area) The geographic area in which the Regional Bell Operating Companies (RBOCs) are allowed to provide long-distance service. At divestiture of AT&T, the U.S. District Court divided the country into LATAs, which established the toll call boundaries for the RBOCs. Because the Modified Final Judgment (MFJ) stated that the RBOCs cannot provide interexchange services, they are permitted to carry toll calls only within LATAs. Interexchange carriers (IXCs) have to carry calls between LATAs. While independent telephone companies are not subject to the MFJ interLATA restriction, most independent territories do fall within a specific LATA.

Lavaliere (or Lapel) Microphone A small microphone that is attached to the speaker's lapel. The microphone is then connected to the audio system directly with a wire, or via a wireless transmitter.

Learning Style The method or methods by which individuals assimilate information and data into knowledge, e.g., visually, orally, tactilely, etc.

LEC (Local Exchange Carrier) A telephone company that operates within one or more local exchanges.

LUX A measurement of light intensity equal to one lumen per square meter. A basis for rating the light sensitivity of a camera.

Mbps A measure of bandwidth — megabits per second.

MFJ (Modified Final Judgement) The consent decree that broke up American Telephone and Telegraph, resulting in the seven RBOC's or Regional Bell Operating Companies.

Microwave A region of the electromagnetic spectrum or radio communication signals transmitted above one gigahertz (billion cycles per second).

MODEM (MOdulator-DEModulator) A device commonly used to transmit digital information over an analog transmission line, such as a telephone line.

Multiconferencing Unit (MCU) A device used to electronically combine three or more videoconference rooms together. See Chapter 2.

Multimedia A variety of media materials consisting of text, sound, still or moving graphics, and/or video stored digitally and viewed with a computer.

Narrowband Network A communications network that transmits voice, fax or data at slow speeds.

NTSC (National Television Standards Committee) Usually refers to the standard in the United States for transmitting composite video signals. PAL (Phase Alternate Line) is the European standard for composite video.

Plant Term used by telecommunications companies to refer to the equipment that is invested either in the ground (cables) or in a central office (switching equipment).

POTS (Plain Old Telephone Service) Traditional analog voice telephone service with a bandwidth of 3000 hertz.

PSTN (Public Switched Telephone Network) Telephone network accessed through LECs and regulated by the FCC and state utility commissions.

Rate of Return A method of federal regulation of local exchange carrier (LEC) earnings which establishes the percentage of net profit that an LEC is allowed to earn on its rate base.

RBOC (Regional Bell Operating Company) One of seven regional telephone companies that was formed from the breakup of the American Telephone and Telegraph (AT&T) corporation, for example, USWest or Southwestern Bell.

Reflector The Internet equivalent of a multi-conferencing unit.

RGB (Red, Green, Blue) The three primary colors of transmitted light. In video, RGB video refers to the division of video information into these three primary colors for transmission, usually to a monitor. RGB is of considerably higher quality than composite video.

Safe Area The area in an NTSC video signal that is guaranteed of being transmitted and displayed on the reception device (e.g., television).

Satellite An earth-orbiting device for relaying communications (voice, video, and data) between terrestrial uplink and downlink sites.

SONET (Synchronous Optical NETwork) A digital hierarchy of bandwidths. Designations have the prefix "OC," such as OC-1 (52 mbps) or OC-24 (1.2 gbps).

T-1 A telecommunications line with a bandwidth of 1.5 mbps, also known as DS-1.

T-3 A telecommunications line with a bandwidth of 45 mbps, also known as DS-3.

Tariff A legal document issued to telephone carriers, both local exchange carriers and interexchange carriers, by either the FCC or state regulatory commission that describes the rates for a particular service and any restrictions or regulations regarding that service. Tariffs for interstate services are filed with the Federal Communications Commission; tariffs for intrastate services are filed with state public utility commissions.

Teleconferencing   The mixing of the audio from three of more telephones for audio conferencing.

Telemedicine   The application of telecommunications technology for remote medical use, e.g., diagnostics, consultation, teleradiology, telecardiology, etc.

Time-Base Corrector (TBC)   A device generally used for synchronizing the phase of a video signal with a device into which the signal is sent (such as a CODEC) which in turn outputs a reference signal for synchronization.

Transponder   A device used to re-transmit communications signals. For example, a transponder in a satellite receives communications from a ground station (uplink) and then relays that signal on a different frequency to multiple ground stations (downlink).

Universal Service   The concept originating in the Communications Act of 1934 that all subscribers – both urban and rural – are entitled to quality telephone service at reasonable rates.

Universal Service Fund (USF)   A federal communications program that compensates local exchange carriers (LECs) whose costs of providing basic local telephone service are higher than the national average, thereby allowing LECs to charge their subscribers reasonable local service rates. The money for the USF is generated by mandatory contributions from interexchange carriers (IXCs) who pay a flat monthly per-line fee based on their number of lines. The National Exchange Carrier Association bills the IXCs for the charges and distributes the funds to LECs on a monthly basis; payments are in direct proportion to the LEC's costs of providing service with the highest cost study areas receiving proportionately more funds.

Uplink   The transmission of information from an earth station to a satellite.

URL (Uniform Resource Locator)   A standard way of referencing the location of files and host computers on the Internet.

VHS (Video Home System)   A standard for recording and playing video cassettes.

Video Dial Tone   The concept of ubiquitous availability of two-way audio and visual communication, similar in ease of use and availability as today's telephone circuits.

Videodisc (or Videodisk or Laserdisk) Player   A device for playing videodisks by reflecting a laser off the surface of the disk and translating fluctuations in the reflected light into standard video and/or audio signals.

VSAT (Very Small Aperture Terminal) Small, portable, and relatively easy to operate ground station for use in satellite-based I-TV transmissions.

Wave Division Multiplexing (WDM) A method of using multiple frequencies as carriers (radio waves or light), thereby increasing the total amount of data that can be transmitted over a communications channel.

Annenberg/CPB Project and the PBS Adult Learning Service. 1992. *Going the Distance: A Handbook for Developing Distance Degree Programs Using Television Courses and Telecommunications Technologies.* Bethesda, MD: Corporation for Public Broadcasting and Public Broadcasting Service.

Apple Computer. 1992. *Multimedia: Getting Started.* Reading, MA: Addison-Wesley Publishing Co.

Barker, B. 1992. "The Distance Education Handbook: An Administrator's Guide for Rural and Remote Schools," Brigham Young University, HI, ERIC Document Number ED 340 547.

Barker, B., Frisbie, A., and K. Patrick 1989. "Broadening the Definition of Distance Education in Light of the New Telecommunications Technologies," *The American Journal of Distance Education,* 3(1): 20−29.

Beare, P. L. 1989. "The Comparative Effectiveness of Videotape, Audiotape, and Telelecture in Delivering Continuing Teacher Education," *The American Journal of Distance Education,* 3(2): 57−66.

Bednar, A.K. et al. 1991. "Theory into Practice: How Do We Link?" in *Instructional Technology: Past, Present and Future.* Gary J. Anglin, ed. Denver, CO: Libraries Unlimited.

Berge, Z. L. and M. Collins, eds. 1995. *Computer Mediated Communication and the Online Classroom. Volume III: Distance Learning.* Cresskill, NJ: Hampton Press.

Bloom, B.S., ed. 1956. *Taxonomy of Educational Objectives: The Classification of Educational Goals. Handbook I: Cognitive Domain.* New York: D. McKay Co.

Bloom, B. S., M. D. Englehart, and E. J. Furst. 1977. *A Taxonomy of Educational Objectives. Handbook I: The Cognitive Domain.* New York: Longman.

Bluestone, B. and B. Harrison. 1982. *The Deindustrialization of America.* New York: Basic Books.

Bond, S. 1987. "Telecommunications-Based Distance Learning: A Guide for Local Educators," Southeast Educational Development Laboratory, NC, ERIC Document Number ED 287 474.

Bourdieu, P. 1977. "Cultural Reproduction and Social Reproduction," in *Power and Ideology in Education,* J. Karabel and A. H. Halsey, eds., New York: Wiley Publishing, pp. 487−511.

Brandt, R. 1990. "On Cooperative Learning: A Conversation with Spencer Kagan," *Educational Leadership,* 47(4).

Bruder, I. 1989. "Distance Learning: What's Holding Back This Boundless Delivery System?" *Electronic Learning,* April: 30−35.

291

Bunting, C. 1994. "Interactive Television in a Rural State," *Connection*, Summer: 22–23.

Caro, A. 1983. *The Years of Lyndon Johnson, The Path to Power.* New York: Vintage Books.

Carlson, R. 1965. *Adoption of Educational Innovation.* Eugene, OR: Center for Advanced Study of Educational Administration.

Chandra, M. 1993. "Parent Involvement in Education and School Sector." Atlanta: Annual Meeting of the American Educational Research Association.

Christianson, J. S. and V. Hobbs. 1995. "Education in Rural Missouri via Two-Way Interactive Television: Evaluation of Learning and Technology." Atlanta: 161st National Meeting of the American Association for the Advancement of Science.

Clark, C. 1989. "Distance Education in the United States Schools," *The Computing Teacher*, 16(6): 7–11.

Clay, M. and R. Grover. 1995. "Throw Me a Rope: A Distance Learning Faculty Guide," *Technology and Teacher Education Annual.*

Coleman, J. S. 1988. "Social Capital in the Creation of Human Capital," *American Journal of Sociology*, 94: S95–S120.

Damyanovich, M. 1987. "Cubism Live–Teaching by Two-Way TV," *Media & Methods*, 24(2): 18–19.

Dillon, C. L., C. Gobson and S. Confessore. 1993. "Interaction in Interactive Satellite Teleconferencing: Can It Be Increased?" *The Journal of Interactive Television*, 1(2): 43–62.

Duffy and Jonassen. 1991. "Constructionism in the Technology of Instruction: A Conversation," ERIC Document Number ED 364 198.

Egan, M. 1988. "Two-way Interactive Television Instruction: Comparative Studies of Instructional Effectiveness in Three Rural/Remote Special Education Courses," American Council on Rural Special Education, VA, ERIC Document Number ED 299 729.

Ellis, Clyde T. 1966. *A Giant Step.* New York: Random House.

Ellis, L. and D. Mathis. 1985. "College Students Learning from Televised versus Conventional Classroom Lectures: A Controlled Experiment," *Higher Education*, 14(2): 165–173.

Galvin, P. and R. Bruce. 1987. "Technology and Rural Education: The Case of Audiographic Telecommunications," Cornell University, NY, ERIC Document Number ED 307 072.

Garrison, D. R. 1987. In "Final Report on the Development, Pilot-Testing and Dissemination of a Comprehensive Evaluation Model for Assessing the Effectiveness of a Two-Way Interactive Distance Learning System," Kabat, E. and Friedel, J., eds. 1990. Eastern Iowa Community College District, Office of Academic Affairs and Planning.

Gehlauf, D. N., M. A. Shatz, and T. W. Frye. 1991. "Faculty Perceptions of Interactive Television Instructional Strategies: Implications for Training," *The American Journal of Distance Education*, 5(3): 21–29.

Gellerman, E. 1994. "Teleconferencing Systems Facilitate Collaboration and Distance Learning," *Technological Horizons in Education*, October: 16–28.

Hakes, B. T., S. G. Sachs, C. Box, and J. Cochenour. 1993. Compressed Video: Operations and Applications. Association for Educational Communications and Technology.

Hart, D. 1995. Electronic mail to authors, December 5, 1995.

Helms, L. 1993. "The World's Networks: The U.S. Still Lags Many Nations in Developing Digital Communications Systems," *Los Angeles Times,* October 24: D-1.

Hezel, R. T. 1994. *Educational Telecommunications: The State-by-State Analysis.* Syracuse: Hezel and Associates.

Hezel, R. T. 1990. "Policies for Educational Technology: A National, State and Local Agenda." Minneapolis: Chief State School Officers' 1990 State Technology Conference.

Hobbs, D. 1995. "Capacity Building: Re-examining the Role of the Rural School" in *Investing in People: The Human Capital Needs of Rural America,* L. J. Beaulieu and D. Mulkey, eds. Boulder, CO: Westview Press, pp. 259–284.

Hobbs, D. 1989. "Relationships between School and School District Size, Educational Costs and Student Performance: A Review of the Literature," Austin, TX: Southwest Educational Development Laboratory.

Hobbs, D. 1986. "Knowledge-Based Rural Development: Adult Education and the Future Rural Economy," Arlington, VA: National Invitational Conference on Rural Adult Postsecondary Education.

Hobbs, V. 1990. "Distance Learning in North Dakota: A Cross-Technology Study of the Schools, Administrators, Coordinators, Instructors, and Students," Mid-Continent Regional Educational Laboratory, CO, ERIC Document Number ED 328 225.

Hobbs, V., D. Pellant, and M. Chastain. 1990. *The School Administrator's Primer on Distance Learning: Two-Way Interactive Television (I-TV) via Fiber Optics.* Denver, CO: Mid-Continent Regional Educational Laboratory.

Holznagel, D. and T. Olson. 1990. "A Study of Distance Education Policies in State Education Agencies," Northwest Regional Education Laboratory, OR, ERIC Document Number ED 319 402.

Institute for Information Studies. 1995. *Crossroads on the Information Highway: Convergence and Diversity in Communications Technologies.* Institute for Information Studies.

Jacobson, R. 1994. "Extending the Reach of 'Virtual' Classrooms," *The Chronicle of Higher Education,* 6 July: 19–23.

Kabat, E. and Friedel, J. 1990. "Final Report on the Development, Pilot-Testing and Dissemination of a Comprehensive Evaluation Model for Assessing the Effectiveness of a Two-Way Interactive Distance Learning System," Eastern Iowa Community College District, Office of Academic Affairs and Planning.

Keller, J.M. 1983. "Motivational Design of Instruction" in *Instructional Design Theories and Models.* Charles M. Reigeluth, ed. Hillsdale, NJ: Lawrence Erlbaum.

Kemp, J., and D. Smellie. 1994. *Planning, Producing, and Using Instructional Technologies.* New York: Harper Collins.

Kendall, J. R. and M. Oaks, 1992. "Evaluation of Perceived Teaching Effectiveness: Course Delivery via Interactive Video Technology versus Traditional Classroom Methods," *The Journal of Continuing Higher Education,* 40(3): 2–12.

Klinger, T. H. and Connet, M. R. 1992. "Designing Distance Learning Courses for Critical Thinking," *Technological Horizons in Education Journal,* 20(3): 87–89.

Koop, C. E. 1994. "Telemedicine: 21st Century Housecalls," *Connections,* Summer: 24–25.

Krebs, A. 1991. "Funding and Policy Initiatives in Distance Learning," *ED: The Official Publication of the United States Distance Learning Association*, 5(3): 9−14.

Kruh, J. J. and K. L. Murphy. 1990. "Interaction in Teleconferencing: The Key to Quality Instruction," paper presented at the *Annual Rural and Small Schools Conference*, Manhattan, KS (ERIC Document Reproduction Service No. ED 329 418).

Krebs, A., and P. Pease. 1993. "Dimensions of Interactivity," *Education at a Distance Journal*, 7(1): 9-11.

Lichter, D. and J. Costanzo. 1987. "Nonmetropolitan Underemployment and Labor Force Composition," *Rural Sociology*, 52:3.

Los Angeles Times. 1994. "High-Tech House Calls Catching on: From the South Pacific to Rural Kansas, Doctors Find Long-Distance Telemedicine Can Save Lives and Money," *Los Angeles Times*, April 28.

Markey, E. J. 1993. "A Legislative Agenda for Telecommunications," *Issues in Science and Technology*, Fall: 59−64.

McGranahan, D. and L. Ghelfi. 1990. "The Education Crisis and Rural Stagnation in the 1980s," unpublished report.

Merrill, M. D. 1983. "Component Display Theory," in *Instructional-Design Theories and Models*. Charles M. Reigeluth, ed. Hillsdale, NJ: Lawrence Erlbaum.

MITN. 1991. "Distance Learning in Minnesota," Minnesota Department of Education.

Moore, M. G. 1989. "Editorial: Three Types of Interaction," *The American Journal of Distance Learning*, 3(2): 1−6.

Moore, M., Thompson, M., Quigley, B., Clark, C., and G. Goff. 1990. "The Effects of Distance Learning: A Summary of the Literature," University Park, PA: The American Center for the Study of Distance Education.

Morris-Lee, J. 1995. "Connecting: How Combining Videoconferencing with Meeting Software Alters Group Dynamics and Improves Learning," *Medical Meetings*. 22(4): 18−22.

Mort, P. 1953. "Educational Adaptability," *The School Executive*, 71:1−23.

NADO Research Foundation. 1994. "White Paper on Telecommunications and Its Impact on Rural America," Washington, DC: National Association of Development Organizations Research Foundation.

Negroponte, N. 1995. *Being Digital*. New York: Alfred A. Knopf, Inc.

Nesbit, D. 1993. "Taking the Road Less Traveled in Evaluating Two-Way Interactive TV Instruction," *Journal of Interactive Television*, 1: 75−84.

Nix, D. and R. Spiro, eds. 1990. *Cognition, Education, and Multimedia: Exploring Ideas in High Technology*. Hillsdale, New Jersey: Lawrence Erlbaum Associates.

O'Keefe, J.W. 1982. "Assisting Student Learning Styles: An Overview," in *Student Learning Styles and Brain Behavior*. Reston, VA: National Association of Secondary Principals.

Olivieri, K. 1993. "The Social Environment Dimensions of a Fiber Optic Distance Education Network as Defined by High School Teachers, Facilitators, Students, and Staff in the Rural South," Ph.D. Dissertation, Mississippi State University.

O'Neil, J. 1990. "Making Sense of Style," *Educational Leadership*, 48(2): 4−9.

OPASTCO. 1994. "Keeping Rural America Connected: Costs and Rates in the Competitive Era," Washington, DC: Organization for the Protection and Advancement of Small Telephone Companies.

Pagel, N. 1995. Telephone conversations with the authors, January 1995–June 1995.

Papert, S. 1992. *The Children's Machine: Rethinking School in the Age of the Computer.* New York: Basic Books.

Perrin, Janet. 1990. "The Learning Styles for Potential Dropouts," *Educational Leadership,* 48(2): 23–24.

Portes, A. and J. Sensenbrenner. 1993. "Embeddedness and Immigration: Notes on the Social Determinants of Economic Action," *American Journal of Sociology,* 98: 1320–1350.

Postman, N. 1992. *Technopoly.* New York: Alfred A. Knopf.

Rheingold, H. 1993. *The Virtual Community: Homesteading on the Electronic Frontier.* Reading, MA: Addison-Wesley Publishing Company.

Rico, D. 1990. "Art: The New International Order," *Mother Jones,* 15(3): 79.

Rifkind, L. J. 1993. "Immediacy as a Predictor of Teacher Effectiveness in the Instructional Television Classroom," *The Journal of Interactive Television,* 1(1): 31–40.

Ritchie, H. and T. Newby, 1989. "Classroom Lecture/Discussion vs. Live Televised Instruction: A Comparison of Effects on Student Performance, Attitude, and Interaction," *The American Journal of Distance Education,* 3(3), 36–45.

Robertson, A. 1987. "Teleforestry: The Application of Videoconferencing to Forestry," *Forestry Chronicle,* 63: 32–35.

Rogers, E. 1983. *Diffusion of Innovations,* 3rd Edition. New York, NY: The Free Press.

Rogers, E. and D. Kincaid. 1981. *Communication Networks: Toward a New Paradigm for Research.* New York, NY: Free Press.

Ryan, B. and N. Gross. 1943. "The Diffusion of Hybrid Seed Corn in Two Iowa Communities," *Rural Sociology,* 8: 15–24.

Sanders, J. H. 1994. "Telemedicine: Challenges to Implementation," Washington, DC: Presented to the Subcommittee on Investigations and Oversight.

Scollon, S. 1981. "The Teacher-Student Role in Instructional Telecommunications," paper presented at the *Annual Meeting of the American Anthropological Association,* Los Angeles (ERIC Document Reproduction Service No. ED 239 792).

Sidak, G. 1994. "Telecommunications: Unleashing the Industry," *The American Enterprise,* September: 42–47.

Stammen, R. M. 1990. *Needs Assessments for Region 1 and Region 2.* Bismarck, ND: Educational Telecommunications Council, North Dakota Department of Public Instruction.

Theuri, E. 1995. "Relationship between Social Capital and Student Achievement: A Review," Ph.D. Dissertation, University of Missouri-Columbia.

Trowt-Bayard, T. 1994. *Videoconferencing: The Whole Picture.* Chelsea, MI: Flatiron.

Townsend, F. and C. Townsend. 1992. "Meeting Learning Needs through Multimedia: A look at the Way Modern Technology Can Help Classroom Teachers Meet the Varied Instructional Needs of Students," ERIC Document Number ED 352 969.

Tyack, D. B. 1974. *The One Best System: A History of American Urban Education.* Cambridge, MA: Harvard University Press.

University of Maine. 1993. *Maine Cite Guidebook for Accessible I-TV Programs.* Augusta: University of Maine.

University of Missouri, 1994. *Missouri Distance Learning Task Force Pilot Project Study, Survey Data Report.* Columbia: University of Missouri.

Vaughan, T. 1994. *Multimedia: Making It Work,* Second Edition. Berkeley: McGraw-Hill.

Wagner, E. and B. McCombs. 1994. *Learner Centered Psychological Principles in Practice: Designs for Distance Education.* Denver, CO: DLS Group

Walsh, S. M., Price, M. S., and D. Robinson. 1992. "User Perceptions of the Ideal I-TV Classroom," *Journal of Interactive TV,* 1: 3–20.

Wedman, J. 1994. *Cross-Analysis of Student Motivation,* Unpublished.

Whittington, N. 1987. "Is Instructional Television Educationally Effective? A Research Review," *The American Journal of Distance Education,* 1(1): 47–57.

Williamson, B. 1979. *Education, Social Structure and Development.* New York, NY: Homes & Meier Publishers, Inc.

Willis, B. ed. 1994. *Distance Education: Strategies and Tools,* Englewood Cliffs, NJ: Educational Technology Publications.

Woronov, T. 1994. "Six Myths about the Uses of Educational Technology," *The Harvard Education Letter,* 10(5):1–3.

VICKI HOBBS is the Director of the Missouri Interactive Telecommunications Education (MIT-E) Network and works directly with many independent rural school districts in Missouri, primarily in the areas of educational technology applications and program evaluation. She has been involved in several distance learning and alternative education studies in North Dakota, South Dakota, and Missouri. Vicki was instrumental in bringing about the first two-way interactive television networks in Missouri. In addition to several implementation manuals for distance learning and other educational technologies, Vicki is the author of *Distance Learning Evaluation Study: An Inter- and Intra-State Comparison; Distance Learning in North Dakota: A Cross-Technology Study of the Schools, Administrators, Coordinators, Instructors and Students;* and co-author of *The School Administrator's Primer on Distance Learning: Two-Way Interactive Television via Fiber Optics.* She can be reached via Internet mail at vhobbs@mail.coin.missouri.edu.

J. SCOTT CHRISTIANSON is the Director of the I-TV Teacher Training Institute at Central Methodist College and the Technical Coordinator for the Missouri Interactive Telecommunications Education (MIT-E) Network. In these positions, he trains teachers in I-TV equipment use, integrates new equipment into I-TV classrooms, and coordinates the resolution of technical problems. In addition, Scott writes about environmental issues in various magazines and newspapers and is a member of the Outdoor Writers Association of America. Scott is working towards his master's degree in Educational Technology Leadership through a distance learning program from The George Washington University. He can be reached via Internet mail at jsc@igc.apc.org.